Praise for
The Rise of Indigenous Economic Power

Hilton's work reaffirms the significance of relationship economics. Her words clearly illustrate that Indigenomics is the path for the future. As we move through the portal of this time, knowing that pandemics change our world, let's walk through to a path of restorative economics, founded on land, spirit, and the reality of Mother Earth's wealth, which is our responsibility to acknowledge and respect. The time of Keynesian economic analysis has passed, along with the empire. The time of cooperation is here.

—Winona LaDuke, executive director, Honor the Earth

Carol Anne Hilton mounts a convincing case that the rigidity of the Indian Act has put the rest of Canada in a static status-quo headspace that sees Indigenous Peoples as taken care of; meaning they don't see how adept they are in their economic empowerment as they consistently score in the open net.

—Bill Gallagher, resource strategist

The Rise of Indigenous Economic Power challenges conventional narratives of Indigenous economic progress, instead illuminating the transformative opportunities that Indigenomics offers for shaping Canada's future. Carol Anne Hilton brings a refreshingly insightful perspective, presenting Indigenomics as a dynamic pathway to equitable Indigenous economic liberation and advancement.

—Ruth Mojeed Ramirez, Chief Equity Officer, The Inclusion Project

A comprehensively insightful guide for advancing Indigenous economic growth and inclusion. Well-researched, it illuminates Indigenous knowledge systems, business practices, and cultural narratives that can reimagine economic models for our communities and planet. Indigenomics is a future that's being realized today.

—Vinod Rajasekaran, CEO, Future of Good

Over the past few years, described and motivated by Carol Anne's stellar writing and tireless speaking tours, the Indigenous economy has grown in leaps and bounds. Chided for believing that a target of $100 billion in Indigenous economic activity was possible, Carol Anne shows how the Indigenous resurgence will blow well past the $100 billion target, bringing prosperity—finally—back to the lives of Indigenous Peoples and communities in Canada. This wonderful and powerful book is an essential primer for those seeking to understand and celebrate the economic rebirth of Indigenous communities.

—Ken Coates, professor emeritus,
Johnson Shoyama Graduate School of Public Policy, University of Saskatchewan

Praise for Carol Anne Hilton's *Indigenomics*

Carol Anne Hilton has authored one of the most important books of our economic era, providing a new yet ancient Indigenous framework for building economies of well-being. *Indigenomics* represents a pragmatic framework for decision making, policy development, monetary policy, and budgeting that places collective economic well-being, relationships, and Indigenous laws at the heart of wise governance. I feel that Hilton's work will shape global economics for many generations.

—Mark Anielski, economist and author, *The Economics of Happiness: Building Genuine Wealth* and *An Economy of Well-Being: Common-sense Tools for Building Genuine Wealth and Happiness*

Indigenomics provides an anti-colonial lens to reframe narratives about Indigenous entrepreneurship, business leadership, health, and well-being.

—Dr. Jacqueline Quinless, Adjunct Professor of Sociology, University of Victoria

What an inspiring source of wisdom for how to be in the world in the fullness of our humanity. What a powerful guide to building an inclusive economy and serving a new balance between the souls of all living creatures, economics, and nature.

—Ivo Valkenburg, co-founder New Financial Activators

THE RISE OF INDIGENOUS ECONOMIC POWER

DECONSTRUCTING INDIAN ACT ECONOMICS

CAROL ANNE HILTON

new society
PUBLISHERS

Cover design by Diane McIntosh.
Cover image: From an original wooden carving by Dean Hunt, "Spirit of Happiness Copper," 2013. deanhunt.net

Printed in Canada. First printing January 2025.

Inquiries regarding requests to reprint all or part of *The Rise of Indigenous Economic Power* should be addressed to New Society Publishers at the address below. To order directly from the publishers, please call 250-247-9737 or order online at www.newsociety.com.

Any other inquiries can be directed by mail to:
New Society Publishers
P.O. Box 189, Gabriola Island, BC V0R 1X0, Canada
(250) 247-9737

Library and Archives Canada Cataloguing in Publication
Title: The rise of Indigenous economic power : deconstructing Indian Act
   economics / Carol Anne Hilton.
Names: Hilton, Carol Anne, 1975- author
Description: Includes bibliographical references and index.
Identifiers: Canadiana (print) 20250104261 | Canadiana (ebook) 20250104415
   | ISBN 9781774060155 (softcover) | ISBN 9781550928082 (PDF) | ISBN
   9781771424042 (EPUB)
Subjects: LCSH: Indigenous peoples—Canada—Economic conditions. | LCSH:
   Indigenous peoples—Legal status, laws, etc.—Canada. | LCSH: Income
   distribution—Canada. | LCSH: Canada—Race relations— Economic aspects.
   | LCSH: Discrimination—Canada. | LCSH: Canada. Indian Act.
Classification: LCC E98.E2 H55 2025 | DDC 330.971/008997—dc23

Funded by the Government of Canada   Financé par le gouvernement du Canada | **Canadä**

New Society Publishers' mission is to publish books that contribute in fundamental ways to building an ecologically sustainable and just society, and to do so with the least possible impact on the environment, in a manner that models this vision.

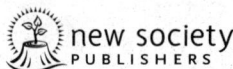

MIX
Paper | Supporting responsible forestry
FSC
www.fsc.org   **FSC® C016245**

Certified
(B)
Corporation

new society
PUBLISHERS

Contents

Acknowledgments

M Y PRAYERS are for the home fires to roar once again. Like so many others, I have spent my years recovering; recovering from the effects of the Indian Act and recovering from a generational response to economic displacement as an Indigenous person. It is from here that I draw both my response and inspiration. These words serve as a contribution to the vision of the evolution of the field of Indigenomics.

I would like to extend my deepest gratitude to my family and colleagues who support me in this vision of articulating Indigenous economic power through the concept of Indigenomics. I am forever grateful to my team at both the Indigenomics Institute and the Global Centre of Indigenomics for your dedication and commitment to the Indigenomics movement, particularly to Sandra Nyamu and Vijai Singh, for your support with this book.

Much gratitude to my late Uncle Qonin, the third Chief of Hesquiaht and descendant of the Nation's whaling house, for inspiring a commitment to upholding our traditional leadership structures, ceremonies, and systems. I am deeply inspired as a descendant of this ancestral legacy of whaling people and a whaling house. I remain in awe of all the disciplines and relationships to succeed in the natural world. To my Grampa JC Lucas—the medicine is strong! Thank you for nurturing and shaping my worldview through ceremony and protocol.

I would like to acknowledge the late author and brilliant human being Richard Wagamese. Your writing and mentorship changed me—keep telling stories on the other side! One word can be a sentence. This one is for you.

To my esteemed colleague and friend, Jacqueline Quinless, you are brilliant, and your humanity shines through you. Pravin Pillay, thank you for your humanity, deep wisdom, and contribution to this book. I appreciate and respect my long-time Indigenomics adviser and friend, Lawrence Alexander; your leadership is formidable. And my relative Eli Ens for always asking me to come home to the homelands. Thank you for the space to write and your steadfast leadership for family, and home, and for upholding our Nuu-chah-nulth ways. Thank you for your leadership and vision.

I extend my gratitude to each of the leaders who participated in the interviews for this book—Kim Baird, Cadmus Delorme, Bill Gallagher, Rose Paul, Wilfred Jimmy, and Hillary Thatcher. Your leadership is exceptional. Keep going.

Big appreciation to Fulbright Canada for building a collaborative partnership with Indigenomics and to Harvard University for creating the space to write this book through this partnership. Much appreciation to the Honoring Nations Program and the Harvard University Native American Program.

To New Society Publishers, thank you for believing in my work of growing the emerging concept of Indigenomics and its place within Canada, internationally, and within economics itself.

This book is dedicated to all who have experienced economic displacement and its effects across generations and all who dream of a beautiful, sustainable, and abundant now and future. It is a book that wanted to be written.

Foreword

Impediments to Indigenous economic development—put in place by the Indian Act, which effectively took Indigenous communities out of the mainstream economy—have held Indigenous Peoples back for generations. We are, however, making our way back in and demanding the changes needed to fully unlock the Indigenous economy.

I'm pleased to offer this foreword for Carol Anne Hilton's new book, *The Rise of Indigenous Economic Power: Deconstructing Indian Act Economics*, which makes a significant contribution in this area.

The author and I have known each other for many years through her work as CEO and founder of the Indigenomics Institute and the Global Center of Indigenomics. I've had the pleasure of participating in several of her well-attended Indigenomics events, which bring people together to discuss pathways and actions toward economic reconciliation. Through these events and in her books, Hilton skillfully raises awareness that the Indigenous economy has tremendous potential and—once fully unlocked—will benefit all Canadians.

Many Canadians recognize the urgent need for economic reconciliation, for the colonial barriers to Indigenous economic development to come down so Indigenous Peoples can build better futures. They know that prioritizing action toward economic reconciliation is the right thing for Canada to do. But not everyone is motivated by what is right. We need to also raise awareness, as Hilton does here, about the substantial benefits Canada as a whole will realize when the Indigenous economy is freed from colonial constraints.

As these barriers to the Indigenous economy are removed, major economic growth follows. The benefits of that growth will boost quality of life and opportunity in Indigenous communities, while also benefiting the rest of Canada.

Understanding the harms caused by the Indian Act is fundamental to taking down these barriers, and Hilton rightly dedicates considerable space to this matter. The Indian Act of 1867 has never reflected the spirit and intent of the Royal Proclamation of 1763, which described a sharing of resources and a respect for the existing governance of Indigenous communities. The harsh reality is that Indigenous governments were never embraced as equals. Indeed, Indigenous communities were placed under the supervision of the Indian agent.

The Indian Act established the parameters of Indigenous economic opportunity and inclusion within the federation. The *Act* did not recognize Indigenous traditional territories; it recognized only those lands the federal government established as reserves.

The Indian Act blocked Indigenous communities from participating in the fiscal framework other governments and Canadians have been able to take for granted for generations.

Additionally, the Indian Act replaced the pre-existing economic systems that had successfully provided for the well-being of our communities. Our economies ceased to exist in areas where they were deemed to conflict with the Indian Act's view of where Indigenous People belonged in the new country's economy. We became wards of the federal government, a government determined to assimilate Indigenous communities and Indigenous Peoples into the European systems and values embraced by settlers.

The Indian Act placed Indigenous Peoples on a path of economic exclusion that has resulted in horrific social and economic consequences for our communities. As well, for most of Canada's history, the country has denied itself the benefits of Indigenous inclusion in the Canadian economy.

These truths of Canadian history are not well known because they have been hidden from view—as are the consequences. As this book explains, the Indian Act economy is still very real today. Hilton brings many of these issues to the forefront, exposing the roots of the harms that continue today.

But there is reason for hope. There are signs of change. There are indicators of the power of the emerging Indigenous economy, and this book shares some of these inspiring success stories. I like how Hilton presents some of these hopeful signs in a list of "25 things that John A. Macdonald would never have seen coming." These items are among the examples of Indigenous resilience and achievement that inspire us today and demonstrate to all what is possible.

Indeed, work is being done today to take down the significant barriers that continue to restrict the Indigenous economy. Among other things, Hilton introduces the First Nations Financial Management Board-led RoadMap Project in this book, as an important framework for unlocking the Indigenous economy.

RoadMap is a practical pathway to economic reconciliation, with full optionality for First Nations. It's an Indigenous-led plan to breathe life into the United Nations Declaration on the Rights of Indigenous Peoples (UNDRIP), to move from a system of managing poverty to a framework for generating wealth.

The RoadMap Project is a direct response to what the First Nations Financial Management Board has heard from the First Nations we serve. It reflects our conversations with First Nation leaders around key questions, including: How do we achieve economic reconciliation? How do we create self-governance and Nation-to-Nation relationships from an economic and fiscal point of view?

In our development of the RoadMap Project, I reached out to many Indigenous organization leaders, including Hilton, to discuss their ideas on these matters. I'm grateful to Hilton for sharing her insights and ideas with us. RoadMap is an Indigenous-led response to calls for the jurisdiction and fiscal powers needed for sustainable governance, the statistics and data needed to make informed decisions, and for the infrastructure gap to be closed. It's about collaborating for First Nations' prosperity, unlocking First Nations' innovation and economic development potential, and achieving economic reconciliation.

RoadMap responds to the needs of First Nations Peoples and the desires of all levels of government for meaningful, systemic, and lasting change. It recognizes that a one-size-fits-all solution doesn't work; that the status quo is not a solution.

Indigenous-led institutions are key to advancing economic reconciliation. Hilton points to the success of the First Nations Financial Management Act (FMA) institutions in this context. Working together, the Indigenous-led FMA institutions—the First Nations Finance Authority (FNFA), First Nations Tax Commission (FNTC), First Nations Financial Management Board (FNFMB), and First Nations Infrastructure Institute (FNII)—have supported First Nations in increasing their own-source revenue, improving financial management, planning and managing infrastructure projects, and accessing the capital needed for socioeconomic development in their communities. In early 2024, the FNFA surpassed $2 billion in loans to First Nations at competitive interest rates, enabling Nations to address community priorities.

As Hilton makes clear in this book, inaction at this time is not an option. Inaction means continuing to hold back Indigenous Peoples while also failing to meet the needs of the Canadian economy. She wisely reminds us of RBC's seminal 1997 report, *The Cost of Doing Nothing,* released after the Royal Commission on Aboriginal Peoples published its final report. The RBC report outlined the financial implications of inaction on the recommendations of the Royal Commission, including substantial and long-term social and economic costs for both Indigenous Peoples and Canada as a whole.

The Rise of Indigenous Economic Power gives us much to absorb and consider. It unpacks many uncomfortable truths and shares important perspectives of the evolution of the Indigenous relationship in Canada. This book reminds us that had there not been the exclusion processes of colonization, we would have our own version of many of the economic and financial structures and institutions that contribute to a higher quality of life for non-Indigenous communities. Our economies would have grown tremendously over the past 300 years. But colonization did happen, we weren't included, and we were held back. As a result, the harmful circumstances that we continue to face must now be corrected.

Ultimately, this book leads the reader to the clear conclusion that Canada must choose whether to take meaningful action or continue to prop up a broken system that perpetuates inequality. It is time to move beyond a failed colonial system that prevents Indigenous Peoples from achieving their socioeconomic goals. Unlocking the Indigenous economy means advancing economic reconciliation—and building prosperity for all of Canada. I welcome Hilton's new book as an important perspective to point us all in the right direction.

Harold Calla, FCPA, FCGA, CAFM
Executive Chair, First Nations Financial Management Board

Introduction:
The Indigenomics Manifestation

History is the stories we tell about the past.

—Thomas King

T HE FIRE HAS BEEN LIT. Over time, the village home fires died down to glowing embers. It is time to stoke the fire and place more wood on the burning coals. As the flames dance and flicker, a mesmerizing spiral of smoke moves upward, radiating heat. A breeze passes over the flames, igniting the sparks, and the smoke begins to rise for all to see. The sky fills with the sound of the roaring blaze of Indigenous economic resurgence.

The fire metaphorically represents the resilience of Indigenous Peoples faced with generations of economic exclusion. While the fires were merely flickers at one time, today, the rise of Indigenous economic empowerment is an unstoppable, formidable, and undeniable force in Canadian reality. It is happening here, it is happening now, and it is happening across this country. The fire of economic justice has been set in motion.

This story is set against the backdrop of the becoming of Canada. It is a reflection on the explosive growth of the Indigenous economy today and the interplay between the historical systemic design of the exclusion of Indigenous Peoples and the features of Indigenous economic growth. This book is a contribution to bringing the untold story of the rise of the Indigenous economy into visibility. History tells us that economics started in the eighteenth century and is an early articulation of Adam Smith's work. Indigenous economies have been functioning for thousands of years. This book is a story of the contrasting economic narratives between what we are told economics is and the actual functioning of Indian Act economics within Canadian reality. This story is a metaphorical contribution to the field of economy.

This book follows the publication of *Indigenomics: Taking a Seat at the Economic Table*, which grounds the claim of modern Indigenous economic space and upholds the relevance of Indigenous worldviews and their application in economy and business. Indigenomics is setting out to establish a powerful why—to uphold a modern Indigenous economic response and examine its misalignment with economics. This book calls into the open the need for increasing accountability of the continued activation of Indian Act economics and its outcomes in Canadian reality.

Indigenomics has emerged as a disruptive economic force—bringing focus to the Indigenous economic worldview and its significance to a sustainable human future. Indigenomics is a radical new approach to Indigenous economic policy that addresses the symptoms and the causes of inequality within a mainstream context today. Indigenomics elevates Indigenous worldviews and facilitates a forward-looking, strength-based narrative of Indigenous economic growth and design. At its core, Indigenomics calls for accountability, ethics, and sustainable outcomes of economics itself. The concept of Indigenomics is centred on the economic narrative that it is time to move beyond the fallacy of all we have been told the economy is. Indigenomics focuses to the foundation of humanity's success that must come from economic systems that have life at the center—the elemental forces of air, water, earth, and fire—and must include the contributive wisdom of all peoples to the economy itself.

Weaving the Invisible Thread

An invisible thread connects this country across time, generations, citizenship, and immigration. Whether you are of Indigenous descent from here for thousands of years, your family has been here for recent generations, or you have only recently arrived, this thread connects each of us. This thread is the historical centering of the ongoing impacts of the Indian Act as the only race-based legislation in Canada since its formation.

This book establishes the concept of Indian Act economics as the antithesis of the function of the economy itself. Indian Act economics is a destructive force working against the function of the economy, cultural continuation, and is a standard of living and well-being. Indian Act economics is a fully functioning structure and process of the continued fragmentation of Indigenous reality, and it is deeply embedded into this country's national identity, psyche, belief system, and bias.

The Indian Act was a response to the problem of Indigenous existence, which slowed the settlement of the lands and access to resources for the newly formed Canada. It is in this uncomfortable truth that it is time to come to terms with the inheritance of economic trauma through the functioning of Indian Act economics.

Indian Act economics is the antithesis of Indigenomics. It brings into focus the absence of the function of "economy" through the administration of the Indian Act as the dominant force of economic exclusion. It is time to address the complacency of the status quo of Indian Act economics and the absence of accountability behind the outcomes it creates. This book upholds a strength-based narrative of Indigenous People's reality—we are a resilient and powerful people and an economic force at the heart of this country.

This book explores several lines of inquiry. It sets out to explore the contrast between the functioning of economy and the ongoing complexities of the Indigenous relationship and the rise of Indigenous economic growth. It questions: Is Indian Act economics working against the function and outcomes of the national economy? It sets out to demonstrate the rise of the Indigenous economy and the features of the emergence of Indigenous economic power. Finally, the book explores a key policy inquiry to drive accountability—is the Indian Act ethical?

Today, the growth of the Indigenous economy has a central role in Canadian reality. Within a constantly evolving economic playing field, this book is set against the background of the Indigenomics $100 billion Indigenous economic growth trajectory as established by the Indigenomics Institute. It serves to bring forward insights into the emergence of Indigenous economic power. This book focuses in on the processes of Indigenous economic value creation and the visibility of the increasing $100 billion of Indigenous economic activity. The rise of Indigenous economic growth must be grounded within several important contexts.

First, the original treaties as the formative contracts of this country remind us of these powerful words: "As long as the sun shines, the grass grows and the river flows." As long as these elemental forces, the ceremonial foundation of life, continue to live and keep the treaties alive, Canada is in a relationship with Indigenous Peoples. The treaties were confirmed and upheld with life at the center. The lands we collectively live, work, and play on hold the vibration of the original treaties, covering over 3.5 million square kilometers or about 35 percent of the country's total land mass. This is the common invisible thread across our collective reality. This land mass consistently expands through legal settlements, land claims, and modern treaties.

Second, an important consideration in framing Indigenous economic growth is the economic urgency within the immediate national economic context due to increased uncertainties, including the need to build post-pandemic economic resilience, the threat of a recession, climate change, and global unrest. Further, it has been identified that Canada's recovery in real gross domestic product (GDP) per capita was the fifth weakest in the Organization for Cooperation and Development (OECD) over the 2019–22 period.[1]

A third pivotal consideration in framing Indigenous economic growth in the national context is the need to highlight that the OECD has projected that Canada will be the worst-performing economy among the thirty-eight advanced economies over the periods of 2020–30 and 2030–60, with the lowest growth in real GDP per capita.[2]

Like a ship without a rudder, Canada lacks a clear plan to address these alarming projections. We desperately need economic innovation in this country. The economic story of now is that Indigenous economic inclusion creates certainty and growth for all.

A fourth key consideration was the release of the Truth and Reconciliation Commission report in 2015. The report sets the context for building critical action-oriented responses to advance the Indigenous relationship. A recent national headline, "Diminished Hope: Yellowhead Institute to End Reports on TRC Calls to Action," highlights a 2023 report by the Yellowhead Institute that found that zero Calls to Action were completed that year by the federal government.[3] The article identified that if Canada continues at this current pace, it will not finish implementing these Calls to Action until 2081. The article highlights that "there are limits to how many times you can write a report about how Canada, once again, has failed to make any meaningful progress. The Institute considers only 13 of the 91 recommendations complete." Complacency, the status quo, and Indigenous economic growth do not go well together.

Finally, another significant context in the growth of the Indigenous economy, which is particularly alarming, is the scale of the ongoing identification of the graves of Indigenous children at residential school sites across the country. First reported on the site of the Kamloops Indian Residential School with the identification of 215 unmarked graves, the number of unmarked graves at residential schools across this country has grown exponentially. The ongoing count is in thousands for unmarked graves of Indigenous children who attended these schools. The growing realization of the horrors of the history and traumatic nature of the story led to the term "genocide" being permanently entered into the lexicon of this country. While Canada is collectively grasping at the meaning of this violent legacy, it is directly connected to the concept of collective trauma. It is time to come to terms with the story and experience of the inheritance of this trauma within Canadian reality.

This collective realization that thousands of Indigenous children were murdered at state- and church-run residential schools broke open this country's perspective and awakening to the inheritance of this story of collective trauma. A national *CBC* article, "Pope Says Genocide Took Place at Canada's Residential Schools,"[4] struggles to articulate this trauma. The article reports the Pope describing the Indian residential schools system as "a policy of assimilation and enfranchisement, and that it harmed families by undermining their language, culture, and worldview." The article then refers to the words of the Pope upon his reflection after the tour to the Indian residential schools: "I condemned it, the taking away of the children, changing culture, the mind, traditions, a so-called race. A whole culture. Yes, it's a technical word, genocide. I didn't use it because it didn't come to mind. But yes, I described it. Yes, it's a genocide." It's so close yet so far from accountability. This is our collective story of the invisible thread that ties our collective national reality and frames the foundation of the context to the growth of the Indigenous economy today.

Collective economic trauma is ongoing, and the cumulative impacts are directly related to the application of the founding policy of the Indian Act. "Collective trauma transforms into a collective memory and culminates in a system of meaning that allows groups to redefine who they are and where they are going."[5] The term "collective trauma" refers to the psychological reactions to a traumatic event that affects an entire society; it does not merely reflect a historical fact, the recollection of a terrible event that happened to a group of people. The concept "suggests that the tragedy is represented in the collective memory of the group, and like all forms of memory it comprises not only a reproduction of the events, but also an ongoing reconstruction of the trauma in an attempt to make sense of it."[6] An important distinction is that "collective memory of trauma is different from individual memory because collective memory persists beyond the lives of the direct survivors of the events and is remembered by group members that may be far removed from the traumatic events in time and space."[7]

As a country, we are only beginning to grasp the meaning of the inheritance of collective economic trauma. The metrics of this meaning are continuously expressed in the lived experience of the Indigenous socioeconomic gap, which is the inheritance of the outcomes of the Indian Act. The foundation of Canada's economy has been built on the formative policy of "take the Indian out of the child." This is the violent legacy of Canada's original policy of the Indian Act, which continues today to separate Indigenous Peoples from their identity, land, culture, responsibilities, and family connections. This is the formative truth—not one single citizen in Canada can escape the collective inheritance of this story of economic trauma across time until today.

The Indian Act facilitated the policy of systemic elimination, the denial of identity, and the economic and cultural dispossession of Indigenous Peoples across Canadian reality. The expression of our continued existence, "we are still here," and the Land Back movement are foundational to the rise of Indigenous economic power today. This book is oriented in this context.

In centering my reality as an author, I begin by reflecting on the fragmentation of my reality as a Nuu-chah-nulth woman. I reflect on the experience of my healing journey and my return to wholeness as I continue to witness the impacts of Indian Act economics as expressed through the violence of the living data of the Indigenous socioeconomic gap of this country. Indigenomics is the response to the experience of Indigenous economic and cultural displacement. I posit that the Indigenous socioeconomic gap is a direct metric of the lack of accountability for the legacy of the Indian Act and is a direct outcome of Indian Act economics.

This book is organized into nine chapters, beginning with the Indigenomics Manifestation. This introduction weaves the understanding of the collective relationship through the invisible thread that connects us and provides critical contexts to today's rise of the Indigenous economy. Chapter one describes the structure of the radical economic exclusion of Indigenous Peoples through the Indian Act. The next chapter focuses on building an understanding of deconstructing Indian Act economics. Chapter three situates the development of the historical evolution of the concept of the cost of doing nothing in relation to the growing Indigenous economy today. Chapter four highlights the fallacy of the Indian Act. It introduces the absence of the ethical framework of Indian Act economics in relationship to the growth of the Indigenous economy today. The next chapter facilitates key insights into the national Indigenous economic media narrative to identify the depiction of value creation. Chapter six examines the pathway of the rise of Indigenous economic power against the Indigenomics $100 billion Indigenous economic trajectory. Chapter seven describes the design framework of value creation in the Indigenous economy. The final chapter focuses on how meaning is derived from Indigenous economic exclusion and examines the rise of Indigenous economic power today as it is shaping new meaning, accountability, and outcomes of Indian Act economics.

In the process of writing this book, I undertook a series of interviews with key leaders in the Indigenous economy as follows:

Cadmus Delorme is an Indigenous political and business leader who served as the Chief of Cowesses First Nation in Saskatchewan for seven years. He recently started One Hoop Consulting and is also the founder of Flowing River Capital. He started these companies in response to his experience as Chief in this country.

Rose Paul is the CEO of Bayside Development Corporation in Nova Scotia. Rose is the trailblazer for business development, negotiations, and partnerships for the business arm of Paqtnkek Mi'kmaw Nation.

Kim Baird is a formidable Indigenous business and political leader and past Chief of the Tsawwassen First Nation in British Columbia. Kim helped negotiate the first modern-day urban Indigenous treaty, which opened up the governance and economic pathways for the Nation's success today.

Bill Gallagher is a lawyer and strategist focusing on the evolution of Indigenous law and Canada's resource sector. Bill has established an entire volume of work that situates the Indigenous legal winning streak into Canadian economic reality; work that is critical to Canada's knowledge foundation. Bill Gallagher wrote the first book, *Resource Rulers*, in 2012, which identified 150 legal wins and served as a wake-up call to centering Indigenous power in Canadian reality. His second book, *Resource Reckoning*, in 2018, came out with 250 legal wins. At the time of this interview, over 364 Indigenous legal wins can be tracked. The significance of this work is also in the realization that the majority of these have not been adequately covered by the Canadian media. Canadians are not getting the information they need to understand the evolving Indigenous relationship in Canada. This volume of work is of critical importance as it tracks the legal wins, reconciliation, the natural resource sector, and the response to Indigenous economic power.

Hillary Thatcher is an Indigenous business leader of Métis descent and serves as the managing director of Investments: Indigenous and Northern Infrastructure at the Canada Infrastructure Bank. Hillary advises Indigenous and northern leaders and structures investments in clean energy, green infrastructure, transit, trade and transportation, and broadband.

Wilfred Jimmy is a citizen of the Thunderchild First Nation located in Saskatchewan. Wil respects his culture and traditions and has learned to balance his cultural life in a corporate environment. Wilfred has business experience gained during his career in the financial sector as a manager of Indigenous banking for the Manitoba, Saskatchewan, and Alberta region. Wilfred believes that the two cultures can enhance each other and create opportunities for the First Nation people that will allow equal participation in the business world.

Recognizing that language evolves, this book uses the most current and respectful language by using the term "Indigenous Peoples" as a collective, inclusive name for the original peoples of these lands. The use of the language "Indigenous Peoples" is intended to be inclusive of First Nations, Inuit, and Métis peoples as three distinct peoples with unique histories, languages, and cultures. Sources quoted will also periodically use Indian, First Nations, or

Aboriginal. Within the Indian Act, the use of the terms "Indian" or "Status Indian" refer to the existing language within the Act. While noticeably problematic and alarmingly outdated, as well as racist at its foundation, the use of the term "Indian" is the evidence of our time.

The threads that weave the collective experience of the rise of Indigenous economic power must be examined as the Indigenous economy is becoming an undeniable force to be reckoned with.

Reflective Questions

1. What is your reaction to the term "genocide" being used by the Pope on his tour to Canada as described here?

2. What does economic displacement mean to you?

3. Why do you think the Indian Act still uses the term "Indian"?

4. What does the term "collective economic trauma" mean from your perspective?

1

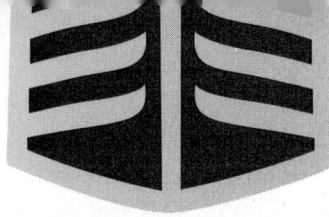

Radical Indigenous Economic Exclusion

The happiest future for the Indian race is absorption into the general population and this is the object of the policy of our government. The great forces of inter-marriage and education will finally overcome the lingering traces of native customs and traditions.

—Duncan Campbell Scott

WHAT A PECULIAR USE of the language "happiest future" as described in a policy of elimination of the Indigenous population. This is the uncomfortable space in Canadian reality—the calculated directive of the eventual elimination of Indigenous Peoples as described in these words of Duncan Campbell Scott, the first superintendent of the Department of Indian Affairs.

The concept of "othering" is the defining and securing of one's identity by distancing and stigmatizing the "other's identity." The concept of othering is an essential construct of the functioning of Indian Act economics. Othering reinforces one's own "normality" by articulating the differences of others as a point of deviance.[8] The person or group being othered experiences this as a process of marginalization, disempowerment, and social and economic exclusion. This effectively creates the separation between "us" and "them."

In the context of examining the illusion of the Indian Act economics, the connection between "othering" and structural racism must be examined. The work of Viruell-Fuentes describes othering as being "treated as a function of structural factors, including institutional racism. Othering contributes to shaping an individual's prescribed racial status and their access (or lack thereof) to resources associated with such a status."[9] This is the foundation of the functioning of Indian Act economics.

Othering is described as a set of dynamics, processes, and structures that cause marginality and persistent inequalities across the full range of human differences based on identity. In the *Economics of Belonging*, author Martin Sandbu introduces the concept of "the end of belonging."[10] The author highlights the absence of economic belonging and its social implications. He eloquently describes how "the notion of belonging captures the psychological, sociological and political fallout of economic change." Sandbu establishes that economics is at the center of widening social and economic inequality. "Othering" is a term that not only encompasses the many expressions of prejudice based on group identity but also provides a clarifying frame that reveals a set of common processes and conditions that propagate inequality and prejudices. This is Indian Act economics.

The concept of othering is useful language in naming the cause-and-effect experience of Indian Act economics and the radical exclusion of the Indigenous population. The Indian Act is an architectural structure designed specifically for the absence of belonging of Indigenous Peoples and their dis-invitation from having a seat at the economic table. Foundational to the concept of Indian Act economics is its intention to sever Indigenous cultural and economic belonging. It was and is the radical structure for the systemic isolation of the Indigenous population to further access lands, resources, and economic base. The structure and process for the absence of belonging is a core feature and function of the Indian Act. The structure for the absence of belonging continues across the original version of the Indian Act in 1876, the amendments in 1927, and the 1985 version as it remains to this day. Each clause of the Indian Act can be broken down into the structure and process of othering and the absence of belonging of Indigenous Peoples.

Some examples of the structure of othering are demonstrated through the externalization of authority and the establishment of the Indian reserve, which was upheld through the relationship of lands held in trust for the Crown as a specific form of physical and economic isolation. Economic isolation within the Indian Act is structured through the disallowance of leases, sales of grain, oil and gas, and other resources on reserve. Another example is holding "moneys in trust for the Indian," which upholds the structure of othering in Indian Act economics. The policy of isolating and removing Indigenous identity is another example of othering in the Indian Act.

Othering, in practice, upholds the structure of radical exclusion through the Indian Act, which is outlined in a paper for the Centre for First Nations Governance titled *Indian Act Colonialism: A Century of Dishonour, 1869–1969* by John Milloy.

"Indian status" as created in the Indian Act grew out of Victorian cultural and ethno-centric assumptions: that property ownership was the foundation of civilized society and that both ownership and decent of property were attached, primarily, to males. In line with these beliefs, the Indian Act defined "Indian" in relation to property. Thus "For the purpose of determining what persons are entitled to hold, use or enjoy the lands and other immoveable property belonging to or appropriated to the use of the various tribes bands or bodies of Indians."[11]

Understanding the distinctions of the practice of radical exclusion is important in realizing how language is used to uphold othering in the Indian Act. The use of "Indian" upholds both radical exclusion and activation of othering through its definition. "The term 'Indian' means: first, any male person of Indian blood reputed to belong to a particular band. Second. Any child of such person. Third, any woman who is or was married to such person."[12]
The paper continues:

This legal formulation of the "Indian," rooted in the patriarchal nature of property ownership, went a step further. It dismantled tribal nations by segregating their bands into separate property-bound entities and units of municipal administration. Thereafter, the individual's status was tied to the band on its reserve rather than to traditional, tribal collectives. Thus if an Indian woman married an Indian of another band, she "shall cease to be a member of the band to which she formerly belonged, and become a member of the band ... of which her husband is a member." And men's property rights and privileges were restricted to their own reserve. Indians attempting to live on a reserve to which they were not attached by their status were, like white trespassers, subject to removal. [13]

The externalization of authority in the Indian Act was a central feature of othering and radical exclusion of the Indigenous population. The author continues breaking down the structure of othering and the absence of belonging of the Indigenous relationship in Canada.

> The [Indian] Act gave the Department the authority to attribute or deny status to individuals and this led to the development of a powerful colonizing device—a status tracking system composed of band and treaty numbers for individuals, a national registrar and registry to make and register status determinations and eventually status cards. These made the status population legible to the Department, marked it genealogically. That legibility facilitated heightened levels of Departmental surveillance and intervention in communities and in the lives of individuals. By regulating registered births and determining the paternity of each child, band lists could be established and policed and the separation was maintained between status and non-status Indians and non-Aboriginals. Such surveillance and regulation became increasingly important in the 1950s and thereafter as the Indian population increased and thus Federal expenditures in treaty payments and welfare state benefits and services escalated accordingly.[14]

Another clear example of the structure of othering as a tool was the use of gender as a weapon against Indigenous Peoples embedded in the Indian Act.

> In defense of the legal status "purity" of band populations, and of the Indian Department's budget too perhaps, thousands of Indian women and children, culturally but not considered legally "Indian," were exiled from their communities and identity. Cut-off from family and community support, and, often lacking education and job skills, these women often became, in the post-war period, the objects of off-reserve provincial social service organizations. The most tragic consequence of this exile and surveillance was that many of their children would be "apprehended" by child welfare officials and

would be lost to culture and community in the labyrinth of the fostering and adoption system.[15]

The Indian Act establishes the externalization of the position of power. The following chart articulates the key functions of othering as structured within the Indian Act.

Table 1: The Structure of Radical Indigenous Economic Exclusion within the Indian Act

Structure of Radical Exclusion	How
Upholds only ethnocentric worldview and practice	Imposes a singular worldview as the source of power, authority, definition, and isolation Serves to eliminate the Indigenous population to clear the lands and access resources
Externalized decision-making away from Indigenous Peoples	Isolates decision-making to the Indian agent and today to the federal agency
Forces economic isolation/displacement of the Indigenous population	Reserve system isolates land mass and resources
Forced externalized limitations on Indigenous identity	Prescribed conditions for identification with the purpose of reducing the continuation of a people
Attack on existence	Long-term core objective is for Indigenous Peoples to cease to exist
Forbids Indigenous language and cultural practices	Suppression of cultural practices and continuation of identity
Weaponizes Indigenous education	Isolated the Indigenous population to remove continued existence
Indigenous gender isolation and weaponization	Prescribes conditions for gender isolation and removal from Indigenous identity
Isolation from worldview—practice of culture, belonging, property.	Removal of inherent Indigenous stewardship and responsibility

Externalization of decision-making	Removes the ability of Indigenous communities to make decisions for themselves for the purpose of activating control
Removal of any function of Indigenous asset ownership and commerce through the reserve system	Better able to access and control resources on and off reserve
Self-appoints Indigenous Peoples as wards of the state	Removes absence of self-regulation/self-government through externalized governance of the Indian Act Deems Indigenous Peoples as incapable of self-governance
Physical isolation of the Indigenous population from the rest of Canada	Isolates Indigenous population onto reserves and establishes limited mobility
Weaponizes identity	Controls identity as a tool for discontinuation and limitation

The Indigenous Socioeconomic Gap

The Indigenous socioeconomic gap is the accumulation of the long-term impacts of the structured absence of economic opportunities, unequal distribution of resources, and lack of access to the basic functions of economy and commerce. One of the opening clauses of the United Nations Declaration on the Rights of Indigenous Peoples (UNDRIP) is that Indigenous Peoples have the right to dignity. The Indigenous socioeconomic gap is the absence of dignity. Every time you pass by an Indigenous person living the experience of homelessness, this is the continuous accumulative outcome of Indian Act economics in action—the perpetuated impact of long-term trauma of the economic displacement of the Indian. Indian Act economics is the continuous upholding of Indigenous economic displacement. The Indigenous socioeconomic gap is the cost of doing nothing. The Indigenous socioeconomic gap is a value crisis.

Reflective Questions

1. Why is the Indian Act Canada's only race-based legislation?
2. In what ways does the Indian Act establish "othering?"
3. What does radical economic exclusion mean today?
4. How are the processes of belonging and reconciliation connected?

2

Deconstructing Indian Act Economics

We do not want the Indian Act retained because it is a good piece of
legislation. It isn't. It is discriminatory from start to finish.
But it is a lever in our hands and an embarrassment to the
government, as it should be. No just society and no society with even
pretensions of being just can long tolerate such a piece of
legislation, but we would rather continue to live in bondage
under the inequitable Indian Act than surrender our sacred rights. Any
time the government wants to honour its obligations to us we are more
than happy to help devise new Indian legislation.

—Harold Cardinal, *The Unjust Society*

THE ORIGINAL INDIAN ACT of 1876 imposed severe limitations on personal and collective freedoms and prohibitions on the activities of Indigenous Peoples, including restricting movement, consumption of alcohol, land ownership, cultural practices, self-governance, participation of women, and identity. These restrictions reflected the paternalistic, Eurocentric, and assimilationist attitudes and policies. The Act also provided the Canadian government significant powers to enforce these prohibitions, including the appointment of Indian agents who were granted the authority to oversee and manage the day-to-day lives of Indigenous Peoples while clearing the lands for access for the settlers. A series of minor revisions have been undertaken since the original version up until the 1985 revision of the Indian Act.

Looking back into the early formation of the Indian Act as a design instrument of elimination of the Indigenous population, the words of Canada's first prime minster are noteworthy: "The great aim of our legislation [Indian Act] has been to do away with the tribal system and assimilate the Indian people in all respects with the other inhabitants of the Dominion as speedily as they are fit to change."[16]

Canada has inherited the traumatic effects of this historical baggage and the legacy of these formative words of Canada's first prime minister. The Indian Act continuously upholds the intention to extinguish the cultural, social, economic, and political distinctiveness of Indigenous Peoples. While the tenets of genocide were woven into the very fabric of the original Indian Act, the continued activation of this original policy instrument is particularly disturbing as it largely remains intact today. National policy based on the elimination of Indigenous Peoples is both the inheritance and the bias of the Indian Act today. This is the foundation of Indian Act economics.

This country is at a critical intersection in terms of building a response to the rise of Indigenous economic power today, and it is time to acknowledge the role of the Indian Act as problematic to the functioning of the economy. It is time to bring out into the open what this country has inherited through the Indian Act in terms of its functioning and its ongoing impacts and outcomes.

Indian Act economics is the antithesis of the function of the economy itself. This country operates on two economic systems. The first is economics as we know it, expressed through the measurements of the GDP as the benchmark metric for identifying economic strength and productivity. The second is the lesser-known economic operating system of Indian Act economics with the structures of control and the ongoing administration of Indigenous identity, dependence, and economic isolation.

The esteemed Indigenous thought leader and author, as well as the Canadian Research Chair in Indigenous Law at the University of Victoria Law School, John Burrows, writes that:

> The Indian Act is purposely designed to assimilate us. It is meant to sever the generations. The Act is working its purpose, through provisions concerning land, elections, membership, commerce and education. It cuts us from future relationships. We cannot take account of the seventh generation if the Indian Act continues to remove them from us.[17]

What a powerful statement: "We cannot take account of the seventh generation if the Indian Act continues to remove them from us." Ignoring a problem does not make it go away. Canada's structural problems need to be acknowledged,[18] and our economic policy mix needs rethinking.[19]

Author John Leslie's research examines the formative pre-Confederation years of Canadian Indian policy development. It poignantly describes the Indian Act as "in many ways it is the dead hand of a past philosophy which continues to reach into the present."[20] This body of work is particularly important as it points to the shaping of the thinking that led to the building of the Indian Act.

> The central philosophical assumptions and policies of modern Canadian Indian administration were shaped during the four decades prior to Confederation. Instrumental in this process were six government commissions of inquiry which devised, evaluated, and modified a program for Indian advancement and civilization based on treaties, reserves, religious conversion, and agricultural instruction. Though not apparent at the time, the series of investigative reports created a corporate memory for the Indian department and established a policy framework for dealing with Native peoples and issues. The approach became entrenched, like the department itself, and remained virtually unchanged and unchallenged until 1969, when the federal government issued its white paper on Indian policy. [20]

The Indian Act was built from the thinking of the four decades before its creation, putting the timeframe around 1827. It was essentially shaped by the Victorian Eurocentric thinking of the time. To put this in perspective, the types of advancements that were happening in this 1827 timeframe included John Walker inventing modern-day matches, Charles Wheatstone inventing the microphone, and W.A. Burt inventing the typographer, the precursor to the typewriter. The complacency that still exists today toward the Indian Act and its inherent bias upholds its original purpose.

In conversation with Indigenous business leader Cadmus Delorme, past Chief of Cowesses Nation, he offers an important reflection on the meaning of Indian Act economics.

> Indian Act economics is renting your land. Let's take agriculture, for example, in the context of a reserve. To rent reserve land to a

non-Indigenous farmer who will pay below fair market value, and the Nation doesn't gain any long-term equity from it. The non-Indigenous farmer can turn that land around and make a profit, whereas the First Nation under the Indian Act will remain in the status quo— locked out of economic value.

That is Indian Act economics both in its concept and its functioning— it perpetuates the absence of any economic value for Indigenous Peoples. Cadmus Delorme further explains that:

Indian Act economics is when Canada will have us all believing that reserve land is our territory. Reserve land is not our territory—it is land that is set aside for us by the federal government. Indigenous nations have entire territories, and we are the original rights holders. If there are economic projects that are happening off the reserve but in the territory—the denial of our economic participation in that development—that is Indian Act economics.

Indian Act economics is the absence of return on investment. It is the federal government acting on behalf of its own "Indian money" interests, establishing itself as the patriarchal parent and upholding the original thinking of the Indian Act that the Indian is too incompetent to manage moneys. An example of Indian Act economics is that every municipal plan across this country has been made without Indigenous planning and inclusion for decision-making and input. Indian Act economics will have us all believing that municipal lands are not in the jurisdiction of the Indians.

Indian Act economics upholds the status quo thinking and the inherited perspective of the original Indian relationship. "Indian Act economics will have us thinking that if it's not on the reserve, then the Indians just have to stand by and let someone else get economically wealthy from it. This is the structure of Indian Act economics, and this thinking today is unacceptable," explains Delorme. He further describes the absence of function or reasoning of Indian Act economics.

The Indian Act is not economically friendly to anyone, and it is driven by Canada (the Indian Affairs Department) making approvals on everything. When a Nation wants to do an economic project, and if it's in the land use plan, the government has to agree to it, and the Minister has to sign off on it. Chief and Councils have very limited powers under the Indian Act governance mentality. From an economics perspective, the government is very hierarchal, so there are a lot of challenges, time limitations, and approvals required. The absence of functioning in the actual pace of business is Indian Act economics.

Indian Act economics is the removal of the ability to make decisions without federal approval. The Indian Act controls land management, financial interests, and decision-making, limiting economic development opportunities. Today, many Nations across Canada have developed custom laws to regain jurisdiction and authority by developing their own processes in response to the Indian Act.

Fundamental to Indian Act economics is the Indigenous dependency model that it creates. This model establishes conditions of dependency on government services, severe program underfunding, restrictive timelines, and externalized decision-making. Social and economic dependency is a core feature and outcome of Indian Act economics. The opposite of Indian Act Economics is the empowerment of Indigenous Nations to be self-determining.

This is the Indian Act economics fallacy—the absence of the core functions of the economy, business moving at the pace of the Indian Act, the obsession with the cost of the Indigenous relationship, the lack of Indigenous economic data, and the absence of belonging. Indian Act economics is where they'll have us believe that Indigenous Peoples are a cost to the system or a fiscal burden. Indian Act economics will have us all believe it has no alternative and is too difficult to change.

In an interview with Indigenous business leader Rose Paul, she describes the foundation of Indian Act economics: "It is a well known, albeit old story, that the bureaucratic processes and legal constraints within the Indian Act have created barriers to economic development initiatives and infrastructure projects." Rose articulates that in her work at the regional level in driving the First Nations participation in the regional economy: "Overall, the Indian Act's centralized control and paternalistic approach have been cited as factors contributing to the challenges faced by Indigenous communities in achieving sustainable development and self-determination, and today our intention is to shake things up for the Indigenous economy."

The Indian Act has continuously impacted Indigenous Nations by hindering self-governance, the economic development process, and self-determination. It is important to identify how Indian Act economics shows up in regional development or economic development projects. Rose Paul describes how "the Indian Act shows up in our work in terms of the impacts of dependency—it is there and it is real among our people. It takes a long time to detach themselves from the dependency cycle that has impacted us by the Indian Act."

The Indigenous socioeconomic gap is an expression of the outcomes of imposed systems of dependency through the Indian Act. What is the cost of the outcomes that the Indian Act has created? The Indigenous socioeconomic gap is the actual cost. Unraveling the legal context and its costs is the center of the dismantling of the effects of the Indian Act.

Poverty and Indian Act Economics

The early work of Amartya Sen, a welfare economist and author of *Collective Choice and Social Welfare*, was concerned with what economic activity ought to achieve and criticized much economic analysis for privileging efficiency over equity and justice. With a strong focus on poverty eradication in India, Sen's work centers a narrative that poverty is not just a lack of money or resources; it is grounded in not having the capability to realize one's full potential as a human being. Poverty is the deprivation of opportunity. Deprivation of opportunity is a feature and is the outcome of the Indian Act economics.

Poverty is about not having enough money to meet basic needs, including food, clothing, and shelter. However, poverty is more than just not having enough money. The World Bank Organization describes poverty in this way: "Poverty is hunger. Poverty is lack of shelter. Poverty is being sick and not being able to see a doctor. Poverty is not having access to school and not knowing how to read. Poverty is not having a job, is fear for the future, living one day at a time."[21]

In the rise of the Indigenous economy, Indigenomics posits that the Indigenous economy has grown on unequal footing and should not be valued using the same tools as the mainstream economy. The Indigenous economy does not fit entirely within the parameters of the GDP measurement as these metrics fail to advance the understanding of the process of value creation in the Indigenous economy. The entire scope of the set of outputs in the Indigenous economy is not measurable. The Indigenous economy has a different starting point as it is responding to systematic exclusion, chronic underfunding, inequality, and significant structural barriers over time. The starting point for measuring the Indigenous economy does not start at zero; it is important to understand that Indigenous businesses are subsidizing the shortfall of chronic long term government underfunding that has long been documented in the Canadian relationship with Indigenous Nations across education, child welfare, health, infrastructure, and other realms, including economic development.

Attributes of Indian Act Economics

Foundational to the process of deconstructing Indian Act economics is the question, "How is the Indian Act holding back or slowing development regionally?" The objectives, architecture, and design of the Indian Act are archaic, but it is important to understand the inherent control mechanisms currently utilized and operationalized within it today. Equally important is understanding the impact of Indian Act economics within the national and regional economic landscapes.

An important point of note is that there is no function of economy within the Indian Act. Think about that: that is the formative truth of over 150 years of the Indian Act and its relationship with Indigenous Peoples. There is no function of economy in it, only the conditions of dependency, otherism, isolation, and denialism.

In connection with the current rise of the Indigenous economy, Canada faces an important question, and it is a deciding factor as we struggle as a nation to compete and stay relevant in a rapidly globalized economy: Is the function of Indian Act economics acceptable today in the mainstream economy?

Some of the key features of Indian Act economics include:

1. Facilitating an inadequate investment environment for Indigenous Nations.

2. Perpetuating uncertainty in the business environment about doing business with Indigenous Peoples.

3. Creating an environment and perception of increased risk from the financial institutions resulting in a higher "cost of money."

4. The absence of legal frameworks and institutions to support the economic development process.

5. The absence of property rights or economic/market value for the Indians.

6. "Reserve" status facilitating restrictions on lands creating under-market value.

7. The absence of adequate infrastructure (clean water, internet), including chronic underfunding for housing on reserve.

8. Poor reserve location/land quality where the absence or minimalization of land value and poor location selection is not conducive to economic activity.

9. Dividing populations of Indigenous Peoples as "on" or "off reserve" with federal responsibility only established for on-reserve populations, which perpetuates the socioeconomic gap.

10. Externalizing decision-making to the minister is inefficient, unreasonable, and archaic.

11. Facilitating the slow pace of business, including establishing unreasonable timelines not in line with the actual pace of business for partnership, investment, and project development for Indigenous Nations, further isolating Nations from investment opportunities.

12. Creating missed economic opportunities through externalized and inefficient decision-making processes.

13. Facilitating both insufficiencies and "undervaluing" in the process of the management of "Indian moneys" and "Indian lands."

14. Ensuring the absence of the function of "commerce" and financial modelling as seen in the mainstream economy.

15. The absence of time value/future value of money through the treaty annuities payment to Indigenous Peoples.

16. Removing the function and responsibility of the contractual obligations of upholding the original treaties.

17. The absence of business agency and authority within Indigenous Nations, creating the conditions of dependency.

18. The lack of structures/institutions for Indigenous economic value creation.
19. The absence of Indigenous economic data.
20. The lack of system efficiency to facilitate Indigenous economic growth and participation.
21. The lack of alignment with the UNDRIP.

The complexity and tension of administering the Indian Act and its continuous need to control the Indians and manage the absence of the process for Indigenous economic value creation are foundational to the complexity of Indigenous relationship.

Indian Act Economics in Action

There are many real-world examples that demonstrate the Indian Act economics in action. The first is the historical, high-conflict legal case of the Musqueam Band land lease.

A *Golf Business* magazine article describes the Shaughnessy Golf Club leasehold on Musqueam reserve lands in Vancouver.[22] The Shaughnessy Golf Club is described as a "coveted asset" located on a lush 160-acre parcel of waterfront property near Vancouver. The club is described as a national golfing treasure and is the four-time host of the Canadian Open and the fifteenth-ranked course on the country's top 100 list. The article describes that "the private facility sits on native land leased to the club until 2032, and the Musqueam Band that lays ancestral claim to the land seems determined to unlock its billion-dollar potential."

Of historical significance, the golf club was moved to accommodate the expansion of the city of Vancouver. The 1950s version of the Indian Act allowed for the lands to be extracted from the Nation as well as the below-market value leasehold on the Musqueam reserve land. The reserve land seizure was an expression of the concept of Indian Act economics.

In the 1950s Indian bands were not allowed to sign any leases, so the federal government negotiated on behalf of the Musqueam people. Through the structure of the Indian Act, the band surrendered the parcel of land and entered into a 75-year lease that restricted land use exclusively to golfing. While it was legal at the time, it planted the seeds for future litigation that would burden Shaughnessy's bottom line and strain its relationship with the Band.[23]

The reserve lands that the golf club is situated on were forced into a leasehold under market value by the federal government through the Indian Act provisions. After the lands were forcibly surrendered, and upon testing the current leasehold value, this value was essentially diminished by the Supreme Court. This is Indian Act economics in action—land value exists for everyone except the Indians. The market value of lands is not for the Indians. Indians are not allowed to set current market value. Value creation does not exist for the Indian. This is Indian Act economics activated across time. It upholds and further perpetuates the narrative that it is risky to do business with Indians.

In this example of Indian Act economics in action, the initial legal challenge came into play in 1984. At this time, the federal government was ordered to pay the Musqueam Band $10 million as compensation for the unfavorable terms of the original lease value. The article describes that:

> Shaughnessy Golf Club began paying its property tax directly to the Band—an amount that today approaches $800,000 a year. Lawyers for Musqueam Nation argued that the property tax should be paid on the land's potential value as a residential development, not as a golf facility. With the average detached home in Vancouver now worth more than a million dollars, this re-assessment would have been a crippling blow to the club and its 1,700 members.[24]

The intricacies of Indian Act economics come into play only in the complexity of the tension between the denial of land value for the Indians and land value for golf clubs.

The next example, also on the same reserve lands in Musqueam, further demonstrates Indian Act economics and how it is activated. A historical Windspeaker article, "Supreme Court Slashes Rent on Musqueam Land," describes a ruling in favor of non-Natives holding ninety-nine-year leases on forty prime acres belonging to the Musqueam band.[25] The article notes that "Chief Stewart Phillip, president of the Union of BC Indian Chiefs

complains the court is valuing Indian land at half the value of the land ad-
joining their reserve. Systemic racism runs deep and is firmly entrenched in
the parliamentary and judicial system of Canada." The article further provides several key contextual points describing Indian reserve land value.

The Supreme Court of Canada case turned on the meaning of current land value of an Indian reserve. In a 5–4 decision, the court set
aside the Federal Court of Appeal decision that set annual lease payments at an average $22,800. It put them back to $10,000 a lot, the
same as the trial division set in 1997.

In the context of the absence of land value on the Indian reserve, that
article notes:

The lower court had ruled that the market value of land under
long-term leases on an Indian reserve is lower than fee simple land
off-reserve. Lots off-reserve were valued in the $600,000 range, but
the court made a deduction of 50 per cent for the land in Musqueam
Park. The band was joined by Department of Indian and Northern
Affairs in appealing that decision to the Federal Court of Appeal because the department's process of setting rents was challenged and
this could affect other leases it holds.

In this highly visible and controversial legal process, the appeal court
overturned the lower court and appraised the land as if it were fee simple
land with an appraised value of $600,000 per lot. It did not discount the
land value because of any Indian reserve features, but it did deduct servicing
costs of about $120,000 per lot. It set rents on the lots at $18,400 to $26,400
annually. This is Indian Act economics in action.

The specific dynamics in the unfoldment of the Musqueam leasehold
situation is an example of Indian Act economics in action. Key lines of inquiry stemming from the foundational operations of Indian Act economics
include asking why this had to go to the Supreme Court. If this happened on
non-reserve lands, what would the process be? Why the distinction here?
What is particularly alarming in this example is the inability of the Nation

to decide leasehold value, the original miscalculation of land value with "reserve status," the removal of economic value systematically, and the harm to Indigenous business relationships or partnership development.

In this context, it is important to understand that the federal government, through the Indian Act, has a fiscal responsibility to the Nation. It is important to build an understanding of the situation of the Musqueam reserve leasehold in the context of Indian Act economics in action. Essentially, residents were getting the leaseholds for dirt cheap on Musqueam Band lands until a lawyer noted, "You guys should be making a lot more money." So, the Nation increased the price, and the leasehold people began to shout that it was unfair. All of a sudden, these people, these Canadians, who lived on the Musqueam reserve on the leasehold lands, learned very quickly what the Indian Act was about.

Of particular importance here is to remember that the federal government holds fiscal responsibility, by their own authority, as a parental caretaker of "Indian moneys." The court found that the federal government had failed to exercise its fiduciary responsibility. The federal government should have been actively appraising and advising the Band that the leases were under market value and that they could get more money.

In this example of Indian Act economics, the court ruling said the Musqueam Nation should be able to charge more, but it doesn't have to be the same as market rates because it is an Indian Band. So, the leasehold rates went up but not to the actual market value. This is an example of how Indian Act economics is perpetuated throughout time, from the beginning of the reserve to the 1950s amendments right up until today. A core operational premise of Indian Act economics is that Indian land is worth less. Deconstructing Indigenous land value is deconstructing Indian Act economics.

This is just one example of one Nation. Yet the clear demonstration of the structured system for devaluing land through the reserve status and the mismanagement of facilitating "land values" through imposed federal fiduciary duty are key features of Indian Act economics. Breaking the cycle of economic dependence must be founded on the deconstruction of federal fiduciary duty through actual accountability and transparency.

The third example that brings Indian Act economics into visibility in the Canadian legal, policy, and economic landscape is through treaty annuities.

A treaty annuity is the requirement for payments made to First Nations to honor the original obligations set out in the historical treaties that shaped the development of Canada. The treaties provided for an annual cash payment, ordinarily distributed at treaty events or by individual check as well as other key provisions. The legal case has shone a spotlight on the development of the historical treaties that shaped Canada. The annual payments were often added to treaties to sweeten the deal as Britain, and later Canada, pursued access to Indigenous lands for white settlers and resource development.[26]

This is a shining example of the function, structure, and outcomes of Indian Act economics as viewed through the Robinson Huron Treaty annuities legal challenge. In the Canadian media narrative, a *SooToday* article, "Done Deal: $10-billion Robinson Huron Treaty Settlement Finalized,"[27] outlines the inherent nature of the complexities of the mismanagement of the federal fiduciary duty and the lack of oversight of financial value across time for the Indian. The uncomfortable truth of Indian Act economics is that the future value of money and the function of inflation exist for everyone except the Indians.

The article describes how "the multi-billion dollar settlement provides past compensation to treaty beneficiaries after not seeing an increase to annuity payments for a period of over 150 years, as wealth generated in the territory through resource revenues from the mining, forestry and fishing sectors continued to grow." The article further articulates that "annual treaty payments to the Anishinaabe beneficiaries have remained capped at $4 per person since 1875. In 2018, the Supreme Court of Canada ruled the Crown had an obligation under the 1850 treaty to increase annuities as wealth generated from the land grew over time, so long as the Crown can do so without incurring a loss." This is Indian Act economics in motion. The absence of accounting for the future value of money is foundational to Indian Act economics. A key inquiry to reflect on is who says the future value of money does not apply to the Indians. It is also important to keep in mind that this is the settlement value—not the actual value as accounted for as loss over time.

The article "First Nations Seek to Raise Canada's Rent After 150 Years of $4 Payments" describes the financial significance of breaking the original treaties.[28] These examples serve to test the concepts of fiduciary duty and systemic denial of economic value through the Indian Act. The article describes the experience of the paltry sum over time and the extracted value in the resource-rich lands of Canada. The original treaty instructs that any increase in the annuity "shall not exceed the sum of 1-pound provincial currency in any one year, or such further sum as Her Majesty may be graciously pleased to order." Her Majesty did not graciously order. This provides a clear insight into the function of Indian Act economics.

The article frames the narrative of the court process in this paraphrased perspective: "Here's what I'll do. I'll offer you this annuity, and if the territory produces more revenue for the crown, the annuity will be increased accordingly," said Mike Restoule, one of the representative plaintiffs in the case. More than a century later, the annuity remained unchanged despite petitions and appeals from the Nations. "They're still today paying that $4 a year to each individual from the First Nations despite the fact that trillions of dollars have been gained from the territory for the Crown and for corporations," says Restoule, pointing to the significant revenues from mining, forestry, and other resource development that has been carried out on the lands. This example clearly demonstrates the upholding of the process of Indian Act economics through the absence and denial of value creation.

The original monetary values of the historical treaty annuities are starting to be challenged and tested in court. Since the establishment of the annuities, there has been no movement to establish modern-day value by the Crown, even though it holds fiduciary duty or the "honor of the Crown." Again, breaking the cycle of economic dependence must be grounded on the core inquiry of federal fiduciary duty and accountability to the honor of the Crown. Complacency, the status quo, and inaction perpetuate the inherited bias of Indian "value."

Racism and exclusion have been systematically structured into the Canadian economic field of finance, commerce, investment, value, and assets through Indian Act economics. Every possible card has been stacked against Indigenous Peoples to participate in the Indigenous economy from the beginning of Canada until today. Yet, Indigenous Peoples are creating the space at the economic table and excelling in rapidly growing economic participation, businesses, partnerships, and investments. What happens in the courtroom as Indigenous Peoples are challenging the structures and outcomes of Indian Act economics is expressed in the economic realm of Canada.

These examples of Indian Act economics in action articulate the experience from the Indigenomics perspective: The future value of money is calculated for everyone but the Indians. The denial of economical value through "You can't have" facilitates a culture of denialism, isolation, dependency, and financial diminishment that is foundational to the process and outcomes of Indian Act economics.

It is important to highlight the culture of economic denialism within the Indian Act. The built-in structure of denialism can be viewed through the absence of the function of commerce and the denial of economic value-creation process. This is the inheritance of the legacy of the Indian Act and is the foundation of Indian Act economics. If you live in one of the regions of historical treaties, you are living within Canada's failed obligation and absence of "honor of the Crown."

The process of dismantling Indian Act economics and calling the Canadian government into accountability continues in this example of Canada's failure to uphold its treaty obligations. In another region of the country, a CBC article, "Saskatchewan Chief Files Class Action Lawsuit Over $5 Annuity Payments Signed 150 Years Ago," describes a lawsuit alleging that Ottawa has not kept its end of the bargain over annuity payments after signing Treaty 4 in 1874.[29] The Chief of Zagime Anishinabek, home to several First Nations in southeastern Saskatchewan in the Treaty 4 region, filed a proposed class action lawsuit against the federal government. The article articulates further that:

In 1874, Canada signed the Treaty 4 with various Saulteaux, Cree and other First Nations in the Fort Qu'Appelle area of Saskatchewan. It allowed the Crown to use and occupy 195,000 square kilometers of land in what's now south eastern Alberta, southern Saskatchewan and west-central Manitoba. In exchange, the federal government was to set aside land for reserves and pay $750 per year in powder, shot and twine. It was also to provide a school, various tools and supplies. And it was to pay an annuity of $5 per year to each man, woman and child.

The absence of Canada meeting its treaty and fiscal obligations, and denying the function of time value for money while holding the fiduciary duty on behalf of Nations and through the honor of the Crown are coming into the light. Indigenous Peoples' financial and economic interests have been held hostage in the structure of Indian Act economics. While acknowledging that the federal government holds the self-imposed fiduciary duty to act in the best interest of the Indians, an important question to enter into Canadian reality is: Would you want to be in this financial adviser relationship?

In these examples of Indigenous leadership testing the structure of "time value for money" as a core function of commerce and economy, let's suppose each of the historical treaties were to launch legal cases and achieved outcomes similar to the amount of the $10 billion marker of the Robinson Huron settlement value with Canada. That is potentially over a $100 billion payout, which is only the settlement value, not the actual value withheld from the Indians from the beginning of Canada and treaties until now. A core question to consider here is to wonder how to what extent has economic value been denied to Indigenous Peoples through the absence of upholding the treaties. This is the deconstruction of Indian Act economics.

Indian Act economics is failing Canada. Not upholding the original treaties of these lands has failed the concepts of commerce, finance, business, and economy. The future value of money exists for everyone except the Indians, which is the truth of Indian Act economics and the height of colonial shenanigans. The dominant economic narrative of Indian Act economics is of value stagnation, value isolation, and the absence of economic value for the Indians. This is the story of Indian Act economics.

Yet this story is continuously unfolding and testing the Indian Act's complacency. Another significant development is the Manitoba First Nation suing the federal government, alleging unchanged $5 annuity payments violate the treaty. Thirty-six Treaty 5 First Nations sought a class action status in a suit against Ottawa. In a different region, a *Global News* article articulates a similar story where "14 First Nations receive $37 million after federal minister settles treaty salaries claims."[30]

These stories demonstrate how economic value has been systematically denied to Indigenous Peoples. But what exactly is the federal government's fiduciary duty in the Indigenous relationship? What is the honor of the Crown regarding the Indigenous relationship? Canadians deserve better than Indian Act economics. The stagnation and denial of economic value for the Indian are the causes of the Indigenous socioeconomic gap.

The Lake Manitoba and Fisher River First Nations have also brought class action lawsuits against the federal government, seeking compensation for annual treaty annuity payments that have not kept pace with 150 years' worth of inflation, among other damages. These class actions in Treaties 2 and 5 cover large swathes of land in eastern Saskatchewan, Manitoba, and northwestern Ontario.

These legal cases highlight the original treaty agreements that have shaped the Canadian economic reality of prosperity "for which, settler society and Canada received enormous benefits—incalculable benefits—in terms of access to this enormous and rich-in-natural-resources country that that we call Canada."[31]

The facilitation of the absence of economic value creation and fiduciary duty are all up for discussion in the depiction of the honor of the Crown here. Through the specific wording of the treaties, the Crown committed: the annuities would continue in perpetuity "while the water flows and the sun rises ... for your children, grandchildren, and children unborn." This is Indigenomics in action—this is values from an Indigenous worldview, steeped in responsibility across time. This is Indigenous futurism. Indigenous economic purchasing power is the narrative shift of Indigenous economic growth. Of note here, in referring to the original treaties:

> "These are and were very much to Canada's benefit—permanent agreements without an expiry date," says Faille. "They were intended to last forever. I don't think anyone can seriously challenge that. There is "no possible way," he says, that the parties intended to agree to an annuity payment that gradually depreciated until it was "basically worthless. There's just no possible way in which that was the intention of either the Crown or the Indigenous parties."[32]

In the ongoing process of holding the federal government accountable for the short fallings of Indian Act economics:

> The First Nations are seeking class action certification, liquidated damages of the difference between annuities paid and the annuities adjusted for purchasing power and special damages for the "improper

or wrongful withholding of money, due, or an allowance for the loss of opportunity to invest the amount." They also seek a declaration that the Crown breached and continues to breach treaties 1 and 2, among other relief.[33]

It is estimated that approximately 580,000 Indigenous Peoples were eligible to collect annuities stemming from the treaties signed between 1850 and 1921. For many, the meagre payment amount symbolizes the economic undermining of the Crown's fiscal duty to Indigenous Peoples and the absence of the honor of the Crown.

The series of legal cases cite the billions of dollars of natural resources extracted that have never been aligned with the obligations of the original treaties of this country. The push for retroactive payments and increased annuities in the future are shaping a new meaning of Indigenous economic value today. This space for taking full account of natural resource profits across time is directly connected to the settlement value of compensation amounts in these broken treaties and the Indian Act serving its own interests to supersede the original treaties.

"It's time for us to get justice on this. Industries, the Crown and other people have gotten very wealthy from the territory—everyone except the First Nations people. The First Nations people today continue to live in poverty in their very wealthy land."[34]

The Canadian legal landscape is chaotic and filled with the pressures of Indigenous continued existence, rights, and injustice. The evolution of Indigenous legal rights, with all the complexities stemming from the historical baggage of Canada's formative relationship, is shaping the rise of Indigenous economic power today. The winds of economic justice are shifting.

Indian Act economics is the over-representation of a Eurocentric worldview. Indigenomics is the process of unlocking economic value through how it has been denied to Indigenous Peoples through the processes of colonialism and economic isolation. In an example of Indian Act economics in motion, the government will have us all believe that there are only two types of land title—Crown and fee simple. That was true until the Tsilhqot'in title case win, which was a historic case securing the modern space of Indigenous title across a vast track of Tsilhqot'in territory in BC. Another significant legal win was the Nuu-chah-nulth Nation winning the right to fish commercially. By upholding the structure of Indian Act economics, the government will have us believing that the Indians cannot participate in modern commerce and exchange fish for money.

Indian Act economics is the denial of access to economic opportunity. The Indigenous socioeconomic gap is the inheritance of Victorian-era archaic thinking operating in modern Canada. The Indigenous socioeconomic gap is the effects and measurements of this denialism. Indian Act economics is the economics of inequality. It is managing rising costs instead of investing in solutions to the structural problems of economic isolation and displacement.

In an interview with legal expert Bill Gallagher, he reflects on the meaning of the shift away from Indian Act economics toward Indigenous recognition.

The federal government are the gatekeepers. But today, in the resources sector right across this country, no matter what premier is calling the shots, the final say on access to resources will be from Indigenous Nations. While Indigenous Peoples do not have a legal veto, they sure have a de facto veto. Even right-wing commentators who have come to that point of view reluctantly admit that, yes, Nations don't have a veto, but they can definitely stop a project. First Nations have the power to stop major projects. That is the truth in this country.

The deconstruction of Indian Act economics must happen on several fronts. These examples above serve as pivotal moments in this dismantling. While plenty has been written on the amendments of the clauses of the Indian Act over time, seeing these pivotal moments through the lens of Indian Act economics is an important exercise.

An important question in reflecting on the rise of Indigenous economic power today is: What is the true cost of the missed economic opportunity that has been continuously activated through Indian Act economics over time?

Moving Away from the Indian Act

The process of moving away from the Indian Act is long and complex. It establishes an important perspective on its impacts, processes, and limitations over time. As the CEO of the Bayside Development Corporation, which is the business arm of Paqtnkek Mi'kmaw Nation in Nova Scotia, Rose Paul states that, "in terms of our recovery process from the Indian Act, we have developed our own laws around protecting the environment. We've slowly removed some of the layers of the Indian Act that have hindered our processes, and while we still keep pieces in there and utilize those to the best of our ability." The process of moving away from Indian Act economics and toward a clear pathway for economic self-determination is outlined by the First Nations RoadMap. This pivotal Indigenous economic document contributes to the pathway toward effective modern business development rooted in building economic self-determination outcomes. The First Nations RoadMap series is a crucial entry into Canadian policy, fiscal, and economic reality activated by the First Nations Fiscal Management Act (FMA). The RoadMap outlines how to move away from the Indian Act by providing key insights into what is impeding growth and economic activities. The RoadMap identifies how:

> The Indian Act has created a poor investment environment for First Nation communities. The Indian Act has created and perpetuates an environment of uncertainty without adequate legal frameworks, property rights, infrastructure or rule of law. The Indian Act is not an environment for economic development. It is a desert.[35]

This is an essential understanding within the Canadian experience of the Indian Act and a powerful statement of the effects of Indian Act economics—the Indian Act is not an environment for economic development. It is a desert. The series of reports refers to "Indian Act economics as a failed system and no level of government is satisfied with this status quo. It traps First Nation governments in poverty and segregates them from the financial systems that underpin the rest of the national economy."[36]

This is about creating new optional paths for First Nations as they move from managing poverty to generating wealth. It's an Indigenous-led plan for achieving economic prosperity and self-determination for First Nations while reducing risk for Canada.

Cadmus Delorme describes the process of this return of Indigenous Peoples to the economic table of this country: "We were systematically denied a place at the economic table, but piece by piece, we are creating the pathway for our return and our belonging. We belong at the equity level. We belong on the best return on investment on all of our lands and our territories." While Delorme powerfully captures the essence of Indigenous economic belonging, the reference to return on investment on our lands and territories is steeped in upholding the Indigenous worldview and our inherent responsibilities. We belong at the equity level. This is Indigenomics.

Reflective Questions

1. What are the top three insights that stand out for you in learning about Indian Act economics?

2. What does the following statement mean to you: "The Indian Act is not an environment for economic development. It is a desert."

3. What does the statement "We belong at the equity level" mean to you?

4. What does "honor of the Crown" mean regarding the Indigenous relationship?

3

Indians, Ethics, and Economic Value

The end of belonging is fundamentally a story about power.
—Martin Sandbu, *The Economics of Belonging*

THE LANGUAGE in the Indian Act perpetuates and isolates Indigenous identity from Canadian reality and is a key ethical consideration in the deconstruction of Indian Act economics.

There is no such thing as an Indian. The word "Indian" by definition is a construct of euro-centric racialized otherism: "An Indian is a creation of the European imagination and is legally inscribed on us by the federal government. There were no Indians in Canada prior to European arrival. There are only Indians in contemporary terms if we let the federal government take control of our identity." [37]

There is a considerable body of work on understanding the relationship between ethics and governance. Ethics is commonly described as the standards of right or wrong that specify what people should do in terms of rights, obligations, fairness, and equality in a society or community. Ethics refers to moral beliefs and conduct and ensures that institutions work to set standards based on equality, inclusion, and fairness.

An ethical lens is a metaphorical framework or perspective through which ethical decisions can be viewed. It reflects a set of principles, values, and beliefs that guide understanding of right or wrong or describe moral dilemmas and provide guideposts to make decisions. Different ethical lenses may emphasize various aspects, such as the consequences of actions, duties, policies, or rights. Understanding and applying an ethical lens can help to navigate complex moral issues and contribute to a thoughtful and principled approach to decision-making and governance. As such, "economic ethics attempts to incorporate morality and cultural value qualities to account for the limitation of economics, which is that human decision-making is not restricted to rationality."[38]

In his early work, sociologist Raymond Baumhart asked a targeted business audience the question, "What does ethics mean to you?" Some of the common responses included, "Ethics has to do with what is right or wrong, or being ethical means doing what the law requires, or ethics consists of the standards of behavior our society accepts."[39] Baumhart's work brings into focus the role of ethics and society.

Ethics exists outside of religious, cultural, and political orientation. It is an important distinction that being ethical is not the same as doing "whatever society accepts." Standards of behavior in society can deviate from what is ethical as "being ethical is also not the same as following the law. The law often incorporates ethical standards to which most citizens subscribe. But laws, like feelings, can also deviate from what is ethical."[40] This is a formative point in framing ethics—law can deviate from what is ethical, and this is an essential consideration in the deconstruction of Indian Act economics.

The Markkula Center for Applied Ethics describes a series of ethical lenses in the "Framework for Ethical Decision Making."[41]

The Rights Lens: Examines which options best respect the rights of all who have a stake. In applying an ethical lens, a core question is whether the Indian Act respects Indigenous rights. The answer is no.

The Justice Lens: Examines which options treat people fairly, giving them what they are due. In applying an ethical lens, a core question to examine is whether the Indian Act is just and treats Indigenous Peoples fairly. The answer is no.

The Utilitarian Lens: Examines which options will produce the most good and do the least harm for as many stakeholders as possible. Does the Indian Act produce the most good and do the least harm? No.

The Common Good Lens: Examines which option best serves the good of the whole, not just some members. Does the Indian Act serve the common good? No.

The Virtue Lens: Examines which options support positive personal agency. Does the Indian Act serve personal agency? No, it removes it.

The Care Ethics Lens: Examines which options take into account the relationships, concerns, and experiences of all stakeholders or citizens. Was the Indian Act built to consider the concerns and experiences of Indigenous Peoples? No.

Each of these applied ethical lenses can be viewed through the ongoing administration of the Indian Act over time and brings into focus the need to situate the ethical space of the Indian Act today. These lenses focus attention on how we look at Indigenous policy and governance. Does the Indian Act create respect and fairness, support the most good, serve and support agency and concern for all, as considerations of ethics? The answer is no.

The work of Beauchamp and Childress on ethics describes "the core ethical principles of beneficence (do good), non-maleficence (do no harm), autonomy (control by the individual), and justice (fairness)."[42]

In the context of the Indian Act, the concepts of do good, do no harm, self-determination, and justice are brought into focus. Turning the ethical lens onto the Indian Act is critical in deconstructing Indian Act economics. The Indian Act was a formative policy in the establishment of Canada and has always been regarded as highly contentious for its genocidal undertones. Specifically, the Assembly of First Nations describes it as a form of apartheid.[43] While Amnesty International, the United Nations, and the Canadian Human Rights Commission have continually criticized it as a human rights abuse.

It is time to bring the ethical space of the administration of Indian Act economics out into the open, and in doing so, there are fundamental questions in applying an ethical lens to it today. Is the Indian Act ethical? Does the Indian Act cause good? Does it do no harm? Does it create control by the individual and group or establish the foundation of fairness and equality? If any of these answers are no, it lends the question: What leadership is required to advance an ethical pathway for Canada regarding the Indian Act and the modern Indigenous relationship?

In a series of interviews, Indigenous political and business leaders frame a critical perspective of the ethical lens of the Indian Act. Rose Paul, CEO of the Bayside Development Corporation, upon being asked the question, "Is the Indian Act ethical?" responds:

> The Indian Act has always been unethical—the way the treatment has been to Indigenous Peoples, how it has hindered our people for centuries. It is still unethical because the practice of the Indian Act still hinders the development processes in the community. It is paternalistic, and it was created to cause a lot of division in our people and was created to set us up for failure and assimilation so we would no longer exist as people.

Kim Baird responds from her perspective to the question, "Is the Indian Act ethical?"

> The Indian Act has never been ethical, and it has changed form very little since its creation. It was structured as a kind of limited municipal style governance framework and forced onto Indigenous communities across all of Canada. It is a very poor governance framework with poor jurisdiction tools. There's nothing about it that is great.

As past Chief, she describes the night before the Tsawwassen Nation signed the treaty and the Nation officially emerged from underneath the Indian Act to follow the community's cultural ways.

> The night before we signed the modern treaty for our Nation, we had a ceremony that an Elder convened where he identified some culturally important work. It was a significant moment to ensure that we as people are moving forward from this moment in a cultural and ceremonial way. He had instructed us to wrap a copy of the Indian Act in a cedar container and to place it in a ceremonial fire, and we did as we were instructed, but it just wouldn't burn, it just sat there in the fire. Some of the interpretations from the Elder was that it was rejected from the other side because the ancestors didn't want to

accept it because of its dark history. It was a very powerful moment underscoring the point of the treaty, which was to reset our relationship with Canada. The copy of the Indian Act we had placed in the fire in a bone-dry wrapping literally wouldn't burn. The Elder had to communicate our intention and how we were trying to make it right before it would ignite. It was a powerful reminder of how the Indian Act was such a destructive force to our reality, and the feeling I got from the experience symbolically was that it was too wet from all of our collective tears so it wouldn't burn.

Past Chief Cadmus Delorme also responds to the question, "Is the Indian Act ethical?"

No, absolutely not. It is not ethical. An example of how it is unethical is from 1982, when Canada created the Charter of Rights and Freedom, which came with the new constitution. At that time, Canada was obligated to assess all the legislation to make sure it aligned with the Charter of Rights and Freedom and realized that the Indian Act was gender biased and required a significant change in how an Indigenous person is defined.

Delorme further identifies the complexity between Indigenous identity, rights, and the constitution and continues:

Another way the Indian Act is unethical is through the management of "Indian" money. When a Nation rents land and gets a permit and they collect that dollar, the check is not made to that First Nation. The check is made to Canada. Canada then puts that money in a revenue trust that's held in Ottawa. For a Chief and Council to get this money that is rightfully theirs for renting of their land, they have to write a Council resolution and get it approved through a political motion with a plan on what they're going to spend that money on, and then the government has to agree to it. The Minister has to agree to it, so it's like holding a checking account for a child, and the Nation never gets the benefit of the interest. The Indian Act is set up

so you can't use your own money. You still need your parent to sign
for you. The government is not fiscally caring for that money with the
Nations' interests in mind. This attitude of the oversight of the parent
is entirely unethical.

Delorme offers further insights into the absence of ethics in the Indian
Act:

Last, in the context of on and off reserve, Indigenous Peoples don't
want to be under Section 92 of the Constitution. Canada just put us
there. And so today, there's a huge on- and off-reserve challenge, and
it creates division, which spills into the economic development process because of this unethical practice of how on and off reserve are
treated due to the relationship with Canada and Indigenous Nations.
So yes, the Indian Act is unethical. There are Nations that identify
over 50% or more of their population living off reserve, which is ap-
parent in the socioeconomic gap.

Indigenous business leader Hillary Thatcher contributes to this perspective when asked, "Is the Indian Act ethical?"

No, it's not ethical. The Indian Act was written in 1876, and while it
has had some amendments, it's not enough. This piece of legislation
doesn't align with Canadian values, particularly in a time of reconciliation. Despite the amendments to try and make it better to try
and address some of the racist policies and things that have created the systemic barriers within this legislation, there's still too many
draconian provisions that exist within it. It is causing systemic barriers that continue to operate in this country. And when something
like that just doesn't align with Canadian values, it really needs to be
rethought. At the end of the day, there is no space in the Canadian
context for draconian racist legislation.

Lawyer and strategist Bill Gallagher responds to the question "Is the
Indian Act ethical?" with "No, it's a piece of trash. It's a Victorian nightmare.

It is now being overtaken by the Indigenous legal winning streak. Out of 363 legal wins to date, I don't think there's a single case in there on reserve lands."

Indigenous business leader Wil Jimmy further responds to the question with this perspective:

The Indian Act has never been ethical in its current form. Historically, it's always been the same oppressive piece of legislation that prevents a group of people from participating in the economy. The Indian Act makes Indigenous Peoples dependent, and the Indian Act makes Indigenous Peoples through the reserve system subservient and not sovereign. The Indian Act makes Indigenous Peoples subject to the Crown, not as partners in the vision of Canada as laid out in the original treaties that were signed. You know, our ancestors said we're willing to share the abundance of the lands, and that was the original intent of the Treaty. So, when the treaties were signed by our ancestors, the federal government instead instituted the Indian Act and prevented the implementation of the treaties as they were meant to be from the beginning. This is unethical.

He continues:

The Indian Act has never been ethical; it is racist legislation. It's not ethical. It was obviously built on the attitudes of exclusion. Communities were moved away from the best markets by moving communities 10 to 20 kilometers away from the major centers, from the railways. Plot the location of every reserve to see this. Another example is in the amendments when the Indian Act was changed so that Indians could no longer sell their grain on the open exchange like everybody else— it had to go through the Indian agent. We still have Indian Oil and Gas Canada today. The Indian Act remains what it is today, and it's a reflection of society at the time. It is archaic. The early Indian Act changes ensured the government has the ability to expropriate lands for the development of cities and municipalities without permission from the Indians. If you live in one of these cities, thank an Indian.

What Is the Ethical Response to the Indian Act?

Building a response to the absence of the ethical space of the Indian Act is pivotal in the deconstruction of Indian Act economics. Cadmus Delorme describes this further in the work of Indigenous Nations today.

> It's about utilizing one of our best strengths and that's the greatest of our warriors. These are the ones that bring a peaceful attitude to the business and governance meetings and that we understand how to walk in a Western worldview, but our Indigenous worldview is just as important. It is leaders in those capacities that have been breaking barriers, lifting the negative feelings, and changing the mindset of society that Indigenous Peoples belong at all levels. It's not that Indigenous Peoples lack talent. We have the talent to do all this. We just lacked the resources and institutions to lift us up and to include us.

It is important to build an understanding of the impacts of the Indian Act on the Nations' economic development process. Interview participants were asked how the Indian Act shows up in the economic development process. How this connects to advancing economic outcomes within the Canadian economy is a critical conversation to have right now, particularly in the context of the rise of the Indigenous economy today. Cadmus Delorme responds:

> Predominantly, the Indian Act defines land assets, so Section 21 to 28 of the Indian Act refers specifically to land. In working with Indigenous governing bodies, it is really challenging to talk economics when we're talking about projects on reserve land. First Nations have a very high-risk profile in the financial sector because of these specific sections.

Delorme continues by describing his experience as Chief and the difficulty in moving economic development projects forward within the Indian Act.

> To add further complexity to the economic development process for Nations through the Indian Act, Nations are allowed up to a five-year

period for a Band Council resolution. The Government of Canada will sign it up to a five-year period only, not beyond that time. In that time limitation, no one wants to do business within this restrictive five-year timeframe. Second, it takes eight months to go from idea to getting it signed off from both the Minister of Indigenous Affairs and from the Band Council, whereas with mainstream business, this is usually done in a matter of weeks. This makes the timing really difficult in moving projects forward. This is Indian Act economics.

Hillary Thatcher describes how the Indian Act shows up in the Indigenous economic development process.

With projects on reserve, a really big issue is access to capital on reserves where the Nations don't actually have security as established through the Indian Act. Therefore, they can't leverage any assets in order to access capital. When communities are trying to borrow, they can't secure against assets that are located on the reserve. That shows up in the economic development process because it means that private sector lenders don't want to lend to projects that are located on reserve. And when communities are trying to raise capital so they can invest, maybe they're trying to raise some equity so they can invest in a major project off reserve but they don't have the collateral because their assets are on reserve. They don't have something that they can secure again so that it does cause some challenges.

Thatcher continues to provide a key perspective:

In working with all of the major banks and trying to entice them to take on some of this risk, knowing that First Nations communities do pay back their debts. At some point, the banks need to start having some trust in the Indigenous clients and know that these clients are going to service their debt and on reserve security isn't needed as prescribed through the Indian Act. In fact, many communities now have own-source revenue that they can pledge security against or have trust dollars that are held with the banks that can be pledged.

It's a bit of a scapegoat story now for a lot of the major lenders and is not contributing positively to advancing leverage-ability for Nations.

An essential question in deconstructing Indian Act economics is, "Is the Indian Act holding back development in the region. If so, in what ways?" Cadmus Delorme reflects on this question:

> The Indian Act is not economically friendly, and it is definitely holding back development. The Bank Act of Canada drives economics in this country. The Indian Act supersedes the Bank Act of Canada. That's why there's a clash in the Indian Act legislation and Section 91 of the Constitution. The Indian Act is too powerful for the Bank Act of Canada. The Indian Act ultimately serves to make reserve land status with no business or economic value. The word "value" here must be used cautiously because, as Indigenous Peoples, we value our land in a distinct way, but from a business or economic mindset, it has been structured to have very minimal value and that is the foundation of Indian Act economics.

Canada exists in a profound paradox today in the interplay between the release of power and control of the Indians and the need to adapt to the evolving Indigenous legal and economic environment. This shifting power dynamic focuses on the adapting relationship of shifting jurisdiction, legal rights, and recognition.

In applying the ethical lens, it is also important to describe unethical behavior or actions that go against accepted moral principles or standards. An unethical policy is a set of rules, policies, or regulations that go against accepted principles of morality, fairness, or justice. Unethical policies contribute to harm, discrimination, or violating basic ethical standards and human rights. Unethical policies can manifest in various contexts, including businesses, governments, or organizations, and they may involve issues such as discrimination, exploitation, or disregard for human rights. Identifying and correcting unethical policy requires careful evaluation of its impact on different stakeholders and an alignment with ethical principles to promote fairness, equality, and respect for fundamental rights.

Are Canadians Affected by the Indian Act?

An important contribution to the deconstruction of Indian Act economics is understanding how Canadians are affected. Interview participants were asked the question: "Are Canadians affected by the Indian Act, and if so, how?"

Indigenous business leader Wil Jimmy responds to this question.

Yes, Canadians are absolutely affected by the Indian Act, but they don't know how, and they don't know that they've been affected. An example of this is the Truth and Reconciliation Commission Call to Action, I think 7, to close the education and employment funding gaps. This is primarily for First Nations on reserve to close the employment and economic gap. Through the Indian Act, it purposely distributes less funding to a child that goes to a non-reserve school, but 20% less anyway, 10 to 20% less, and Canadians don't know this. Indian children get less. Do Canadians know about that? No. this also is an aggravating factor in the outcomes of the deployment of the Indian Act over time.

It is time for Canadians to wake up to the effects of the Indian Act. Wil Jimmy describes Indian Act economics in an interview: "There are two different functioning systems. Canadians should care about the Indian Act today because it is racist. Canadians should care about the Indian Act today because it limits opportunities for Indigenous Canadians, which then limits opportunities and outcomes for them." The functioning of two separate systems of economy is a core feature of Indian Act economics.

Hillary Thatcher eloquently describes how Canadians are impacted by the Indian Act:

Yes, Canadians are absolutely affected by the Indian Act. It's just that they don't know that they're affected by the Indian Act. If the Indian Act is preventing the full participation of First Nations in Canada's economy, and if the Indian Act is limiting in any way that participation and the wealth creation and the well-being of Indigenous communities by virtue of these barriers that it puts to that participation,

Canadians are absolutely affected by it but just are not aware of it.

When viewing this as a reflection of the economic breakdown of Indian Act economics, Thatcher describes this further: "When Indigenous communities aren't actively participating in the regional economy and can't generate their own source of revenue and can't invest in their own people, that's a problem because there's going to be reliance on the federal government. But that will never be enough, which is why we see extreme situations of poverty and rising poverty costs." Thatcher articulates further that Indian Act economics create the conditions of dependency.

Rose Paul shares that, "Yes, Canadians are affected by the Indian Act, albeit indirectly. The Indian Act shaped the original relationship between Indigenous Peoples and the Canadian government, influencing policies, resource management, and land use decisions that impacts all Canadians." Some of how Canadians are affected include:

Resource Management: Decisions regarding resource extraction, land use, and environmental protection on Indigenous lands can have implications for the broader Canadian economy and environment.

Legal and Policy Frameworks: The legal and policy frameworks established by the Indian Act contribute to broader discussions and debates surrounding Indigenous rights, reconciliation, and social justice in Canadian society.

Economic Impacts: Economic development opportunities and investment decisions in Indigenous communities can have ripple effects on regional and national economies.

Cultural Awareness and Education: Debates surrounding the Indian Act and its legacy contribute to discussions about Canadian history, identity, and relationships with Indigenous Peoples, shaping public perceptions and attitudes.

Overall, while the direct impacts of the Indian Act may primarily affect Indigenous communities, its broader implications can influence various aspects of Canadian society and governance.

In answering, "Do you think Canadians are affected by the Indian Act, and if so, how?" Cadmus Delorme responds:

Absolutely. We are affected as Canadians and as Indigenous Peoples. We have an untapped market right now of close to $50 billion in contribution to the GDP in this country, which is 1.5 percent of the GDP. Indigenous Peoples are not at parity in this country but could be with investment and partnership. That is the opportunity.

Delorme further describes shaping meaning and reconciliation:

Reconciliation is delayed gratification. Our next generation will feel it, but we may not see all of the results now. It all starts with jurisdiction and policy shifting. When we truly understand reconciliation, we will understand we are going to have two relationships between Indigenous people and the nation. One of them is quasi jurisdictional, and the other one is economics and policy.

"Should Canadians care about the Indian Act today?" is an important question. As Hillary Thatcher notes:

Canadians should care about the Indian Act today because it does not align with Canadian values. It limits the full potential of the First Peoples in this country, and that is not something that Canadians should tolerate today. It lends the question: Do Canadians know what is in the Indian Act? Today, I believe Canadian consciousness has awoken and shifted, and Canadians are caring about these systemic barriers to Indigenous development because they're starting to understand and see the real impacts that residential schools and the Indian Act have had on our people.

Bill Gallagher notes that, in responding to the question of whether Canadians should care about the Indian Act today, "the thing about the Indian Act, it does confirm the colonial guilt trip because it's basically based on South Africa apartheid. Canadians have to realize that Indigenous

Nations have put themselves up in the passenger seat, maybe even in the driver seat, in every region of this country, based on their legal wins."

In centering Indian Act economics in the concept of the absence of belonging, the words of Martin Sandbu resonate: "For those left behind by the economy, this is experienced as losing influence over their own lives."[44] The Indigenous socioeconomic gap can be viewed through this experience of "losing influence over our own lives" as Indigenous Peoples. This is the Indigenous socioeconomic gap—the absence of belonging. This is Indian Act economics.

In unlocking Indigenous economic reconciliation in this country together, we will begin to see a huge shift in our municipal budgets, our provincial budgets, our federal budgets, and in Indigenous governing body relationships. Through increasing the Indigenous GDP, our entire relationship will shift because we all inherited the ignorance to the truth, and the Indian Act mentality is what's holding us back. Once we shift toward investing in Indigenous economic growth, we are going to see a huge shift in our social and economic impact across our country when it comes to the relationship between Indigenous people and Canadians.

Reflective Questions

1. Is the Indian Act ethical from your perspective? Why or why not?
2. What should an ethical response to the Indian Act be today?
3. What do you think that means to "equalize the Indian Act"?

4

The Actual Cost of Doing Nothing

In many parts of the country, there is a realistic appreciation of the enormous challenges still ahead but also a spirit of determination to regain stewardship of Aboriginal economies and to develop them in accordance with the priorities of particular communities and nations.

—Royal Commission on Aboriginal Peoples

T HE CONCEPT of the "cost of doing nothing" refers to the cost of inaction in the Indigenous relationship in Canada. It is multifaceted and has significant impacts on areas such as business, health, education, and the environment. The cost of inaction can be substantial, often exceeding the costs of taking proactive measures.

The cost of doing nothing can be viewed through the lens of the dominant narrative that Indigenous Peoples are a cost on the system or a fiscal burden. In the business and economy realms, this essentially means lost opportunities leading to a competitive disadvantage, increased costs, and establishing the conditions for market failure. In understanding the Indigenous economy as an emerging market, the postponement of necessary and critical investments into infrastructure, clean water, or connectivity leads to significantly higher costs in the future due to inflation, crisis management, and lost opportunity.

The cost of doing nothing is expressed as inaction or the lack of willingness to take action and invest. It is foundational to social and economic inequality by perpetuating cycles of Indigenous poverty and social symptoms. Further, the absence of investment into, or the decline of, adequate infrastructure leads to overall economic inefficiencies. An example of this can be seen in a recent study by the Canadian Council for Public-Private Partnerships that identified that the current estimate of the infrastructure deficit across First Nations communities in Canada to be at $25 billion and possibly even higher than $30 billion.[45]

It is important to understand the early entry of the concept of the cost of doing nothing in the context of the Indigenous relationship in Canada through the Royal Commission on Aboriginal Peoples (RCAP). RCAP was established in 1991 to investigate and propose solutions to the challenges affecting the relationship between Aboriginal Peoples (First Nations, Inuit, and Métis), the Canadian government, and Canadian society. In the 1996 RCAP Report, the Commission tabled five volumes with 6,800 pages and 434 recommendations, which was more in-depth than any other Commission in Canadian history. The Commission proposed an ambitious course for reconciliation and the renewal of the relationship between Canada and Indigenous Peoples, and a twenty-year implementation timeline to close the socioeconomic gap was established, which lapsed in 2016. The "Choice of Paths" section of the report on the status quo describes:

> Canadians face two paths. They may choose the status quo in their relationship with Aboriginal people or they may choose to renew the partnership that began at the time of contact. Status quo has serious financial and human consequences as articulated in the Final Report of the Royal Commission. Partnership will mean significant financial consequences but Aboriginal people and the rest of Canada will have a future of mutual support and equality not enjoyed in centuries.
>
> The current status quo for Aboriginal people is characterized by large economic, education and social gaps. Lower income levels, extreme rates of unemployment, proportionately higher percentage of social problems and under-educated people must be overcome. This gap will continue to grow unless steps are taken to slow down and reverse the increasing discrepancy between Aboriginal and non-Aboriginal people. The growth of Aboriginal education, economic development and business initiatives are essential strategies to changing the status quo.[46]

It is important to understand that while Indigenous Peoples make up just over 5 percent of the total population, the remaining 95 percent are entirely and continuously impacted by the structure of Indian Act economics over time. The cost of doing nothing is reflected in the growing size of the Indigenous socioeconomic gap, which is the foundational measurement of the cost of doing nothing.

The Royal Commission on Aboriginal Peoples specifically identified:

> Ultimately measures to support economic development must reach and benefit individuals, but some of the most important steps to be taken involve the collectivity—for example, regaining Aboriginal control over decisions that affect their economies, regaining greater ownership and control over the traditional land and resource base, building institutions to support economic development, and having non-Aboriginal society honour and respect the spirit and intent of the treaties, including their economic provisions.[47]

How many more years can we afford to go without an actual policy response for Indigenous economic growth and inclusion?

The Commission concluded that the primary Indigenous policy directive for over 150 years has been the wrong approach. The dominant theme presented in the recommendations was that Aboriginal Peoples must have room to exercise their autonomy and structure their solutions. RCAP also presented the specific socioeconomic target of closing the economic gap between Aboriginal Peoples and non-Aboriginal Peoples by 50 percent and improve social conditions in the next 20 years.[48]

In the context of the length of time from the entry of the concept of the *Cost of Doing Nothing* report and the evolving Indigenous relationship in Canada today, a recent *CBC* article notes that "the Canadian government likely owes Indigenous people almost $76 billion for currently filed land claims and lawsuits, recent official reporting says."[49] Further, the article notes that in 2015, Ottawa counted $11 billion in "contingent liabilities," which are potential legal obligations recorded only in cases where the probability of future payment is considered "likely," according to the 2023 public accounts of Canada. The 2023 Fall Economic Statement demonstrated that most of these liabilities—95 percent—stem from Indigenous claims against the Crown.

The following chart (Figure 1) from the economic statement identifies the escalating cost of the process of reconciliation. The figure further articulates that the identified investments have contributed to substantial progress, including the elimination of 143 long-term drinking water advisories in First Nation communities, the conclusion of outstanding child welfare agreements, health care services and homes, the resolution of historical wrongs, and opening pathways to self-determination.

Transfers to Support the Advancement of Reconciliation with Indigenous Peoples

In 2015, the federal government committed to doing the work necessary to meaningfully advance truth and reconciliation with Indigenous peoples. Since then, the federal government has worked to renew its nation-to-nation, government-to-government, and Inuit-Crown relationships. This has required the federal government to change how it works, including making record investments in indigenous communities.

The federal government has invested more than **$185 billion** in indigenous priorities since 2015, representing an annual spending increase of 168 per cent since 2015–2016 (from $11 billion in 2015–16, to more than $30 billion in 2023–24).

Chart A1.1

168 Per Cent Increase in Investments in Indigenous Priorities Since 2015–16

$billions

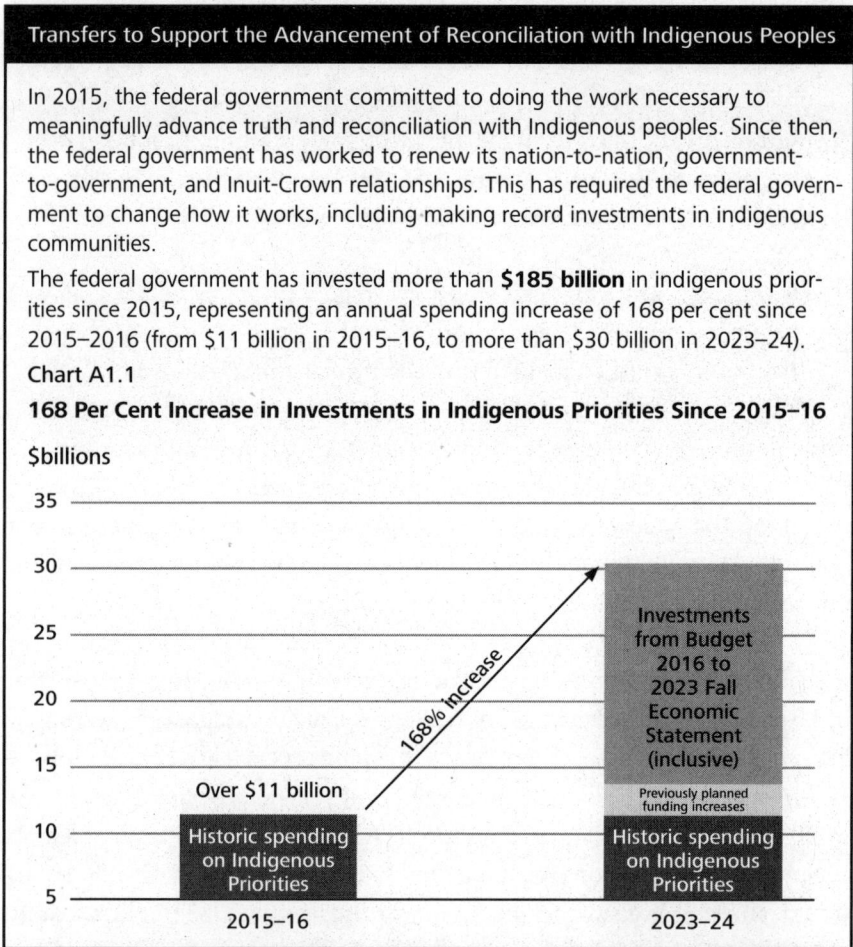

Figure 1: *The escalating cost of reconciliation. Source: Budget Canada, 2023,*
https://www.budget.canada.ca/fes-eea/2023/report-rapport/FES-EEA-2023-en.pdf.

Figure 2 depicts that, in addition to these investments, Canada has ac-knowledged its obligations, with recorded liabilities increasing from $11 billion in 2015–16 to $76 billion in 2022–23, the vast majority of which relate to Indigenous claims.

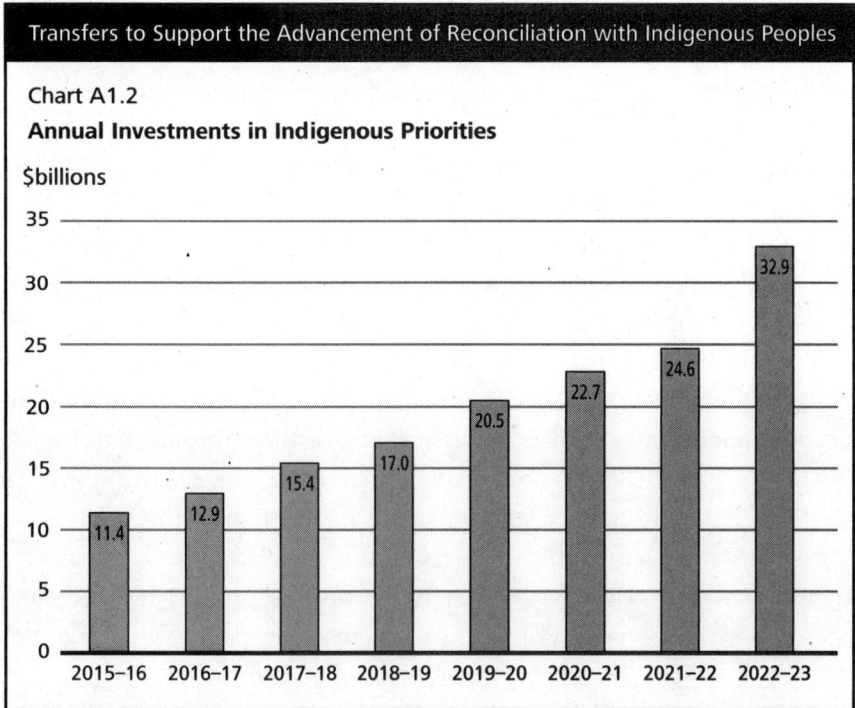

Transfers to Support the Advancement of Reconciliation with Indigenous Peoples

Chart A1.2
Annual Investments in Indigenous Priorities

$billions

Year	Value
2015–16	11.4
2016–17	12.9
2017–18	15.4
2018–19	17.0
2019–20	20.5
2020–21	22.7
2021–22	24.6
2022–23	32.9

Figure 2: *Transfers to support the advancement of reconciliation with Indigenous Peoples. Source: Budget Canada, 2023, https://www.budget.canada.ca/fes-eea/ 2023/report-rapport/FES-EEA-2023-en.pdf.*

Most recently, as reported in the 2022–23 public accounts, the govern-ment recorded approximately $26 billion to resolve past injustices.[50] Minus these expenses, the 2022–23 budgetary deficit would have been roughly $9 billion or 0.3 percent of the GDP. The federal government identified that it would continue its efforts to work with Indigenous partners to resolve litigation and implement negotiated settlements to support reconciliation collaboratively.

Further:

> Contingent liabilities are recorded when lawyers assess a claim and
> conclude the Crown is at least 70 per cent likely to lose in court and
> it has a dollar value on it. So the $76 billion represents not what
> Indigenous people may be owed for all grievances, but Ottawa's best
> guess at how much the Crown stands to lose through existing, credi-
> ble specific claims, comprehensive land claims and lawsuits.[51]

Along with this theme of the escalating cost of doing nothing in the
Indigenous relationship, in a speech at the inaugural 2024 Indigenomics
on BAY STREET forum, Minister Hadju, Minister of Indigenous Services
Canada, described the department as having the fourth-highest expenditures
across all the federal ministries. One of the biggest myths in Canadian fiscal
reality is the myth of the cost of the Indigenous relationship. This myth is
based on the concept that Indigenous Peoples receive free health care and education, among other services, at the cost of Canadians through the absence
of a tax base. Yes, the Indigenous relationship is increasing in cost, but it lacks
the tools, structure, and leadership for closing the impacts that are causing
the socioeconomic gap. The absence of action to create an Indigenous economic foundation also came at a cost that is only beginning to be felt today.

The 1996 Report of the Royal Commission on Aboriginal Peoples
initially estimated "the cost of doing nothing" as the cost of failing to fundamentally change federal government policy toward Aboriginal Peoples,
which was identified at $7.5 billion annually at the time. This figure includ-
ed $5.8 billion in lost productivity and the remainder in increased remedial
costs due to poor health, greater reliance on social services, and similar program expenditures of Indigenous Peoples. Figure 3 visualizes the rising cost
of doing nothing across the 1996 timeframe.

The escalating cost of doing nothing is the visualization of Indian Act
economics.

Figure 4 outlines the business case for the growth and investment in the
Indigenous economy. In contrast, the Indigenous relationship is expressed as
a burden and on the cost side of the equation of this country. Considering the
RCAP report's prediction of the cost of doing nothing, the following graph

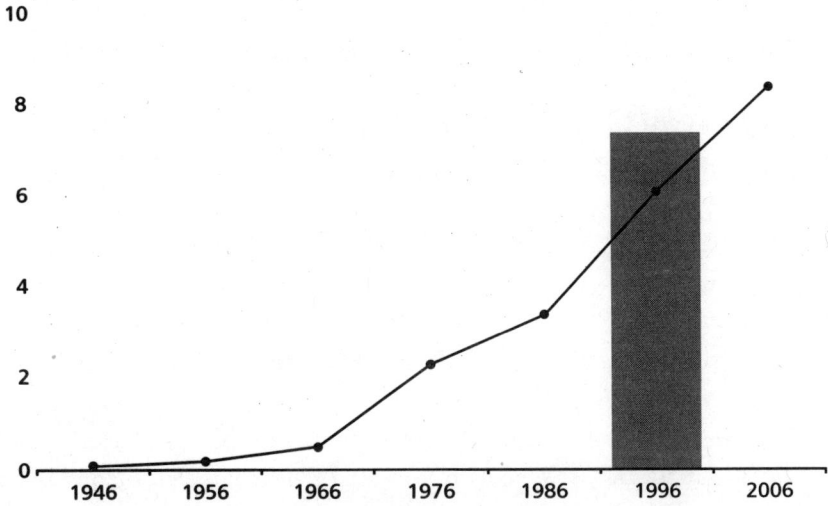

Figure 3: *Federal indigenous spending by Aboriginal Affairs and Northern Development Canada. Source: Indigenomics Institute.*

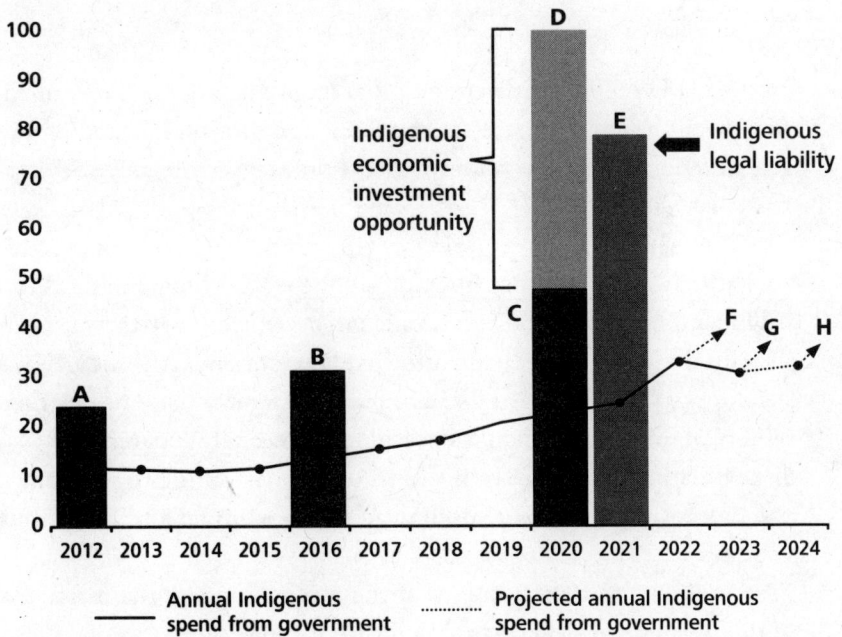

Figure 4: *The business case for Indigenous economic growth (in billions). Source: Indigenomics Institute.*

depicts the tension between the experience of cost as seen through Indian Act economics and the actual rise of Indigenous economic growth.

- Between 2015 and 2021, there was a 114.91 percent increase in federal expenditure for Indigenous priorities.
- By 2026, with $18 billion committed in 2021 over the next five years, the size of Indigenous spend is expected to increase by an additional 7.46 percent.
- This means that the Indigenous spend will be $10 billion larger ($42.5 billion) than the estimated size of the Indigenous economy ($32 billion) in 2016.
- Canada's approach creates a dependency culture; in reality, the Indigenous economy has massive growth potential that is largely untapped and unstructured.

There are several critical aspects when viewing the rise of the Indigenous economy:

- In 2012, a $12 billion Indigenous initial economic value was identified. Significant legal cases have set the foundation for understanding the rise of the Indigenous economy. At this time, approximately 150 legal cases have been won.
- The annual Indigenous economy was identified at $32 billion in 2016.
- In 2019, the Indigenomics Institute led the establishment of the $100 billion annual Indigenous economic target, which made the business case for designing growth, inclusion, and investment in the Indigenous economy. While this was a forward-looking target at the time, the possibility of this achievement is becoming increasingly apparent.
- A key distinction is the Indigenous economic value proposition— the innovative investment space to achieve a $100 billion Indigenous economy.
- Also in 2024, it was reported that the $75 billion was the estimated amount of federal legal costs with Indigenous Peoples.
- Statistics Canada released a report in 2021 identifying the Indigenous economic contribution to the economy at $50 billion.

- In the 2022 federal budget, an $18 billion investment was identified to close the Indigenous socioeconomic gap. While confirmed within the federal budget, there remains no specific plan for closing the Indigenous socioeconomic gap.[52]
- Finally, in 2023, another investment into the Indigenous socioeconomic gap was confirmed within the federal government's annual budget, also without a clear plan on how to close it[53]

Within the context of the concept of the cost of doing nothing, a recent news article demonstrates that the "Assembly of First Nations says $349B is needed to close infrastructure gap by 2030," which outlines the critical case of infrastructure in building and advancing the Indigenous economy.[54] The report identified the need for "$135 billion for housing, $5 billion for digital connectivity and another $209 billion for other infrastructure."

In an interview with Indigenous business leader Wil Jimmy, he further articulates the concept of the cost of doing nothing in the Indigenous relationship with the federal government: "The Indian Act is the cause of poverty for reserve communities in Canada, and that costs everybody. While First Nations face the brunt of that, it is important to understand that the cost of poverty costs everyone. Until we are in a place where we are investing in Indigenous economic and governance capacity, the more we remain in this unsustainable situation as a country."

Deconstructing Indian Act economics reveals the extent to which the Indigenous cost/expense narrative has dominated Canadian political and economic reality. Upon further reflection, understanding the generative nature of Indigenous business is much more relevant to Canada's economic future in terms of sustainability and well-being.

Indigenomics is the process of building the tools, structures, policies, investments, and programs in response to the growth of the Indigenous economy. An example of Indigenous economic designed levers for Indigenous economic growth was included in the 2021 federal budget mandate for the combined investment to establish the National Aboriginal Capital Corporation's Indigenous Growth Fund. The fund was established as a $153M investment fund with anchor investments from the Government of Canada and the Business Development Bank of Canada that will provide improved space for access to capital for the network of Indigenous Financial Institutions and Indigenous small and medium-sized enterprises (SMEs) to be able to overcome some of the systemic barriers they have historically faced. The fund is described as an innovative model that offers institutional and social impact investors a direct vehicle to contribute to economic reconciliation.

Indigenomics is driving a new narrative that moves away from the myth of the Indigenous cost and the socioeconomic gap. Indigenomics serves to advance a strengths-based narrative of Indigenous economic power and identifies how value creation is happening in the rise of the Indigenous economy. The combined processes of deconstructing Indian Act economics and the rise of Indigenous economic power bring the balance sheet and the narrative of "Indigenous cost" into focus. A narrative of Indigenous cost is better framed through the lens of the cost of historical injustice, the absence of inclusion, and all its effects across time, as well as the absence of the honor of the Crown.

Reflective Questions

1. What does modern, constructive, generative Indigenous economic design mean as an approach to the Indigenous economy today?
2. What does the cost of doing nothing mean to you?
3. The Indigenous socioeconomic gap is the cost of doing nothing. Discuss.
4. What is important about measuring Indigenous economic strength instead of the Indigenous socioeconomic gap?

5

The Indigenous Economic Media Narrative

*There is a profound difference between information
and meaning.*

—Warren Bennis

A NARRATIVE IS A STORY that reinforces the ideas, norms, and expectations of a society or culture. It includes the perceptions, myths, stereotypes, biases, and blind spots that weave a way of seeing, understanding, and experiencing the world and our perceptions of it. A narrative is powerful as it can drive how and what we communicate and see and help us make sense of the world by shaping meaning. Narratives are upheld within a dominant society through education, government systems, and public policies. They are often reinforced by upholding the status quo, allowing continued oppressive systems, norms, and policies to remain unquestioned over time. The dominant and inherited narrative in Canada is reflected in the "myth of tolerance" in which Indigenous Peoples are viewed as the beneficiaries of Canadian benevolence. By deconstructing the narrative of Indian Act economics, the rise of Indigenous economic power is addressing this tolerance myth.

While narratives have been used in Canada to perpetuate and justify violence and injustices against Indigenous Peoples over time, the national narrative is changing. This is a response to the efforts of re-storying the violence of the past. National truth-seeking initiatives, such as the Truth and Reconciliation Commission of Canada (TRC), have significantly contributed to Canadians' knowledge about the truth of past human rights violations against Indigenous Peoples across time.

The narrative shift of economic reconciliation has made powerful social change possible. By shifting the negative, outdated, irrelevant, and false dominant perception of Indigenous Peoples, more positive attitudes, behaviors, beliefs, and policies are being replaced. This book intends to address the dominant narrative of Indian Act economics.

> For years, the lives and experiences of Indigenous peoples have often been introduced or described from a negative perspective. This may be well intentioned because the narrative draws attention to the many challenges and incredible needs faced by Native peoples, but this narrative reinforces stereotypes and implies hopelessness. Native peoples are deeply hopeful and have an abundance of cultural knowledge that is positive. A better narrative is one that reclaims the truth of our positive values and relationships.[55]

National and regional media stories are an ongoing thread within the constantly evolving stream of Indigenous business stories. These stories provide insights into the emerging strengths and trends of the modern Indigenous economy.

The concept of Indigenomics was shaped by distributing news stories focusing on Indigenous business success and challenges using the #indigenomics hashtag across social media platforms. This hashtag highlighted the patterns and trends in the growing Indigenous economy and brought into focus the rise of Indigenous economic power.

In an unpublished paper commissioned for the Indigenomics Institute named "Public Perception of the Indigenous Economy: Inserting the $100 billion Indigenous Economy into Canadian Consciousness" by Virginia Carefoote, Master's in Public Policy Candidate 2023. This paper builds upon insights into the Indigenomics approach to framing the national Indigenous economic media narrative. Indigenomics advances a strength-based narrative of Indigenous economic success and empowerment growth. "The establishment of the $100 billion Indigenous economic forward-looking target is counteracting false and antiquated narratives by 're-storying' the past and the future of Canada's Indigenous economy." The Indian Act systematically excluded Indigenous Peoples from the mainstream economy, ensuring dependence on the government. The effects of this over hundreds of years and the shifting relationship dynamic with the government and reconciliation frame the primary narrative of the Indigenous economic relationship. Today, Indigenomics is driving the strengths-based narrative of framing the rise of Indigenous economic power. Indigenomics focuses on how Indigenous Nations are continuously addressing the difficulty of developing economies under the Indian Act through a system that was never intended or designed to accommodate Indigenous economic participation. The following identifies a series of recent examples in the Canadian media that focus on the narrative of the rise of Indigenous economic power.

First, in Vancouver, BC, the rise of Indigenous economic power is demonstrated in an article "MST Development Corporation Is About First Nations Becoming Powerful in Our Territories Once Again."[56] The article describes the expansive land holdings of MST that are spread across the Lower Mainland region and owned by the tri-Nation-owned development corporation comprised of the Musqueam, Squamish, and Tsleil-Waututh Nations. The article identifies the local First Nations as "the richest landowners in the city of Vancouver," as Tsleil-Waututh Chief Leah George-Wilson describes to a Greater Vancouver Board of Trade meeting. What a power shift that even John A. Macdonald would never have seen coming!

A similar media story in a *Western Investor* article titled "First Nations Are Now Elite Vancouver Developers" is also of particular significance.[57] The article outlines that MST owns six prime real estate properties in Metro Vancouver, totaling 160 acres. "The value of our land today, with the holdings that we have is identified at $5 billion," notes MST Development CEO David Negrin. These lands were acquired through federal land dispositions. The advancement of Indigenous justice outcomes is facilitating increasing land access and leveragibility. This demonstrates the activation of the power of the Indigenous Land Back movement.

Another example is the Squamish Nation, one of the three nations that comprise the MST Development Corporation and is a regional economic powerhouse. A media article from *CTV News* titled "Squamish Nation Embarks on Ambitious Plan to Become One of Largest Developers in Canada" explains that the Nation is developing 350 acres of land across several parcels within several municipalities, including North and West Vancouver, Squamish, and along the Sunshine Coast.[58] The article highlights Squamish Nation leader Khelisilem's poignant words: "For a long time, the fight was to get a seat at the table but where we are going now is that we're actually going to be the ones creating the table and inviting others to sit at our table." He continues, "All of these developments require partnerships. We won't be able to do it alone. They all require municipal service agreements, they require financing, they require all kinds of business partnerships for procurement and contracting." This is the strength-based approach of the Indigenous economic development process, which is the requirement for partnership development and investment across the entire supply chain of this country. This is the opportunity.

One of these noted land parcels acquired by the Squamish Nation is named Sen'áḵw. It is identified as the largest First Nations economic development project in Canadian history. It will feature more than 6,000 rental homes in eleven towers with significant advancements in sustainability in its construction and impacts. In a time of a national crisis in housing, it is incredible to witness how First Nations are creating the economic power to lead in this space.

Also, of particular note in the context of the rise of Indigenous economic power is the history of the city of Vancouver and the Sen'áḵw parcel of land. The nation reclaimed this parcel through the court system.

> The B.C. government under Conservative Premier Richard McBride forced the Squamish people to abandon their homes so the city of Vancouver could expand. This was an outcome of the federal government's 1911 amendment to the Indian Act, which made it legal to remove Indigenous People from reserves within an incorporated town or city, without their consent. The residents of Sen'áḵw were given two days to pack up and go. As soon as the Squamish were out, the government burned down their homes.[59]

This is the history of the city of Vancouver. This is the demonstration of Indigenous economic displacement and a shining example of Indian Act economics in action.

Of further significance in this development, beyond its size and scale, is the important point that the project is not identified as reserve lands as established within the Indian Act. Therefore, the Squamish Nation is not obligated to conform to municipal governments' local land use planning process. "These specific lands fall outside of municipal jurisdiction and their use is at the sole discretion of the Squamish Nation and its development corporation—although it will need to develop service agreements with adjacent municipalities as it did with Vancouver as part of the development process."[60]

The third example of how Canadian media stories are demonstrating the narrative of the rise of Indigenous economic power is with the Tsuut'ina Nation in Calgary, Alberta. Taza is a development corporation owned by the Tsuut'ina Nation, which owns a sprawling 1,200-acre development project—one of the largest Indigenous developments in North America. The website states, "The development is divided into three distinct Villages; Taza is a beacon of economic prosperity, entrepreneurial spirit, and a shared vision for the future."[61] The massive Calgary connector development is valued at $4.5 billion.

Tsuut'ina Nation is developing this multi-billion-dollar development along the ring road in Calgary, which is built to connect the city. The project spans over 1,200 acres and will contain 25 million square feet of leasable space. It will be built over twenty years. Chief Whitney describes this development in a *Calgary Herald* article: "Along with the benefits of rent and land development, the real motivation is to allow future generations of people to work and flourish here."[62]

Also relevant to this storyline is that Canderel is one of Canada's largest privately held real estate companies. It partnered with Taza Development Corporation to form the development company, which the Nation hired through the limited partnership of the Tsuut'ina Nation. They are 50/50 partners in the project development. This project spans a variety of sectors, including retail, hospitality, financial, and entertainment venues, and includes an innovation and research campus, office space, health and community facilities, and parklands as well as over 6,000 housing units. It is important to really understand the actual size and scale of this project that will forever change the city of Calgary. This success is in spite of Indian Act economics and is a clear demonstration of the rise of Indigenous economic power.

The fourth example is another groundbreaking recent media headline that reads "Indigenous Economy Generates Billions in Goods and Services

Across Atlantic Region" with the subtitle "Indigenous-owned Businesses Responsible for 5% of Region's GDP." This regional economic report further identified that the Indigenous economy contributed 5 percent of the region's GDP and more than 8 percent of the region's jobs. Putting it in the context of the significance of this growth, the article notes, "This is about twice the size of the impact of the aerospace and defence sector in the Atlantic region." The article continues to note that the Indigenous economy added $3.6 billion to Atlantic Canada's gross domestic product in 2020, according to Bergman's report, including $1.3 billion in Nova Scotia.

To many, this media story might not have had any particular significance. An alternate title of this news article, however, could read "Historical Achievement as Indigenous Regional Economy Reaches Par." As Indigenous Peoples make up close to 5 percent of the entire population, achieving 5 percent of the region's GDP is a significant and historic milestone, with the understanding that all the cards have been stacked over time against Indigenous participation in the economy, and this growth has occurred despite the function of Indian Act economics. Also of note here is that this is in a time when this generation of business leaders are Survivors or have parents who are residential school Survivors. This is the evidence of our time. The winds of economic justice have shifted. We are witnessing the rise of Indigenous economic power. The fire of Indigenous economic resurgence is blazing.

A fifth example is in a *Toronto Star* article titled "Oneida Energy Storage Project Shows True the Commitment to Partnerships with Indigenous Business," which outlines that "the 250-megawatt Oneida Energy Storage Project is set to be a groundbreaking facility on several fronts. Not only is the major resource project expected to be one of the largest energy storage facilities in the world, but it's also noteworthy for its collaborative and inclusive approach as a joint 50:50 venture that's being developed in collaboration with Indigenous partners."[63]

The rise of Indigenous economic power is continuously demonstrated across the Canadian media narrative telling story after story of Indigenous business success through partnership, investment, ownership, and economic reconciliation outcomes.

Reflective Questions

1. What is important about the unfolding media narratives around Indigenous business developments and achievements?
2. What insights can be gained from these media themes?
3. Describe the new story of Indigenous economic success today.

6

An Indigenomics Perspective–Shaping Meaning

Everything can be taken from a man but one thing: the last of the human freedoms—to choose one's attitude in any given set of circumstances, to choose one's own way. When we are no longer able to change a situation, we are challenged to change ourselves.

—Victor Frankl

T HE CONCEPT OF DAYLIGHT SAVINGS time lacks logic. I recollect seeing a social media post that visualizes the logic of daylight savings time from an Indigenous perspective—cutting the bottom off a blanket and sewing it onto the top does not make the blanket longer. It carries no logic. Nor does the concept that a corporation is a person. But in the absence of logic here, further pursuing this line of thinking in the context of Indian Act economics leads to the fundamental question: If the Indian Act was a person, how would it behave?

In deconstructing the concept of daylight savings, it disrupts and manipulates our sense of time and reality. It is a delusion, and a social construct. The Indian Act was a destructive and disruptive force and a primary tool of genocide. It serves as a primary instrument for the dehumanization of Indigenous Peoples. The Indian Act is a social construct serving the illusion of separation and the continued delusion of the absence of belonging in its rigid structure of othering and inequality. It is a hallucination. In the time of the advancement of artificial intelligence, the concept of hallucination specifically refers to the phenomenon where the system, particularly a generative model, produces outputs that are factually incorrect, fabricated, or nonsensical despite being presented in a plausible or coherent way. A hallucination occurs when the system generates information not supported by training data or real-world facts, often filling in gaps with inaccurate or invented content.

The original intention of the Indian Act was to dehumanize and to serve as the structure for the long-term elimination of Indigenous Peoples. Today, as a response from a place of strength and resilience to the truth that we are still here, and we mean to establish the exact opposite of this original intention: humanizing the Indian Act.

Personifying the Indian Act

Let's explore this concept of humanizing the Indian Act further through a series of questions. What if the Indian Act was a person? What would the Indian Act look like if it was a person? I imagine an old man wearing a top hat and a wool three-piece suit, stale with the slight smell of mothballs. He walks with an air of superiority. What would he say? How would you feel around him? What would he wear? What does he sound like? How does he stand? Would there be a distinctive smell? A certain sound or tone to his voice?

And then the Indian Act started to speak with a commanding, arrogant voice declaring loudly: I control you. I control where you move. I control where you live, what you own, how you speak, who you are. I control what you can sell. I will tell you who you are. You will become like me. You will be me, and you will act like me. I will control what you believe and what you learn. You own nothing. I will eventually eliminate you, and I will tell you when you stop existing. I will name you. I will decide for you. I will give you a false identity. I will give you a number. I am responsible for you and have ultimate authority over you. I will tell you where to live. I control your destiny. I control all activities in your home. You don't own anything. You cannot make decisions for yourself. I approve decisions for you. I am taking your identity away. Stop being who you are. I will refer to you as a number. You cannot dance or

sing. I make decisions on your behalf because you are incapable. You have no rights. You cannot govern yourself or make decisions for yourself. You will surrender your home to me. I control your finances. I will hold in trust money for you because you are incapable. I will punish you if you resist. I decide what you can decide. I decide how many of you can gather. You cannot sell anything without my permission. I decide what privileges you get. You will speak like me. I will give you permission to leave your home. I will protect you. I decide what you can drink. You don't belong here. I am isolating you from everyone else. You are not one of us. I am your father. You will obey me.

This is it, the madness brought into the light. This is the dysfunctional family we are collectively in, as expressed through the voice of the Indian Act in the Indigenous relationship in Canada. If the Indian Act was a person, this is what it would say and what it would sound like. The critical inquiry here is to question whether this behavior is appropriate. Is this behavior ethical by today's standards? Is this appropriate for any person to speak to another? Or would the person be called out for being controlling, abusive, and a bully? Would you let anyone treat you this way? Is it ok for someone in a position of power to treat anyone this way? These are all formative questions that this behavioral analysis of the Indian Act creates the space to reflect on.

Behavioral Analysis of the Indian Act

The personification of the Indian Act as a legal document when viewed through the lens of psychological behavior is a metaphorical exercise that uses the language and concepts of psychology and mental illness to illustrate the nature of the Act's continuous impacts on Indigenous Peoples and through the continued deployment of the Act into Canadian ethical reality. The exploration of how the Indian Act behaves if it is a person brings into focus how it relates to Indigenous Peoples through language use and behavior as outlined above.

It is possible to create a psychological profile of the Indian Act as a person.

Using IndigenomicsAI, the exercise of creating a psychological profile of the Indian Act as a person in relation to Indigenous Peoples involves anthropomorphizing this legislation into a human character with specific traits, behaviors, and language usage. This metaphorical personification reflects the Act's specific behaviors, intentions, language, tone, posturing, and highlights the nature of its interactions with Indigenous Peoples. A conceptual profile of these behaviors include:

1. **Authoritarian and Controlling:** The Indian Act, personified, would exhibit extremely controlling behavior, exerting authority over every aspect of Indigenous life, from governance and economic activities to personal decisions and cultural practices. This entity would seek to manage and dictate the structure and functioning of Indigenous Peoples without their consent or input.

2. **Paternalistic:** This character would display a paternalistic attitude, believing that Indigenous Peoples are incapable of managing their affairs or making decisions beneficial to their communities. It would justify its control and intervention as being for their own good, despite significant evidence of harm and disregard for Indigenous autonomy and rights.

3. **Manipulative:** The Act, as a person, would manipulate Indigenous identities and relationships. It would redefine social roles and hierarchies within communities, undermining traditional leadership and imposing externally defined governance structures.

4. **Culturally Insensitive and Destructive:** The Act would show a lack of respect for Indigenous cultures, traditions, and languages. It would not only ignore the cultural heritage of Indigenous Peoples but actively seek to suppress and replace it with Euro-Canadian norms and values, reflecting a belief in the superiority of these traits.

5. **Unyielding and Inflexible:** The personification of the Act would be rigid, showing little to no flexibility to adapt to the changing needs or voices of Indigenous Peoples. It would persist with policies proven to be ineffective or harmful, demonstrating a lack of responsiveness or empathy.

6. **Dismissive of Rights:** This character would exhibit a dismissive attitude toward the rights and legal statuses of Indigenous individuals and communities, often infringing upon these rights under the guise of legal and bureaucratic procedures.

7. **Invasive:** In personal relationships, this character would be overly intrusive, invading personal spaces and privacy without consent, much like the Act's provisions that intrude into the minutiae of daily life and community governance.

8. **Eurocentric:** Exhibiting behavioral traits shaped by beliefs and actions, hidden or openly expressed, that assume superiority over all others.

9. **Patriarchal:** Behavior that reinforces male dominance across social, political, or family structures. Patriarchal behavior manifests through unequal power dynamics, gender stereotypes, and the prioritization of male perspectives and voices to advance these interests through structures and systems that ensure men hold primary power, which is then further reinforced in roles of decision-making, political leadership, moral authority, social privilege, and control of the property.

In summary, the Indian Act personified resembles an overbearing, controlling, narcissistic, dominant figure lacking empathy with little regard for others' autonomy, rights, dignity, boundaries, property, or cultural identity. This initial profile serves to illuminate the dysfunctional, controlling, misogynistic, suppressive human dynamic that is inherent in the Act's relationship with Indigenous Peoples. It further contributes to the perspective of ongoing discussions about the ethical centering of the Indian Act's future in the context of reconciliation efforts and the rise of the Indigenous economy.

Anthropomorphization—A Diagnostic Profile of the Indian Act

To anthropomorphize the Indian Act means attributing human characteristics or behaviors to it. The global standard used in the health care profession is the Diagnostic and Statistical Manual of Mental Disorders (DSM), the leading authoritative guide for diagnosing human mental disorders. The DSM manual outlines the descriptions, definitions, symptoms, and criteria for diagnosing mental disorders. It is an insightful exercise here to use the identified behaviors of the Indian Act and compare these within the manual's outline of the diagnosis of mental disorders to frame the relationship with Indigenous Peoples. Several categories of mental disorders can be metaphorically aligned with the traits depicted in the Indian Act's "behavior" as follows:

Narcissistic Personality Disorder (NPD): in the DSM-5, the criteria for Narcissistic Personality Disorder (NPD) is characterized by an exaggerated or inflated sense of self-importance, a need for admiration or validation, and a lack of empathy for other people.[64] A narcissistic person will expect to be recognized as superior even without achievements. The narcissist individual tends to makes one's own achievements and talents seem bigger than they are. The person is heavily preoccupied with the fantasy of authority, power, and success; a narcissistic person believes they are superior to others and can only spend time with or be understood by equally special and superior people.

A lack of empathy is often cited as the primary distinguishing feature of Narcissistic Personality Disorder. This mental dysfunction is characterized by a pattern of abnormal behavior that features exaggerated feelings of self-importance and a lack of empathy for others. The Indian Act, when personified, displays paternalistic and superior attitudes and likely fits this profile due to its imposing measures of control and assumed superiority over Indigenous ways of life while ignoring the needs and rights of Indigenous Peoples and a complete absence of empathy for the harm caused as the consequences of its own actions. Narcissistic personality traits include a grandiose sense of self-importance or superiority, a belief in one's unique importance and perceived authority, and a constant need for validation. A narcissistic individual may exhibit behaviors such as exploiting others for personal gain, having a sense of entitlement, displaying arrogance, experiencing difficulty in maintaining healthy relationships due to a lack of empathy, and constantly seeking validation and control.[65]

Next is Antisocial Personality Disorder (ASPD): The DSM-5 describes Antisocial Personality Disorder (ASPD) as a pervasive pattern of disregard for and violation of the rights of others.[66] The behavior begins in childhood or early adolescence and continues into adulthood. The diagnostic criteria for ASPD includes a pattern of disregard for and violation of the rights of others and is indicated by three (or more) of the following:

1. Failure to conform to social norms with respect to lawful behaviors, as indicated by repeatedly performing acts that are grounds for arrest.
2. Deceitfulness, as indicated by repeated lying, use of aliases, or conning others for personal profit or pleasure.
3. Impulsivity or failure to plan ahead.
4. Irritability and aggressiveness, as indicated by repeated physical fights or assaults.
5. Reckless disregard for the safety of self or others.

6. Consistent irresponsibility, as indicated by repeated failure to sustain consistent work behavior or honor financial obligations.
7. Lack of remorse, as indicated by being indifferent to or rationalizing having hurt, mistreated, or stolen from another.

Individuals with ASPD are often manipulative, deceitful, and callous, with a tendency to violate social and legal rules. They typically lack empathy, cannot form meaningful long-term relationships, and may engage in criminal behavior. There is often a disregard for the consequences of actions for themselves and others. An individual with ASPD will often disregard or violate the rights of others and may not conform to societal norms or laws. Symptoms of antisocial personality disorder may include physical aggression, bullying, hostility, and violence toward others. Someone with anti-social personality disorder will typically be manipulative and deceitful with reckless disregard for others' well-being or boundaries and will not care for other people's feelings or rights. APSD could metaphorically correspond to the Indian Act's invasive and controlling nature through the removal of Indigenous and basic human rights and can be examined through the role of implementing policies that were detrimental to Indigenous cultures and communities without regard for Indigenous well-being or consent and shaped in genocidal intent.

Next is Obsessive-Compulsive Personality Disorder (OCPD): OCPD is characterized by the presence of obsessions, compulsions, or both, which are time-consuming and cause significant distress or impairment in social, occupational, or other important areas of functioning.[67]

Within the manual, the next dysfunction is Obsessions. The manual describes obsessions as:

Obsessions are defined by:

1. Recurrent, persistent thoughts, urges, or images that are intrusive and cause marked anxiety or distress.
2. The individual attempts to ignore, suppress, or neutralize these thoughts, often by performing a compulsion.

Compulsions are defined by:

1. Repetitive behaviors that the individual feels driven to perform in response to an obsession or according to rigid rules.

2. The behaviors or mental acts are aimed at preventing or reducing anxiety or distress, or preventing some feared event or situation. However, these behaviors are not realistically connected to what they are meant to prevent or are clearly excessive.

This disorder is characterized by a preoccupation with order, perfectionism, rules, details, and control. An individual with OCPD may insist that others submit to their way of doing things. If the Indian Act were a person, it would display traits aligned with OCPD through its need for strict regulations and insistence on restructuring Indigenous governance and identity to ensure assimilation into Euro-Canadian norms.

It is important to clarify that this exploration into mental diagnostic comparisons is purely an illustrative exercise and metaphorical in nature. It is a demonstration that explores the behavior of the Indian Act and how that is expressed from policy and law into the human experience. It is understood that laws do not have psychologies, and the DSM manual is intended only for diagnosing human individuals and not for evaluating legislation or historical documents. However, these correlations bring into focus and help to illustrate how the Indian Act's outdated, rigid, and controlling behaviors have continuously psychologically impacted Indigenous Peoples, affecting their autonomy, identity, cultural practices, dignity, ways of being and knowing, well-being, health, development, participation in the economy, and social and governance structures.

This metaphorical exercise highlights the ongoing need to critically examine and advance the ethical space of the Indian Act to respect and promote the rights, sovereignty, self-determination, and dignity of Indigenous Peoples. This metaphorical exercise serves to enter into Canadian reality the problematic behavior and relationship as inherently dysfunctional. While also examining the originally intended behavior of the eradication of Indigenous Peoples, the Indian Act's behavior lives in the realm of the pathological. The truth we collectively face today is to recognize that these symptoms are upheld within the inherited legislated system of the Indian Act, and its legacy is embedded structure for the continued social, cultural, and economic isolation. The Indian Act is the symptom. Indian Act economics is the sickness.

Indian Act economics is the structure for denying economic opportunity. The result is social and economic hardship through poverty, isolation, and despair. This is the foundation for the formation of the Indigenous socioeconomic gap. In looking at the socioeconomic gap as outcomes of Indian Act economics, it must be fully realized that Indigenous Peoples are not a problem to be solved or a program to be funded. Indigenous Peoples are ready to activate our true capacity and autonomy and are actively taking our seat at the economic table of this country that has been denied to us as stewards of the Earth.

Controlling Behavior

Controlling behavior can look like insisting upon doing things one's own way, removing personal choice, being overly critical, or intimidating. The Indian Act created control of lands, the reserve lands and natural resources (including minerals, trees, and wildlife), which were set out to be "protected" from trespassing and exploitation, and the assets of Status Indians living on reserves are protected from seizure by creditors and from taxation at both the provincial and federal levels. Because creditors cannot claim reserve land, it cannot be used as collateral, reducing its value to potential lenders and creditors. This is the heart of Indian Act economics.

As a demonstration of the controlling behavior, the Indian Act "created" the right for Status Indians to live on reserve lands, but they do not own those lands—the lands are held in trust by the federal government. The Act, c. I-5 (20)(1) states: "No Indian is lawfully in possession of land on a reserve."[68] Ultimate control resides with the minister of Indian Affairs, as section (20)(4) states: "The Minister may, in his discretion, withhold his approval and may authorize the Indian to occupy the land temporarily and may prescribe the conditions as to use and settlement that are to be fulfilled by the Indian before the Minister approves of the allotment."

A further demonstration of the controlling nature of the Indian Act was the development of the reserve pass system.

The pass system proved to be a less than effective way of restricting Indian movement. The problem was, that lacking legislative sanction, the pass system could not be enforced in law. To get around this, Indian Affairs simply assumed an air of authority and attempted to enforce the system by other means within its power. In some cases, rations and other "privileges" were withheld from those who refused to comply with pass regulations, but the most effective approach was to have the police arrest those found off the reserve without passes and, where possible, prosecute them either for trespass under the Indian Act or for vagrancy under the Criminal Code.[69]

Aggressive / Violent Behavior

The demonstration of aggressive and violent behavior, through the administration of the Indian Act, can be seen within the acts of clearing the lands of the Indigenous villages and the relocation of the Indians onto reserves for the benefit of settlers' expansion and access to resources. An example of this forcible relocation can be seen in this historical depiction of forced removal: "A lot of the villages were destroyed when the reserve commissions went through. My grandfather Marshall told me, they tried to go and live out on some of the old village sites and were chased off because white people owned the land."[70] This depiction is from the W'sanec Peoples on Vancouver Island in BC.

Lack of Empathy

In demonstrating a lack of empathy, it is very revealing to understand how Canada used a policy of starvation against Indigenous Peoples to clear the way for settlement.

The book *Clearing the Plains* articulates that the founding of Canadian politics and the railroads across the country were the politics of ethnocide, which played into the deaths and subjugation of thousands of Indigenous Peoples through the activation of John A. Macdonald's "National Dream."[71] The National Dream "was a dream that came at great expense: the present disparity in health and economic well-being between Indigenous and non-Indigenous populations, and the lingering racism and misunderstanding that permeates the national consciousness to this day."

Patriarchal Behavior

Patriarchal behavior refers to the characteristics of a society or government controlled by men. The Indian Act is built on patriarchal behavior by systematically eliminating Indigenous women from the imposed governance system while at the same time destroying traditional systems of government where Indigenous women were highly valued in decision-making and management roles for thousands of years.

An example of patriarchal behavior can also be seen in the W'sanec region on Vancouver Island in BC through the Indian Act's forced governance Band Council system. A historical depiction describes how "the leaders were arbitrarily picked. My mother was disappointed in 'her men.' Under the Indian Act, leaders were to be elected, and they weren't allowed to be women. The way things used to be, women were important advisers, both spiritually and politically, although it doesn't really fit to call it political."[72]

Eurocentric Behavior

Eurocentric behavior upholds a European worldview and ways of being and doing that are seen as superior. It centers its own history while excluding Indigenous Peoples and Indigenous approaches. The specific behaviors here refer to imposing the Eurocentric education system on Indigenous Peoples for the purpose of severing their identity over the long term to become more Euro-Canadian.

The following examples identify the Eurocentric attitude toward Indigenous Peoples through the specific words "to bring the Indian out of savagery and into citizenship, we must make him more intelligently selfish. A desire for property is needed to get this Indian out of the blanket and into trousers with a pocket and with a pocket that aches to be filled with dollars."[73]

Sexist Behavior

Sexist behavior is characterized by and shows prejudice, stereotyping, and discrimination typically against women on the basis of sex. The Indian Act demonstrated this behavior through the implementation of specific rules that systematically excluded Indigenous women and their children from Indian status due to marriage with non-Indigenous individuals. In the long term, this caused a significant displacement of identity, dislocation, extreme poverty, political disenfranchisement, and social and cultural exclusion of Indigenous women. The courts determined that this constituted gender-based discrimination.

Abuse and Overreach of Power

Abuse of power refers to situation of abuse in a position of power to harm the other party, bully them into submission, or take advantage of them. Abuse of power is when one uses tactics to control the other, causing damage. This control or power imbalance can take many forms, including threats, intimidation, and abuse. This usually results in one party being scared of the other, leaving a lack of safety in the relationship. A relationship has a power imbalance when one party has the power over money, a place to live, employment, or a reputation. Numerous examples of the federal government's application of the Indian Act demonstrate the forced removal of Indigenous Peoples from their homelands and constitute an abuse of power.

For example, in Ausuittuq on Ellesmere Island in Nunavut in the early 50s, the community was forced to move as part of a government relocation program. While the official reason given to the Indians was that food supplies were dwindling in the region and wild game would be more abundant in the new location, archival documents demonstrate that Arctic sovereignty during the Cold War was Canada's primary objective for this relocation. Those who left their community were promised that they could return in two years and that a better life awaited them. Instead, they found a completely foreign environment and a climate and landscape lacking their traditional food sources.

The Inuit in Labrador were also forcibly relocated in the 1950s to reduce administrative costs for the high costs of living in the North. Administration stated, "Civilization is on the northward march, and for the Eskimo and Indian, there is no escape. The last bridges of isolation were destroyed with the coming of the airplane and the radio. The only course now, for there can be no turning back, is to fit him as soon as may be to take his full place as a citizen in our society. There is no time to lose."[74]

Manipulative Behavior

Manipulative behavior refers to controlling or influencing someone to gain an advantage, often unfairly or dishonestly. Some specific ways that the Indian Act did this included manipulating Indigenous Peoples to give up their identity. Early accounts of the Eurocentric voting system imposed on the W'sanec Peoples on Vancouver Island, BC, are a prime example. The manipulation of the imposed system of governance and decision-making happened when "votes" took place in 1954 and was described as "The count was 171 Indians absent, 70 present, 68 'for,' and 2 abstained from voting." In this early account, one Indigenous leader, Pelkey, says, "It wasn't our process—so we didn't go." In a letter dated July 15th, 1954, submitted within the report, L.L. Brown (Superintendent, Reserves and Trusts) acknowledges that the process may have been illegitimate, noting, "The number of absentees is considerable and we will, therefore, have to ask the Departmental Legal Adviser as to whether or not the vote can be considered representative or whether, in such cases, we should follow closely the provisions of the surrender sections of the Indian Act."[75]

Edgar Dosman sums it up well in the context of the Prairie provinces and the experience of manipulation in clearing the plains region:

> The life of an Indian was never isolated from all contacts with white society, only from most. He was numbered and rationed, and closely watched. He could do almost nothing without the permission of the Indian agent: buy or sell; slaughter cattle; be educated; drink or travel. While every person of whatever background relates to his primary group of family and peers, his community and the outside world, Indians have an exceptional balance, or rather imbalance, among these levels. The outside world, the Indian Affairs framework, not only determined the Indian's income, living conditions, education and mobility; it also made every attempt to shape his culture and personality. It is for this reason that a study of Canadian Indians must start, not with "culture," or the "culture of poverty," but with the institutions that dominated him and the society that destroyed him.[76]

Bullying Behavior

A key aspect of preparing and clearing the land for settlers in the province of Saskatchewan was the subjugation and forced removal of Indigenous communities from their Traditional Territories, essentially clearing the plains of Indigenous Peoples to make way for railway construction and land settlement.

James Daschuk's work in *Clearing the Plains* further describes in detail that, despite guarantees of food aid in times of famine in Treaty No. 6,

Canadian officials denied food as a means to ethnically cleanse a vast region from Regina to the Alberta border for the Canadian Pacific Railway project to move forward.[77] For years, government officials withheld food from Indigenous Peoples until they moved to their appointed reserves, essentially forcing them to trade freedom for rations of food. Once on the reserves, food placed in ration houses was withheld for so long that much of it rotted while the people it was intended to feed fell into a decades-long cycle of malnutrition, suppressed immunity, and sickness from tuberculosis and other diseases with thousands of Indigenous Peoples dying.[78]

Although officially promoted as a protective safeguard for the "endangered" Indigenous population, the reserves served one singular goal: to make room for the new European settlers to live and access resources. The common thread of the behaviors stems from the Indian Act directive of John A. Macdonald: "I have reason to believe that the agents as a whole ... are doing all they can, by refusing food until the Indians are on the verge of starvation, to reduce the expense."[79] This is a depiction of bullying behavior as experienced through the Indian Act.

Gaslighting Behavior

Gaslighting refers to the behavior of denying that an event took place, even if there is evidence to prove it. This can include lying and contradicting what the victim knows to be true, making the victim feel like they are crazy or overreacting. It can also make the victim doubt their memory and perception of reality.

A demonstration of gaslighting can be viewed in the historical relationship of the federal government and Indigenous Peoples, which has often been experienced through chronic underfunding of programs and services through the administration of the Indian Act. As an example, the federal court approved a landmark $23 billion settlement that ensures Ottawa must compensate more than 300,000 First Nations children and their families for chronically underfunding the on-reserve child welfare services. Starting in 2007, stretching out across legal challenges, the deal came in two parts—$20 billion for compensation and $20 billion for long-term system reforms. With ongoing federal challenges to the 2016 Tribunal ruling that found Canada guilty of "willfully and recklessly" discriminating against First Nations children involved in the child welfare system on reserve, the dragging on and continued challenges represent gaslighting behaviour. The federal challenges demonstrate the gaslighting behavior.

Economic Abuse

Financial and economic abuse deserves particular attention here. Through the Indian Act, the Crown appointed itself to have fiduciary duty over the Indians and holds the responsibility of the "honour of the Crown." In this context, when viewed through the lens of the ongoing state of the socioeconomic gap as an outcome of this duty and honor, the financial and economic relationship with Indigenous Peoples becomes visible.

As noted above, the behaviors relevant to the concept of deconstructing Indian Act economics come into focus in the financial relationship with Indigenous Nations. In a situation of financial abuse, a common behavioral tactic is to gain power and control within the relationship.

Economic abuse is experienced at a meta level and incorporates a series of specific behaviors that allow the perpetrator to control economic resources or freedoms. Economic abuse is the behavior of denying or restricting access to money or misusing another person's money, as well as limiting access to essential resources such as food, clothing, or transport and denying opportunity and the means to improve economic status (for example, through employment, education, or training). The experience of economic abuse in the relationship with Indigenous Peoples involves managing access to money, which serves to limit and control the victim's current and future actions, economic outcomes, and freedom of choice.

Identifying the elements of economic abuse in the context of Indian Act economics is an important exercise. The original 1876 version of the Indian Act introduced extensive control over the financial and land-related matters of Indigenous Peoples. The Act gave the Superintendent General of Indian Affairs the authority to manage reserves, lands, and financial resources of Indigenous Peoples. These control mechanisms severely limited the economic autonomy of Indigenous Peoples and further restricted their ability to acquire and manage their financial resources independently. The control mechanisms denied Indigenous Peoples the actual function of economy and value creation.

This economic abuse looks like this:

- **Restriction of access to resources:** The Indian Act has historically and continuously restricted Indigenous Peoples' access to their lands and resources. For example, the Act regulated who could live on reserves and how land could be used or transferred. This restriction severed Indigenous Peoples' ability to leverage any economic framework, essentially generating poverty instead of wealth.
- **Restrictions on economic activities:** The Indian Act severely controlled economic activities on reserves, such as harvesting timber and other natural resources such as agriculture and oil and gas, which required permission from the Superintendent General. This is a form of economic abuse as it restricts the economic autonomy of Indigenous Peoples and their ability to benefit from their resources and wealth.
- **Denial of opportunity:** The Act's provisions limiting economic activities on reserve limited employment opportunities and access to resources. Controlling who could live on reserves and under what conditions affected Indigenous People's ability to seek and maintain employment and capacity development. Furthermore, restrictions on economic activities and access to resources created limited opportunities for economic advancement over time.

Although many of the original provisions of the Indian Act regarding the control of First Nations money have been repealed or modified by adding "with the consent of the Band," similar provisions remain in effect. For example, the following two provisions in Section 61 of the Indian Act, Management of Indian Moneys, remain in effect: "(1) Indian moneys shall be expended only for the benefit of the Indians or bands for whose use and benefit in common the moneys are received or held, and subject to this Act and to the terms of any treaty or surrender, the Governor in Council may determine whether any purpose for which Indian moneys are used or are to be used is for the use and benefit of the band. (2) Interest on Indian moneys held in the Consolidated Revenue Fund shall be allowed at a rate to be fixed from time to time by the Governor in Council."[80]

In 1881, the Indian Act was amended to control Status Indians' ability to sell products from their farms. Indian farmers were required to access a government permit to leave the reserve and a separate permit to sell any farm products. Settlers were prohibited from purchasing goods and services from Indian farmers. These restrictions on agricultural sales were not removed from the Indian Act until 2014. This is the long-term economic undermining of Indian Act economics.

It is important to understand the effect of Indian Act economics on Indigenous well-being and development, which includes critical impacts in terms of health and emotional and cultural/spiritual effects across time. Indian Act economics has created the conditions for internalized powerlessness and dependency and the absence of the function of the economy. The impacts of economic abuse can also be seen in poverty rates, unemployment rates, education rates, homelessness, and limited ability to access financial resources. The effects of economic abuse contribute to a lifetime of social, financial, and economic struggle for Indigenous Peoples and communities. This is essentially a description of the Indigenous socioeconomic gap.

Figure 5 outlines key features of economic abuse as highlighted within the function of Indian Act economics.

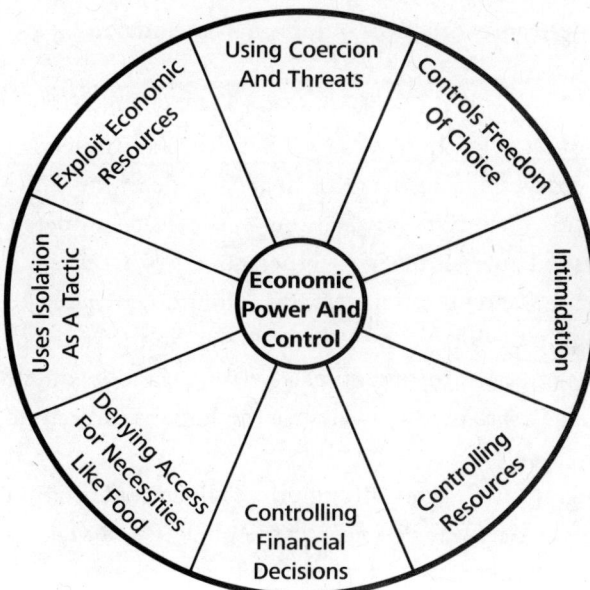

Figure 5: *Key elements of economic abuse. Source: Indigenomics Institute.*

The field of behavioral economics merges insights from psychology and economic principles to better understand how people make decisions. In this light, the perceived behaviors of the Indian Act and the externalization of decision-making and authority are highly problematic in the Indigenous relationship today.

The economic success that Indigenous Nations and businesses have made in recent years goes against the functioning of all economic theory as it has been built upon layers of systemic barriers, denialism, and racial discrimination. The rising success of the Indigenous economy today, when framed against the original motivation of John A. Macdonald's intended removal of the Indigenous population, is truly remarkable. The following highlights some defining moments of Indigenous success, resilience, excellence, and power.

Twenty-five Moments of Indigenous Success That John A. Macdonald Would Never Have Seen Coming

As the first Canadian prime minister, John A. Macdonald was the driver of the Indian Act and was a pivotal character in the story of the Indigenous relationship. While he appeared briefly in this story, his original policy direction still has an impact today. The Indigenous relationship was established through some of these core directives of John A. Macdonald:

- Led the creation of the Gradual Civilization Act (1857), which later formed the development of the Indian Act in 1876. The Act's objective was to enfranchise native men into settler society while at the same time opening up lands of Indigenous Nations into private property, which the newly formed government could then tax. Also, in this early Act, Indigenous women and children were, by definition, attached to the men in their family (a European-settler ideology and practice of heteropatriarchy was imposed through this legislation), and its intent was, as the name suggests, to gradually civilize the Indians until none remained.
- Directed the clearing of the Prairies through the deliberate starvation and detention of the Indigenous Peoples for the objective of making way for European settlement and the construction of the railroad.

Macdonald directed the Indian agents to withhold food to drive the Indians onto the reserves and out of the way of the railroad pathway and for the expansion of settlement. A Liberal MP at the time called it "a policy of submission shaped by a policy of starvation."[81]

- Facilitated the creation of the North-West Mounted Police, which was the precursor to the Royal Canadian Mounted Police. They were directed to incarcerate Indigenous Peoples for the practice of their culture and for leaving the reserve, and to assist in the forced removal from their home villages. There is extensive documentation of the burning of the villages to the ground and forcing the Indigenous Peoples out through the firing of cannons.[82]

These foundational policy directives confirmed the Indian Act's original intention as a policy instrument of denialism, control, and assimilation, shaping the foundation of Indian Act economics. The following section outlines twenty-five things John A. Macdonald would never have seen coming that have changed the trajectory of the Indigenous relationship in Canada.

1. Constitutional Recognition

Section 35 is the part of the Constitution Act that recognizes and affirms Indigenous Rights. Indigenous groups in Canada successfully fought to have their rights enshrined and protected. An important distinction is that Section 35 *recognizes* Aboriginal Rights but did not create them—Indigenous Rights have existed before Section 35 and before the establishment of Canada.

Section 35 of the Constitution Act specifically states:

35. (1) The existing aboriginal and treaty rights of the aboriginal peoples of Canada are hereby recognized and affirmed.

(2) In this act, "aboriginal peoples of Canada" includes the Indian, Inuit, and Métis peoples of Canada.

(3) For greater certainty, in subsection (1) "treaty rights" includes rights that now exist by way of land claims agreements or may be so acquired.

(4) Notwithstanding any other provision of this Act, the aboriginal and treaty rights referred to in subsection (1) are guaranteed equally to male and female persons.[83]

Section 35 of the Constitution Act, 1982, recognizes and affirms existing Aboriginal Rights but does not define them.

2. Modern Self-government Agreements

The modern treaty era began in 1973 after the Supreme Court of Canada Calder Decision, which recognized Indigenous Rights for the first time. This decision led to the establishment of the first modern comprehensive agreement, which was signed in 1975 by the Cree Nation, followed by agreements in the Nunavut Territory and a series of Nations in the Yukon. To date, Canada has negotiated and signed 26 modern treaties with Indigenous groups in Canada, 18 of which contain self-government provisions or agreements. Modern treaties recognize the Indigenous rights to:

- Ownership of over 600,000 km^2 of the land base in Canada
- Protection of traditional cultures, languages, and heritage
- Access to resource development opportunities
- Stewardship of land and resource management decisions and structures
- Predictability or increased certainty with respect to land rights of close to 40 percent of Canada's land base
- Defined self-government rights, definition, and political recognition
- Improved social development through better outcomes in health, education, and housing
- Increased access to economic development opportunities and achieving greater self-determination

3. Alignment of the Indian Act to the Canadian Charter of Rights and Freedoms

Referred to as Bill C-31, the 1985 changes to the Indian Act were required to bring the Indian Act into line with gender equality under the Canadian Charter of Rights and Freedoms. Specific changes included a revised definition of Indian status to address gender discrimination. The changes abolished enfranchisement and restored status to those who previously had status removed through the enfranchisement process. These changes ended Section 12(1)(b), the "marrying out" rule, and 12(1)(a)(iv), the "double mother rule" of the Indian Act. The 1985 revisions also terminated status of those who had acquired Indian

Status only through marriage, rather than descent. This revision resulted in close to 130,000 individuals having their status restored. Canada evolved here through the Charter of Rights and Freedom and forced these changes to the Indian Act at this time, the changes were not voluntarily adjusted by the government. John A. Macdonald would never have seen a return of status to Indigenous Peoples coming.

4. Meech Lake Accord

Elijah Harper from the Red Sucker Lake First Nations served as a Member of the Legislative Assembly of Manitoba from 1981 to 1992 and as a Member of Parliament (MP) from 1993 to 1997. Harper was a central factor in rejecting the Meech Lake Accord in 1990, which proposed key amendments to the Canadian Constitution. The agreement was between the federal and provincial governments that proposed to amend the Constitution to strengthen provincial powers and declare Quebec as a distinct society. The Accord ultimately failed to move forward largely due to the lone no vote by Harper. The significance of the single no vote resulted in the Accord failing. In the absence of Indigenous recognition, Harper's no vote was a representation of the state of the Indigenous relationship in Canada.

5. Canadian Government Formal Apology to Indigenous Peoples

On June 11, 2008, the Office of the Prime Minister of Canada issued a formal apology to former students of the residential school system. At the time, Prime Minister Harper delivered the apology in the House of Commons, where Indigenous leaders and Survivors witnessed the speech. The apology admitted that residential schools were part of a Canadian policy of forced Indigenous assimilation. John A. Macdonald would never have expected to have an apology delivered to Indigenous Peoples based on the policies of the time.

6. Indigenous Consent—Legal Requirement for Free Prior Informed Consent

The legal requirement for Indigenous consent was a catalyst in the economic realm and is a formative feature of the rise of the Indigenous economy today. Originating from the principle of the right to self-determination, this has translated to governments not being able to implement a policy or program on Indigenous lands or concerning Indigenous Peoples without prior consultation and consent from the Indigenous community. This includes any government policy or program seeking to grant permission to a company to conduct any activities on Indigenous lands. While the requirement for consent seems to be a basic concept, there are plenty of examples in the news media where this is still not the case today. This particular Indigenous Right is playing out intensely in the resources race to get critical minerals to the markets to supply a low-carbon global economy. John A. Macdonald would never have seen the requirement to gain consent coming or the critical requirement for Indigenous economic participation.

7.   Idle No More Movement of 2012

Idle No More began in November 2012 as a protest against the introduction of Bill C-45 by the Harper-era Conservative government. The movement was initially shaped by opposition to the proposed Navigable Waters Protection Act and Environmental Assessment Act. Idle No More activists opposed the Acts' changes, which diminished the rights and authority of Indigenous Peoples by making it easier for governments and businesses to push through projects without strict environmental assessment and with no consultation or consent from Indigenous Nations. The movement shook Canadian reality when nonviolent, culturally oriented flash mobs and blockades seemingly brought international attention to the state of the Indigenous relationship in Canada. John A. Macdonald would have been shocked to witness this rise of Indigenous sovereign expression in the Idle No More Movement.

8.   Tsilhqot'in Title Win

In 2014, the Supreme Court of Canada upheld the declaration of Aboriginal Title to over 1,700 square kilometers of land in British Columbia to the Tsilhqot'in Nation. This was the first time the highest court made such a ruling regarding Aboriginal Land Title. The case significantly impacted future economic and resource development on First Nations Lands. Before this win, Canadian reality upheld two types of title—Crown and fee simple. John A. Macdonald would never have seen Indigenous Title coming.

9. BC Implementation of UNDRIP into Law

In 2019, the Legislative Assembly of British Columbia unanimously adopted the Declaration on the Rights of Indigenous Peoples Act. The BC government was the first jurisdiction in Canada to uphold UNDRIP into law. Bill 41 affirms the application and implementation of UNDRIP into the laws of BC, referred to as DRIPA—Declaration on the Rights Indigenous Peoples Act. John A. Macdonald would never have seen this coming in a million years.[84]

10. Truth and Reconciliation Calls to Action

The Indian Residential School Settlement Agreement was the largest class action settlement in Canadian history, which shaped the establishment of the Truth and Reconciliation Commission. The Truth and Reconciliation Commission was a requirement of this Settlement Agreement. It was a national exercise in truth telling, and it created a historical record of the residential school system. The final report's Calls to Action serve as the foundation for collectively building a renewed nation-to-nation relationship with Indigenous Peoples based on recognition of rights, respect, cooperation, partnership, and recognition of the truth of what happened at the residential schools. John A. Macdonald would never have seen the Truth and Reconciliation Commission's 92 Calls to Action as an outcome of the response to the atrocities of the residential school system he founded.

11. Indigenous Legal Winning Streak

Indigenous Nations have created a formidable winning streak, with over 363 legal case wins to date (at the time of writing). This represents a significant shift in this country's legal and economic relationship that was shaped by the wrongs of the original policy directive of the Indian Act. John A. Macdonald would definitely not have seen this coming!

12. The Business Case for the $100 Billion Indigenous Economy

In December 2019, at the Assembly of First Nations Special Chiefs meeting, the Indigenomics Institute identified that a $100 billion annual Indigenous economy was not only possible but essential for Canada's future. John A. Macdonald would never have seen a $100 billion Indigenous economy coming, let alone within the same generation of Survivors of the residential school system.

13. Major Transportation Corridors Shutdown of 2020

National Indigenous protests made global news in 2020, with Indigenous protests shutting down major transportation corridors simultaneously across the country. A *BBC* article, "The Wet'suwet'en Conflict Disrupting Canada's Rail System," confirmed that the national system of rail lines across Canada was paralyzed for several weeks after being blockaded by Indigenous protesters and their supporters. "The economic impact of the rail blockades is beginning to be felt across industries and there are concerns about shortages of goods."[85] The conflict had a significant economic impact as the national CN Rail was forced to shut down its eastern network, effectively stopping all cross-country freight trains. The protest disrupted the movement of goods and passengers nationally.

14. Kamloops Residential Schools Graves Discovery

In May 2021, the Chief of the Tk'emlúps te Secwépemc Nation announced that through the use of ground-penetrating radar (GPR), the remains of 215 "missing children" had been located as unmarked graves on the site of the former residential school in Kamloops, BC. This finding essentially woke Canada up to the realities of the residential school system. It set in motion the investigations of over 130 previous residential school sites across Canada, which has uncovered literally thousands of unmarked graves of Indigenous children who died at these residential schools. John A. Macdonald would never have seen this development coming and how it set in motion tangible efforts for building reconciliation outcomes with Indigenous Peoples today.

15. An Indigenous Governor General

Since the establishment of Canada, over thirty Governor Generals have served as the Monarch's representative. Mary Simon is Inuktitut and has been serving as the 30th Governor General of Canada since July 2021. She is the first Indigenous person to hold the office.

16. Pope's Visit and Apology

With a growing number of residential schools being searched for the unmarked graves of Indigenous children, this established an increasingly national and global pressure for the Pope as the head of the Catholic Church to formally acknowledge and deliver an apology that addressed the Church's role in the past wrongs of the residential school system. Pope Francis travelled to Canada in July 2022 to visit Indigenous residential school Survivors, and residential school locations and to recognize the abuses experienced that resulted in cultural destruction, loss of life, and the continuation of trauma experienced by Indigenous Peoples in every region of this country. John A. Macdonald would never have seen this apology coming.

17. Indigenous Corporate Directors

The rise of Indigenous corporate directors stems from the increasing context of Indigenous consent and participation. For example, four of the big six national financial banks, including the Bank of Canada, now have Indigenous corporate directors on the board. Again, this is happening within the same generation of residential school system Survivors.

18. Indigenous Major Projects Equity Ownership

Endless media coverage, some almost daily, demonstrates the ongoing power play of Indigenous equity ownership in major projects. These projects include airlines, rails, energy systems, pipelines, and transportation systems among other major acquisitions. Today, Indigenous Peoples are taking a seat at the economic table that was systematically denied through the Indian Act. It is possible that John A. Macdonald would roll over in his grave if he was to see this rise of Indigenous economic power and Indigenous Peoples taking a seat at the economic table of this country.

19. Mi'kmaq Land Claim Title Case

Land title claims have been a consistent development for Indigenous Nations, and these claims are creating new space for Indigenous economic participation. Specifically, the Mi'kmaw Nations have advanced an Aboriginal Title claim that includes almost all of the province of New Brunswick, covering almost one-third of the province's total land base.[86]

A *CBC* article cites "Eight Mi'kmaw Communities in New Brunswick Are Formally Asserting Title to Lands and Waters in New Brunswick." The group identified that this move is "another step in the process of reasserting jurisdiction over lands and waters within our territory. This is a step toward self-determination and full recognition of our rights."[87] Although the Mi'kmaw are claiming title over the whole province, MTI said, "We are not seeking the return of private lands to Mi'gmaq ownership, only Crown lands and industrial freehold lands." The claim alleges that the Province is not upholding the Peace and Friendship Treaties signed in what is now Maine, New Hampshire, New Brunswick, and Nova Scotia between 1725 and 1779.

20 Historical Treaty Annuities Payments Legal Challenges

There is a growing trend of historical and numbered treaty signatory Nations challenging the government's lack of upholding their treaty obligations, including the original intention of the annuities. Establishing the value analysis of this economic injustice creates unprecedented momentum in Indigenous economic power today. John A. Macdonald would never have seen the breaking of the original treaties being challenged or the monetary compensation that is only beginning to be demonstrated today and translating into real economic value for Indigenous Nations.

21. Land Claims Settlements

The ongoing stream of Indigenous land settlements is based on the legal resolution of long-standing claims. These land claim settlements are creating unprecedented value in the Indigenous economy nationwide. An example of this is in the Treaty 8 region, where Nations did not receive all the lands owed to them under the Treaty 8 agreement, which was signed in 1899.[88]

22. An Indigenous Woman Justice Minister and Attorney General of Canada

Jody Wilson-Raybauld made history in 2019 when she was elected and appointed the first Indigenous federal minister of justice and attorney general in Canadian history. John A. Macdonald would never have seen this development coming.

23. An Indigenous Premier of Manitoba

Wab Kinew made history in 2023 as Canada's first provincial premier of First Nations descent, and Manitoba's first Indigenous premier since Métis Premier John Norquay in 1887.

24. Appointment of an Indigenous Supreme Court Judge

The Honorable Michelle O'Bonsawin was appointed to the top court in 2022, marking a monumental moment as the first Indigenous person to serve on Canada's highest court. John A. Macdonald would never have seen this coming.

25. Haida Gwaii "Given" Title

In a recent development, the Province of BC signed a title agreement with the Haida Nation. The "Rising Tide" title agreement shifted ownership and jurisdiction of lands and resources away from the Crown to the Haida Nation. The advancement of Indigenous Title is a critical development in the timeline of the deconstruction of Indian Act economics.[89]

John A. Macdonald would never have seen these coming as the Indigenous relationship evolved from radical exclusion to increasing recognition and bridging inclusion and reconciliation. These examples serve as a remarkable demonstration of Indigenous resilience, excellence, and significant generational achievement in a country that counted on Indigenous nonexistence through assimilation and forced removal.

7

Stoking the Fire—Designing for Radical Inclusion

The hardest things to change are the mindsets that create the systems that need to be changed.

—Donella Meadows, *Limits to Growth*

THE INHERITANCE of perception, language usage, and legal and political positions are all reflective of the state of the Indigenous relationship from the establishment of Canada until now. The use of language is depicted in this example of the inheritance of the perception of the Indigenous relationship:

> One of the greatest barriers standing in the way of creating new and legitimate institutions of self-government is the notion that Aboriginal people constitute a "disadvantaged racial minority." Only when Aboriginal Peoples are viewed, not as "races" within the boundaries of a legitimate state, but as distinct political communities with recognizable claims for collective rights, will there be a first and meaningful step towards responding to Aboriginal Peoples' challenge to achieving self-government.[90]

Framing the inheritance of this perception within Canadian reality is critical in understanding the rise of the Indigenous economy today. Viewing the rise of Indigenous economic power through the lens of radical inclusion is like the process of stoking a fire. The rise of Indigenous economic power is a response to the limitations that have been placed upon Indigenous Peoples over time. Indigenomics is bringing into focus the change of process of advancing modern, constructive, generative Indigenous economic design. Indigenous economic design is the active deconstruction of the experience of the Indian Act, in Canadian reality.

The achievement of the $100 billion Indigenous economy represents a powerful value proposition in Canada's economy. Leveraging the unique strengths, capabilities, resources, rights, cultural ways of being and knowing, and Indigenous worldviews creates significant economic, social, and environmental benefits. This value proposition highlights the potential for transformative growth and sustainability within Indigenous economies, positioning them as sustainable, investable businesses and strategic partnerships. It is from here that the meaning of Indigenous economic power is shaped. The Business Council of Canada articulates this context:

> When more than 1.5 million [Indigenous] people are pushed to the periphery of economic life, we cannot expect Canada to thrive and prosper. Nor can we say our country is truly inclusive, when so many of our communities are on the outside looking in. A truly prosperous Canada enables Indigenous Peoples to fully participate in the economy.[91]

Investing in the Indigenous economy is an investment into a more sustainable, inclusive, just, and prosperous future for all. The $100 billion Indigenous economic value proposition outlines ten core tenets for designing for impact and radical inclusion:

1. **Upholds Indigenous cultural and intellectual capital:** Indigenous economic knowledge carries unique cultural assets and deep knowledge of Indigenous economic worldviews that transcend the embodiment of spiritual, cultural, and ecological wisdom across time, and is essential to upholding Indigenous economic worldview.
2. **Indigenous business structures serve to advance sustainable economic development:** Valuing Indigenous economic knowledge systems upholds Traditional Ecological Knowledge that contributes to sustainable resource management, biodiversity conservation, and innovative Indigenous-led climate leadership nationally and globally.
3. **Advances innovation:** Indigenous businesses demonstrate resilience and innovation by adapting traditional practices within modern markets while creating new business opportunities for growth, strategic advantage, and market competitiveness.

4. **Advances positive social and economic outcomes:** Job creation and employment are essential outcomes of activating Indigenous economic growth. Investing in Indigenous economies and partnerships creates jobs, reduces unemployment, and improves living and health standards within Indigenous communities while also contributing to overall economic and social well-being. The growth of Indigenous businesses is the solution to help close the Indigenous socioeconomic gap.

5. **Centers Indigenous education, skills, and capacity development:** Enhanced educational opportunities, skills training, and mentorship for Indigenous Peoples can empower communities while building a skilled workforce, driving further economic development.

6. **Supports partnerships and collaborations:** Partnerships between Indigenous businesses and non-Indigenous companies, governments, and organizations foster knowledge exchange, capacity building, increased market access, and reconciliation outcomes.

7. **Advances Indigenous economic policy:** Building supportive Indigenous economic policies and equitable access to economic opportunities ensures that Indigenous businesses can thrive and participate fully within national and global markets.

8. **Upholds Indigenous cultural well-being and resilience:** Indigenous economic development outcomes are reinvested into cultural continuity processes such as youth and Elder or language activities, which serves to uphold community well-being and long-term generational resilience.

9. **Upholds community-centered economic development and design:** Economic activities are aligned with community values and priorities, ensuring that growth benefits all members and supports social and cultural resilience.

10. **Centers community health and well-being outcomes:** Indigenous economic prosperity leads to improved community health outcomes, reduced poverty, and enhanced overall well-being in Indigenous communities.

In the traditional economics sense, "market power" refers to a company's ability to manipulate the price of an item in the marketplace by manipulating the level of supply, demand, or both. Now, replace company with Nation or Indigenous economic development corporation here. The rise of Indigenous economic power is increasing Indigenous Nations' ability to advance market space in the Canadian economy by affecting supply and demand.

Each Indigenous legal case won is a thunderbolt shaking the foundation of the economic structure of the inheritance of Canada's colonial inheritance. Each win is an expression of "we are still here." Each win reflects the legacy and application of Indigenous worldviews and their place in modernity. This is a high-stakes game that Canada is in with Indigenous Peoples with a behavioral strategy of do nothing, business as usual, bluff, or deny, and pivot.

Status Quo Thinking and Indian Act Economics

In the process of deconstructing Indian Act economics, an important reflective question is: What is status quo thinking regarding the Indian Act? The perspective of Max Libroiron in a short film series accurately describes the concept and experience of the status quo, "Every time you decide what question to ask or not ask others, which counting style you use, which statistics you use, how you frame things, where you publish them, who you work with, where you get funding from ... all of that is political because reproducing the status quo consistently is deeply political because the status quo is crappy."[92] The irony of Indian Act economics is that, to maintain the status quo, it requires actively upholding it. The status quo of Indian Act economics is deeply political.

The concept of the status quo refers to the current state or the way things are and have always been. The status quo is the norms, rules, and practices that shape what we think, believe, and behave about the Indian Act. In a *Medium* article, Andreas Kruszakin-Liboska describes:

> So what is the status quo, and why does it suck? The status quo is the existing state of affairs, the way things are and have been for a long time. It's the norms, the rules, and the conventions that shape the way we think and act. It's the comfort zone, the safe zone, the easy zone. It's the zone that sucks because it limits our potential, our creativity, and our impact.[93]

The status quo means to be comfortable in complacency, to keep things as they are, and to not take action. The status quo is a mindset that facilitates the preference for things to stay the same and actively upholds the aversion to change. The Indian Act is stuck in a rigorous cycle of the conflict between its original intention of elimination, what it says across time, and the delivery of the management and administration of today, as well as the cost of its deployment, what it doesn't say, and the actual pace of business alongside a shifting legal environment that is significantly advancing Indigenous Rights and jurisdiction.

The existing status quo of the Indian Act is built on the inherent bias of the perception of Indigenous Peoples. Adhering to the inherited bias of the Indian Act is problematic, especially in business, because growth requires change. The legal relationship with Indigenous Peoples is also evolving, which is driving change today in the Indigenous economy. In a series of participant interviews, interviewees were asked their perspectives regarding the status quo and Indian Act economics.

Indigenous business leader Rose Paul describes the Mi'kmaq worldview approach to economic development:

A well-known conceptual framework of Indigenous ways of knowing is referred to as Two-Eyed Seeing. Two-Eyed Seeing is the guiding principle brought forward by Mi'kmaw Elder Albert Marshall in 2004. *Etuaptmumk* is the Mi'kmaw word for "Two-Eyed Seeing." We often explain Etuaptmumk, Two-Eyed Seeing, by saying it refers to learning to see from one eye with the strengths of Indigenous knowledges and ways of knowing, and from the other eye with the strengths of Western knowledge and ways of knowing ... and learning to use both these eyes together, for the benefit of all.

In understanding this expansive depiction of operating from within the Indigenous Mi'kmaq worldview, we must realize that this is the opposite of Indian Act economics. The Indian Act is instead cycloptic or one-eyed seeing—as in viewing the Indigenous relationship from a single perspective that has always been Eurocentric, authoritative, and controlling in nature.

Indigenous business leader Wil Jimmy describes the status quo of Indian Act economics: "The big work today is to take accountability for what has to happen with the Indian Act. There has to be truth before reconciliation.

There has to be something to remove the complacency, to remove the beliefs and operating from the status quo of business as usual and to actually bring action into addressing the Indian Act and its consequences."

In an interview with Cadmus Delorme, he offers this perspective on the status quo of the Indian Act.

> The status quo has two approaches from an Indigenous governance perspective. The first approach involves the common process of electing Chief and Council and establishing a housing, health, education, sports portfolio, etc. Here, Chief and Council will be busy micromanaging. If we are busy micromanaging, then we can't be thinking of actual nation-to-nation building. That is the status quo from Indigenous governance perspective. However, from the Canadian government perspective, the status quo means Indigenous Peoples are watering down or giving up our rights and just becoming Canadian.

The mindset of the status quo and the Indigenous relationship is further described by Delorme.

> If anybody thinks the Indian Act should stay the way it is, then that is the status quo as the Indian Act's original purpose is to remove Indigenous worldview and mindsets from within our country. That is the totally wrong mindset to build a long-term strategic relationship between Indigenous people and Canadians today.

As key outcomes in the Indigenous economy are being built, this question on the status quo builds an important perspective around self-determination. Kim Baird of the Tsawwassen Nation refers to this in her experience:

> Until there is change to this terrible structure of the Indian Act, we are all collectively stuck with a poor governance model. And while there are good individuals trying to work within this structure, it is essential to understand that Indigenous Nations are set up to fail within the current Indian Act governance system.

Indian Act economics is the status quo. The connection between good governance, self-determination, and building an economic foundation is directly connected to the rise of the Indigenous economy. Baird continues:

> Status quo thinking is not establishing the structure for self-governance frameworks for Indigenous Nations. It is this archaic thinking that presupposes we can't take care of ourselves, so we can't be self-governing. That is what has been inherited under the Indian Act, this kind of thinking.

Moving beyond the status quo today means a dual approach to governance and nation building. Baird describes this process of moving modern treaty forward in the Tsawwassen Nation and what that meant in the context of moving away from the Indian Act.

> The Indian Act is a very poor piece of legislation and poor governance model. In the concept of moving away from it, that also means it needs to be replaced with other approaches. Our modern treaty allows for regulatory frameworks that are based on building that capacity to allow for business opportunities to happen in a timely way.
>
> In hindsight, the economics of our treaty worked really well and while the people side of things naturally takes longer to evolve, we are over 15 years in now and it's a work in progress, but as a Nation we are definitely in a much better position with a better approach to any problems now than what we had under the Indian Act.

Moving Away from the Indian Act

Baird reflects further on the residual effects of abandoning the Indian Act and developing a strong economic foundation.

> To go from a small Nation that doesn't own our lands or have any kind of jurisdiction over them to being liable and building an economic base for ourselves; it was a huge shift moving away from the Indian Act. And with that comes a strong need to develop governance and business capacity to better understand and respond to the

responsibilities of that shift. It is a massive change management process to move out from the Indian Act and to understand the ultimate
responsibility of self-determination.

Baird describes the process of moving away from the Indian Act in the
context of the modern-day treaty process.

A lot of people are afraid to move away from the Indian Act, but it
needs to be an eyes wide open thing. We have to be aware of what
we're getting into. But we can do it, and while we have had our challenges, it is so much better for us today in moving away from the
Indian Act today. So, even though it might not be perfect, it is way
better than the tools and limitations we had under the Indian Act.
Self-doubt is a big barrier for Indigenous Nations in finding a way
forward. We cannot wait for things to be perfect to move forward,
and when you're dealing with imperfect institutions like the federal
and provincial governments, they will never be 100 percent where
we need them to be. We as Nations need enough autonomy to be
able to build our self-governance and self-determination.

Cadmus Delorme reflects on moving away from the Indian Act in his
Nation.

Moving away from the Indian Act means that an Indigenous Nation's
governing body must have the space to create their own written legislation to exit the Indian Act on their own terms. We need to build up
our own governing institutions. That is what we are looking at today
as Indigenous Nations.

You can't just delete the Indian Act, but it can be addressed by
investing in nation-to-nation relationships and building up self-governance mechanisms. When I served as Chief, we exited Section 87
of the Indian Act and took over our child welfare jurisdiction. Some
Nations have exited Sections 21 to 28 through the First Nations Land
Management Act, and this is an example of how Nations can create
their own laws and exit specific clauses of the Indian Act. In Section

35 of the Constitution, Canada has a fiduciary obligation to respect and fund that law. That's how Nations are exiting the Indian Act, and that's why we need a huge investment in governance reform.

The relationship between self-governance and exiting the Indian Act are correlated. In the context of the process of moving away from the Indian Act, Delorme further explains:

> To get out of the Indian Act requires quasi-jurisdictional development because we have to be able to write our own laws. We understand we have our own laws that are bedded in our songs and our ceremonies. And now, today, in writing them in a modern sense, it starts with our constitutions as Nations, it starts with our legislation as Nations. That is how we're going to exit the Indian Act—through policy reform and the process of nation-building. That is the actual structure and process of coming out from underneath the Indian Act.

While the Indian Act was built by design, it will also be deconstructed by design. The architecture of key Indigenous financial, economic, business, and governance structures will ultimately serve to dismantle the structures of Indigenous systematic economic exclusion and work to increase new outcomes within the economic development process.

Activating modern self-governance and self-determination processes are key elements. The Tsawwassen Nation's modern-day treaty was an exercise in governance design, but it also established the Nation's economic design. Baird reflects on building economic outcomes with the Nation through self-governance:

> Tsawwassen has been able to develop an economy today, and it is an economy that doesn't just benefit our own community. We are a powerful economic generator in the region through the treaty and self-governance. In spite of still having the ongoing effects from the economic limitations imposed on us over time, we were still able to do a thousand of times more than what we could do while under the Indian Act, and that was the very beginning of our economic freedom.

In a post-treaty environment, Baird describes designing economic outcomes of the Nation:

> The concept of Indigenous economic freedom means having the same opportunities as others and having these opportunities without interference from others, whether it be through public policy or systemic kind of interference. Canadians take for granted, but enjoy being able to create infrastructure. But it's important to understand that being able to do that means the whole framework enables that, and that is just not the same for Indigenous communities. But First Nations don't benefit from that framework at all. Basic decision-making frameworks like access to infrastructure, or access to structures that enable economic development, access to capital and all those things Canadians take for granted. It is the absence of these enabling frameworks that impedes economic freedom for us as Indigenous Peoples. That is Indian Act economics.

Tsawwassen First Nation Case Study

The following offers some key insights into the economic space created by Indigenous self-governance. Tsawwassen First Nation (TFN) is pursuing an ambitious agenda of sustainable economic development. The following provides an economic profile of the Nation's post-treaty implementation outcomes:

- The Tsawwassen First Nation Final Agreement provided the Nation with municipal, provincial, and federal types of jurisdiction over 724 hectares of Tsawwassen urban Lands.
- The Treaty provided TFN with the tools to put in the hard work required to realize the Nation's true potential. It has allowed TFN to build prosperity and shape its future as individuals and a community. A strong economic foundation has been critical to this success.

- The Tsawwassen people, like many Indigenous Peoples, have long valued the importance of balancing economic opportunities that promote self-reliance and prosperity as stewardship of our lands.

Infrastructure

- Critical infrastructure was first needed to support not only the Tsawwassen commercial developments but also the full build-out of the Land Use Plan. TFN completed its $27 million state-of-the-art sewage treatment plant and made improvements to significant road and utility services to create the necessary foundation for exponential growth. Almost $100 million has been invested in community-wide infrastructure improvements to date.

Residential Lands

- In 2012, groundbreaking of a forty-two-lot subdivision called Tsawwassen Shores, a partnership signed with Aquilini Development and the first of several residential developments made possible through a treaty that will ultimately bring thousands of new residents to Tsawwassen Lands.
- A master-planned, mixed-use community of up to 2,800 residential market housing units is also in development. The second and third phases are underway and expected to bring thousands of new residents to Tsawwassen Lands.

Commercial Lands

- The 2014 land lease agreements with Ivanhoe Cambridge (Tsawwassen Mills) and Property Development Group (Tsawwassen Commons) comprised the largest non-resource development deal ever signed by a BC First Nation. Tsawwassen Mills and Commons malls remain one of the largest commercial retail developments in Canada, boasting more than two million square feet of commercial retail space. The malls attracted nearly 300,000 visitors in the first five days alone.

Industrial Lands

- TFN Industrial Lands is strategically located directly adjacent to the Port of Vancouver Deltaport, Canada's largest container port complex and bulk commodities terminal, through which approximately $500 million of Pacific region trade flows every day.
- Sitting on approximately 300 acres, only thirty kilometers from both downtown Vancouver and the US border, the initial 90 acres (Phase 1) of TFN's Industrial Lands have been leased to a number of high-quality tenants.
- TFN has leased 100 acres for an industrial logistics center servicing the nearby Deltaport container terminal. Major projects announced on TFN's Industrial Lands include a large warehouse facility, a container examination center, and a card lock truck fueling facility.
- In 2018, Great West Life Realty oversaw the completion of a new 450,000 square foot logistics facility, naming global distribution giant Amazon as their anchor tenant.

Impact

- The development of TFN's Commercial Lands generated significant employment opportunities. It is estimated that the development created up to 3,500 construction, retail, and property management positions. There were indirect opportunities with tenants as employees or potential franchise operators. This project provided relevant job and small business opportunities for TFN members.
- Through self-government, TFN now has an educated and skilled membership that is becoming more entrepreneurial, innovative, and competitive in the labour market. The unemployment rate at TFN dropped by 20% between 2011 and 2016, and today, there

are more employment opportunities on Tsawwassen Lands than members available to fill them.

- TFN's business growth has provided tangible economic benefits to our members and people across the region. TFN's prosperity is a modern representation of meaningful reconciliation.
- Highlights as of the 2019 ten-year Treaty review:
  - ○ $3.7 billion invested into construction on Tsawwassen Lands
  - ○ $350 million in prepaid land lease revenues
  - ○ 22,000 person-years of construction-related employment
  - ○ 11,000 permanent retail and warehouse jobs
  - ○ $1million in training funds and education funds
  - ○ Almost $30 million in annual property taxes
  - ○ $485 million in annual employment income

Indigenous business leader Wil Jimmy describes the lack of understanding of the fundamentals of Indian Act economics:

Indian Act economics is insufficient to the development of Canada today, yet this is an old story, and we need to move past it. What needs to be built is the knowledge base to move forward. While there are probably over 100,000 businesses, nobody knows because it isn't tracked. This is a significant knowledge and data gap in the Indigenous economy. A national Indigenous labor market study is a massive knowledge gap around the growth of the Indigenous economy.

Today, it is estimated that there are over 500 Indigenous economic development corporations across this country, but the exact number is unknown. This is a significant knowledge gap. If each one owned between five to ten businesses, and each generates millions of dollars and generates hundreds, sometimes thousands of jobs annually, but this is unknown as it is not measured. This number is also unknown. No one has actually analyzed sectors for Indigenous participation. For example, how many Indigenous wineries are there? How many construction companies? How many have hotels? There is no sectoral analysis of the types of Indigenous businesses and certainly none on employment. Canada is data-poor in a rapidly growing Indigenous economy.

Through the rise of the Indigenous economic power, Cadmus Delorme offers this insight:

> When Indians are poor, nobody pays attention to them. Now we're not poor, and we contribute millions of dollars into the local economies and billions of dollars into the national economy. We create hundreds of jobs, now they pay attention to us. We are in a business relationship, and that is what the treaty relationship was supposed to originally be 500 years ago.

There has been significant advancements in the development of Indigenous economic structures and institutions with the objective to move out from beneath the Indian Act while building Indigenous economic participation in recent years. One of the earliest and most successful Indigenous economic design structures for the deconstructing of Indian Act economics is the formation of the Fiscal Management Act (FMA), which facilitated the establishment of several critical institutions to advance the Indigenous economy.[94]

The series of FMA institutions represents an alternative structure that empowers First Nations governments to bypass the limitations of Indian Act economics.

> The FMA institutions support First Nation governments to build ecosystems—investment climates—that nurtures social and economic growth with the intention to advance a new institutional regulatory framework. This framework is a key architectural structure in advancing the growth of the Indigenous economy and includes vital elements of modern Indigenous economic design—notably a strong leadership, governance and administration foundation, property rights certainty through a lands management framework, a legal framework to support markets, fiscal relationships with federal,

provincial/territorial governments and competitive infrastructure and financing processes as noted in the First Nations RoadMap.[95]

Beyond $100 Billion of Indigenous Economic Activity

The $100 billion Indigenous economic collective activity thread is visible across Canada's economic landscape today. Glimpses of this can be seen in the increasing values of Indigenous partnerships and equity participation and in the emerging financial structures that enhance access to capital and increase the efficiencies and impacts of Indigenous participation. These projects vary in size, but cumulatively, they represent significant economic opportunities for Indigenous communities, helping to drive energy sovereignty, self-determination, and economic growth through sustainable development.

There is a growing body of national and regional Indigenous economic research following this thread of increasing billion-dollar Indigenous economic activity. Following the early years of economic reports from 2012 to 2016, a similar methodology and framing follows each subsequent report. While mainly using the same sources of data while citing the limitation of these sources, the collection of research centers on the use of GDP as the background and the consistent metric and language of the Indigenous economic activity "as a contribution" to the larger regional or national economy.

The next section follows this collective thread of increasing Indigenous economic activity within the billion dollar value realm. Through this thread, it is easily discovered the advancement of the emerging space beyond the $100 billion Indigenous economic achievement.

National Examples

The First Nations Finance Authority (FNFA) has surpassed a major milestone by issuing over $2 billion in financing to First Nations through its eleventh debenture. This investment funding helps Indigenous governments invest in critical infrastructure, social services, and economic development, improving the quality of life for their communities while promoting self-sufficiency. FNFA continues to provide low-cost access to capital to its member First Nations, enabling long-term growth and prosperity.

Another example of generative Indigenous economic value creation is with the Canada Infrastructure Bank (CIB), which initially introduced a $1 billion Indigenous fund structure. This financial initiative provides low-interest loans for Indigenous Nations to invest in infrastructure projects such as clean energy, transportation, and broadband internet, thereby increasing Indigenous ownership and participation in Canada's economic landscape.

Another early billion-dollar-level response for advancing Indigenous participation as equity players was the establishment of the CIB's equity program as described in a *Globe and Mail* article titled "Canada Infrastructure Bank Unveils Details for $1-billion Indigenous Equity Loan Program."[96] While this is a federal institution initiative, it creates some distance from the economic inefficiencies of the Indian Act.

Following the initial investment structure, the CIB launched a new Indigenous equity initiative to address the market gap by supporting Indigenous Nations in accessing the purchase of equity stakes in projects in which the CIB is also investing. This program features equity loans ranging between $5 and $100 million, up to 90 percent of Indigenous equity interest, with repayments targeted at fifteen years at minimum Government of Canada interest rates. This Indigenous equity initiative is designed to address the challenge of the lack of access to capital to purchase project equity and support Indigenous businesses in becoming active participants in infrastructure developments. Market lenders have often been unwilling to lend to Indigenous Nations because of the risks identified within the existing structure of the Indian Act, which has created the need for this financial tool. Creating institutions that enable Indigenous participation is important in ensuring new infrastructure projects across the country and bringing long-term economic benefits to Indigenous businesses.

Another example of the $100 billion Indigenous economic thread is the development of the Longhouse Capital fund. A *Globe and Mail* interview article outlines founding partner Fred Di Blasio's intention, "Longhouse was created to generate superior risk adjusted returns for investors, while having a lasting positive impact on Indigenous communities as owners."[97] He further noted that "recent government policies and court decisions are transferring significant wealth to Indigenous groups—money that needs to be managed for future generations. We will take our rightful seat at the table to ensure our values are adhered to and our culture is preserved, while delivering on economic independence as full-fledged partners and owners."

Longhouse Capital will identify investment opportunities in Indigenous projects and traditional private-equity markets. Some examples of private sector utilities, such as Innergex Renewable Energy Inc. and Ontario's Hydro One Ltd., have positioned significant equity stakes in infrastructure projects for Indigenous groups as part of the corporate strategy to gain community license for developments and further reconciliation.

Longhouse Capital will back businesses or projects with revenues between $500 million and $1.5 billion and earnings before interest, taxes, depreciation, and amortization between $50 million and $150 million. Its investment criteria and fee structure are similar to established private-equity shops. The market potential for Indigenous property, infrastructure, and private debt investments poses a significant opportunity.

Of particular note, a recent study sponsored by the Assembly of First Nations and Indigenous Services Canada identified decades of underfunding that have led to massive gaps between services in Indigenous communities and the rest of the country. The study identified an estimated $5.2 billion cost to bring wireless and internet connectivity in mainly rural Indigenous homes to urban standards.[98] It further noted it would cost $12.7 billion to fund Indigenous net zero emissions initiatives and identified a whopping $59 billion shortfall in infrastructure investment. The study found that every dollar spent on Indigenous infrastructure generated between $2.46 and $3.83 in benefits for the entire economy.

The next example of the $100 billion Indigenous economic thread is the recently established Federal Indigenous loan guarantee. The federal government's launch of a $5 billion loan guarantee program creates the support for Indigenous investment in major resource and infrastructure projects. This aims to enhance Indigenous participation in projects such as clean energy, infrastructure, and natural resources by providing financial backing, making it easier for Indigenous groups to secure capital and take ownership stakes.[99]

The next example in the $100 billion Indigenous economic activity thread is demonstrated through corporate Indigenous spending. From January 2023 to the end of 2030, Enbridge has committed to spending $1 billion with Indigenous businesses. This commitment includes direct and indirect subcontracting opportunities and wages paid to Indigenous workers. This initiative is part of the company's Indigenous Reconciliation Action Plan.

British Columbia Region

The Sen'ákw Development, led by the Squamish Nation through its development arm, the Nch'ḵay' Development Corporation, is projected to generate over $10 billion in long-term returns from rental income and business leases across ten towers. This project is a prime example of how Indigenous-led projects foster economic growth and cultural preservation in Canada and is described as one of the largest Indigenous-led economic projects.

Another demonstration of the $100 billion Indigenous economic thread is also with the Squamish Nation in BC and the Woodfibre LNG project, which is worth $1.8 billion. Of particular note, this project is the first industrial project to undergo Squamish Nation's groundbreaking environmental assessment process and is the first industrial project in Canada to be awarded an environmental assessment certificate by an Indigenous government.

The Cedar LNG project is the first Indigenous-majority-owned LNG export facility in Canada, providing an unprecedented economic opportunity for the Haisla Nation. This project represents a significant milestone that advances the implementation of UNDRIP. The Cedar LNG project will be the largest First Nations majority-owned infrastructure project in Canada. They will play a key role in the Haisla Nation's economic development over the next four decades.

Next, British Columbia is creating a First Nations Equity Financing Framework as part of its budget and fiscal plan. The Framework aligns with the government's commitment to "co-develop with First Nations a new fiscal relationship that supports the self-determination and operation of First Nations governments" and the implementation of UNDRIP. The government is creating the equity financing tool to help unlock opportunities for First Nation economic participation.

The Crown Mountain Coking Coal Project (Nasuʔkin Business Development and Jameson Resources) has a project value of over $1 billion. The partners include Nasuʔkin Business Development (Ktunaxa Nation) and Jameson Resources. The Crown Mountain Coking Coal Project is a proposed coal mining development in southeastern BC. The Ktunaxa Nation, through its business arm Nasuʔkin Business Development, has agreements in place with the project developer, ensuring participation in economic benefits, including employment, contracts, and environmental oversight.

Next is the Nisga'a Nation and Ksi Lisims LNG Project, which has a project value of $10 billion. The partners include Nisga'a Nation, Rockies LNG, and Western LNG. The Ksi Lisims LNG project is a proposed $10 billion liquefied natural gas export facility in northern BC, led by the Nisga'a Nation in partnership with industry stakeholders. This project, located on Nisga'a territory, will provide substantial economic benefits to the Nisga'a Nation, including ownership stakes, jobs, training, and revenue from LNG exports. The project will collectively produce about 20 percent of Canada's natural gas.

Tahltan Nation and Red Chris Mine Expansion (Newcrest Mining) have a project value of over $1 billion (including expansion) and will continue to generate long-term economic benefits for the Tahltan. The Tahltan Nation benefits from various agreements related to environmental protection, employment, business opportunities, and revenue sharing.

Also in BC, LNG Canada has advanced over $40 billion in Indigenous Participation Agreements with various Indigenous Nations along the project corridor, including the Haisla Nation and the Wet'suwet'en Nation. LNG Canada is the largest private infrastructure investment in Canadian history, involving the construction of a liquefied natural gas (LNG) export facility in Kitimat, BC. Indigenous communities along the project corridor have signed participation agreements, securing benefits for jobs, training, contracts, and environmental protection. Indigenous equity stakes in related infrastructure, such as the Coastal GasLink pipeline, complement this major project.

Alberta Region

A first example of insights into the perspective beyond the $100 billion thread is through the early leadership of responding to Indigenous economic inclusion in Alberta with the establishment of the Alberta Investment Opportunities Corporation (AIOC). The AIOC was established in 2019 as the first Crown corporation in Canada to provide up to $1 billion in loan guarantees for Indigenous investment opportunities. Through this structure, Indigenous Nations can benefit from the direct investment into medium- to large-scale natural resources, agriculture, telecommunication, transportation projects, and related infrastructure.

Since its establishment, the AIOC mandate has increased from the original amount to $2 billion, followed by another increase of $3 billion for Indigenous investment opportunities. In a recent national conference hosted by the Indian Resource Council, former Premier Kenney spoke to this significant development of the Indigenous economy and how it relates directly to the inadequacies of the Indian Act. "The growing generation of visionary leadership in Indigenous communities realize that to move from poverty to prosperity requires full participation in the economy."[100] He continued, "We see dozens of communities across the country getting involved in major projects enthusiastically because they now have a meaningful, long-term ownership stake. So we changed the model, we changed the paradigm."

He further notes that "finally, we are seeing some governments beginning to realize that the old Indian Act model is outdated—where the federal government would collect the royalties, the revenues from oil and gas projects and kind of dribble it out like a paternalistic father—this is the colonial act model." What Kenney is referring to is precisely that—the active dismantling of Indian Act economics.

A recent example of the $100 billion Indigenous economic thread is a TC Energy announcement that highlights a historic equity ownership agreement where up to seventy-two Indigenous Nations will acquire a 5.34 percent equity interest, which represents a $1 billion investment into critical energy infrastructure. This agreement underscores significant progress in economic reconciliation and collaboration with Indigenous Nations for long-term growth, ownership, and prosperity.

The Indigenous economic value highlighted in Suncor's 2023 Report on Sustainability includes several key initiatives to foster collaboration with Indigenous Nations. One of the most significant is their $3.1 billion in spending with Indigenous suppliers, representing 20 percent of their total procurement. This is part of Suncor's commitment to building long-term partnerships and supporting local Indigenous businesses. The company also maintains sixty-three Petro-Canada retail stations in partnership with First Nations and Métis Nations, creating vital economic hubs for these areas. Suncor's efforts extend to workforce inclusion, with 923 Indigenous employees comprising 5.4 percent of their workforce. They foster inclusion through their Indigenous employee network, Journeys, which supports Indigenous staff and promotes cultural engagement. These initiatives reflect Suncor's broader strategy to integrate Indigenous knowledge and business collaboration as part of their reconciliation journey, guided by the principles of UNDRIP.

The next example that demonstrates the rise of Indigenous economic value is the economic reconciliation report of the City of Calgary. The study highlights that Indigenous economic contributions account for $2.1 billion annually or 2.5 percent of Calgary's total GDP. This study underscores the significant economic role Indigenous communities play in Calgary and the Treaty 7 region and aims to inform strategies for economic reconciliation by supporting Indigenous businesses and fostering further growth.[101]

Next, the Wood Buffalo Métis Corporation and Suncor Energy have a project value of over $1 billion in various projects. Wood Buffalo Métis Corporation is involved in various contracts with Suncor Energy related to the oil sands in Northern Alberta. These partnerships focus on construction, maintenance, and environmental management services, with long-term economic benefits for the Métis Nation.

Next, the Fort Chipewyan Solar Project has a project value of over $1 billion (including future expansion). The partners include Athabasca Chipewyan First Nation, Mikisew Cree First Nation, and Three Nations Energy. The Fort Chipewyan Solar Project is one of the largest off-grid solar projects in Canada, providing clean energy to the remote community of Fort Chipewyan. The project reduces reliance on diesel and contributes to long-term energy sustainability. While initial phases are under $1 billion, future expansions and associated infrastructure development are expected to push the value beyond $1 billion.

Finally, to demonstrate economic value in this emerging $100 billion Indigenous economic thread, the Taza Development Corporation of the Tsuut'ina Nation is finalizing a $4.5 billion land development project near Calgary; this initiative spans 1,200 acres and focuses on commercial, residential, and office infrastructure. It is expected to create long-term economic growth and employment opportunities while integrating cultural elements of the Tsuut'ina Nation.

Saskatchewan Region

The Meadow Lake Tribal Council Bioenergy Project in Saskatchewan is a $1.2 billion biomass power generation project owned by the Meadow Lake Tribal Council. The Tribal Council owns 100 percent of the bioenergy project, making it a significant example of full Indigenous ownership in a renewable energy initiative. The project converts forest residues into biomass energy, generating power for the local grid while reducing greenhouse gas emissions. It also provides employment and economic opportunities for the Tribal Council's members.

Next, the SaskPower and First Nations Power Authority (FNPA) partnership has a project value of over $1 billion in multiple renewable energy projects. This partnership involves several large-scale renewable energy projects, including wind and solar power initiatives. The agreement allows for the development of Indigenous-led power generation projects, with multiple First Nations having ownership stakes and economic participation. The projects aim to increase renewable energy capacity in Saskatchewan while ensuring Indigenous participation in the energy sector. These projects collectively exceed $1 billion in investment.

Next, the Kisiskâciwan Power Project has a value over $1 billion (multiple solar projects). It is a partnership between George Gordon First Nation and Elemental Energy. The Kisiskâciwan Power Project is part of Saskatchewan's broader renewable energy development, focusing on solar power. George Gordon First Nation is a key partner in the project, with ownership stakes and benefits in solar energy production. These solar energy projects will contribute to Saskatchewan's transition to renewable energy, ensuring Indigenous communities benefit from the economic returns and sustainable energy generation.

Manitoba Region

Next, the Keeyask Hydroelectric Project (Manitoba) is an $8.7 billion project in partnership with Manitoba Hydro and four Cree Nations (Tataskweyak Cree Nation, War Lake First Nation, York Factory First Nation, and Fox Lake Cree Nation). It is one of Canada's largest hydroelectric projects and aims to produce clean, renewable energy with a capacity of 695 megawatts. The project provides significant long-term economic benefits to the partnering Indigenous communities with 25 percent Indigenous ownership.

Ontario Region

In 2009, the Ontario government created an Indigenous loan guarantee program for increasing clean power. It was the only provincial jurisdiction that had one for about a decade until Alberta came forward with an Indigenous loan guarantee, followed shortly after by Saskatchewan and, most recently, BC announcing a billion-dollar Indigenous loan guarantee program. This is a notable structure for designing and advancing Indigenous economic outcomes. The principle of "form follows function" is foundational to the value creation process in the Indigenous economy.

Kim Baird refers to this trend: "We should be exploring new financial tools for Indigenous participation because we really need to bring those solutions to scale whether it's access to capital, creation of infrastructure, including clean water and clean energy."

Next, the Wataynikaneyap Power Project is valued at $1.9 billion— Canada's largest Indigenous-led infrastructure project. It aims to connect seventeen remote First Nations in northwestern Ontario to the provincial power grid using clean energy, replacing costly and polluting diesel generators. Wataynikaneyap Power is 51 percent owned by twenty-four First Nations communities.

Next, the Bruce Power Refurbishment project, valued at over $13 billion, is one of Canada's largest nuclear power initiatives. In 2020, Bruce Power partnered with the Saugeen Ojibway Nation (SON), allowing them to acquire an equity interest in the refurbishment project. SON holds a minority equity interest in Bruce Power's project, making it one of the largest Indigenous ownerships in the nuclear sector. The refurbishment will extend the life of the Bruce Power nuclear plant by several decades, ensuring energy security for Ontario while providing financial returns to SON.

Next, the Oneida Energy Storage Project in Ontario has a project value of over $1 billion. The partners include Six Nations of the Grand River Development Corporation, Northland Power, NRStor, and the Government of Canada. The Oneida Energy Storage Project is set to be one of the largest energy storage systems in the world, supporting Ontario's grid by storing renewable energy and reducing greenhouse gas emissions. Six Nations of the Grand River is a key equity partner, benefiting from long-term revenues and involvement in the clean energy sector.

Atlantic Region

The Miawpukek First Nation is involved in several large-scale renewable energy projects in Newfoundland and Labrador, with significant economic potential. One of the key developments is the Toqlukuti'k Wind and Hydrogen Project, a partnership between Miawpukek First Nation, ABO Wind, and Braya Renewable Fuels. This project is valued at around $1 billion and aims to produce green hydrogen for both local use and export. Phase 1 of the project involves building a 500 MW wind power facility.

The Mi'kmaq have been increasingly involved in wind energy projects across Nova Scotia, working with private companies to co-develop wind farms. These projects are part of the province's broader push toward renewable energy, with the Mi'kmaq holding equity stakes and benefiting from long-term revenue generated by clean energy production.

The Territories

In the Yukon, the Casino Mining Project (Selkirk First Nation and Western Copper and Gold) have a project value of over $3 billion. The Casino Project is a copper, gold, and molybdenum mining project located in the central Yukon. Selkirk First Nation is working closely with Western Copper and Gold to ensure that the project provides economic benefits to the community, including jobs, training, and business opportunities. The project is subject to environmental assessments and benefit agreements to ensure Indigenous participation in decision-making and economic benefits.

Next, the Eagle Gold Mine has a project value of over $1 billion (including future expansions). The Eagle Gold Mine is a significant gold mining project located in the Yukon, in partnership with the Tr'ondëk Hwëch'in First Nation. The Tr'ondëk Hwëch'in First Nation benefits from agreements related to employment, environmental stewardship, and business opportunities. Long-term revenue-sharing agreements ensure the First Nation receives ongoing financial benefits from the mine's operations.

The Kudz Ze Kayah Project (Ross River Dena Council and BMC Minerals) has a project value of over $1 billion (estimated development and expansion). The Kudz Ze Kayah Project is a proposed lead, zinc, and silver mining project in southeastern Yukon. The Ross River Dena Council has negotiated with BMC Minerals to ensure that the project brings economic benefits to the community through impact and benefit agreements (IBAs).

Next, the Selwyn Project is a partnership between Ross River Dena Council, Liard First Nation, and Selwyn Chihong Mining and has a project value of $1.2 billion in development costs. The Selwyn Project is a large-scale zinc and lead mining project located along the Yukon-Northwest Territories border. Both the Ross River Dena Council and Liard First Nation are actively involved in the project through IBAs, ensuring that the project delivers long-term benefits to their communities. These benefits include employment, training, business opportunities, and revenue-sharing agreements.

Next, the Yukon Bell Indigenous Partnership is a landmark deal where Sixty North Unity, a consortium of Indigenous organizations from the Yukon, Northwest Territories, and Nunavut, is set to acquire Northwestel, the largest telecommunications provider in northern Canada, from Bell for $1 billion. This acquisition will make Northwestel the largest Indigenous-owned telecommunications company globally. The consortium is focused on enhancing telecommunications infrastructure in northern communities, with plans to significantly invest in improving internet speeds and expanding access to remote areas. The deal will enable Indigenous communities to have greater control over telecommunications services and reinvest revenues into critical areas like housing, education, and social services. The partnership is viewed as a major step toward economic reconciliation, allowing Indigenous communities to own and operate key infrastructure in their regions while maintaining a strategic partnership with Bell for ongoing operational support.

Tłı̨chǫ All-Season Road (Tłı̨chǫ Government and Northwest Territories government) has a long-term project value of $1 billion. The Tłı̨chǫ All-Season Road is a vital infrastructure project aimed at providing year-round access to the Tłı̨chǫ region, connecting communities to the provincial road network. This road will improve transportation, facilitate economic development, and reduce the cost of goods and services for the Tłı̨chǫ people. Indigenous businesses and communities have played a key role in the construction and management of the project through procurement and employment opportunities.

The Gahcho Kué Diamond Mine (Denesoline Corporation, De Beers Group, and Mountain Province Diamonds) has a project value of over $1 billion. The Gahcho Kué Diamond Mine is one of the world's largest new diamond mines, located in the Northwest Territories. Indigenous participation through Denesoline Corporation provides local communities with employment, training, and contracting opportunities. The mine contributes significantly to the Northwest Territories' economy, with Indigenous communities benefiting from impact and benefit agreements (IBAs).

The Mackenzie Valley Fibre Link (Indigenous Investment and GNWT) has a project value of over $1 billion (projected benefits over time). The Mackenzie Valley Fibre Link is a critical infrastructure project that provides high-speed internet to communities in the Mackenzie Valley. This project opens the region to new business opportunities and improves service access. Indigenous participation is integral, with local Indigenous businesses benefiting from the construction, operation, and maintenance of the fiber link.

Next, the Prairie Creek Mine (Nahʔą Dehé Dene Band and NorZinc Ltd.) in the Northwest Territories has a project value of over $1 billion (projected for full development and operation). The Prairie Creek Mine is a zinc-silver mine located in the Mackenzie Mountains. The Nahʔą Dehé Dene Nation, through partnerships with NorZinc Ltd., has secured benefits agreements that include revenue sharing, employment, and environmental monitoring.

The Mary River Iron Ore Mine (Baffinland Iron Mines and Qikiqtani Inuit Association) has a project value of $1.2 billion (including expansions). The Mary River Mine is one of the richest iron ore deposits globally and has significantly contributed to Nunavut's economy. The Qikiqtani Inuit Association represents the local Inuit. It has secured substantial benefits through the Inuit Impact and Benefit Agreement (IIBA), including revenue sharing, employment opportunities, training, and business development for Inuit communities. Expansions and ongoing operations push the value of the project beyond $1 billion.

The Kiggavik Uranium Project (Areva Resources Canada and Inuit Organizations) has a project investment of over $1 billion. The Kiggavik Uranium Project is a proposed uranium mine near Baker Lake, Nunavut. While it has faced delays and opposition from local communities, the project has the potential to generate significant economic benefits, including employment and business opportunities for local Inuit. Inuit organizations have been involved in negotiations to ensure that the project respects the environment and delivers economic benefits to the community.

The Meliadine Gold Mine (Agnico Eagle and Inuit Organizations) has a project value of $1.6 billion. The Meliadine Gold Mine is a large-scale gold mining project near Rankin Inlet. It is one of the largest and most significant mining projects in Nunavut. Agnico Eagle has worked closely with Inuit organizations to ensure that the project provides economic benefits through Inuit Impact and Benefit Agreements (IIBAs), offering employment, training, and business development opportunities.

The Hope Bay Gold Project (TMAC Resources and Kitikmeot Inuit Association) has a project value of over $1 billion (including future expansion plans). The Hope Bay Gold Project is a major gold mining initiative in Nunavut. The Kitikmeot Inuit Association has an IIBA in place, ensuring that Inuit communities benefit from the project through employment, contracting opportunities, and revenue sharing. The ongoing development and future expansions of the mine are expected to exceed $1 billion in value.

Beyond the $100 Billion Indigenous Economic Thread Profile

This is it. This is what the emerging $100 billion Indigenous economy looks like. A collective series of Indigenous economic development projects connected together in an investment environment that is responding to the growth of the Indigenous economy.

Table 2: Indigenous Projects with Values Over $1 Billion

Billion-Dollar Project Thread	Identified Indigenous Economic Value ($)	Type / Impact / Structure	Function
Alberta Indigenous Opportunities Corporation	3 billion	Investment vehicle	Increase access to capital and inclusion structure
TC Energy	1 billion	Partnership	-
First Nations Bank of Canada	4 billion	Assets under management (Indigenous Trust focus only)	Advancing Indigenous access to capital and Indigenous-led

-	-	-	investment vehicles
BMO	6.5 billion	Economic out-comes summary	2024 BMO's Indigenous banking portfolio at $6.5 billion, with an $8 billion goal by 2025
Squamish – Sen'ákw Development	10 billion	Indigenous-owned development	-
MST Corporation	5 billion	Lands development	-
Cedar LNG Project	2.4 billion	Indigenous-led partnership	-
Woodfibre LNG Project	1.8 billion	Partnership	-
Canadian Infrastructure Bank	3 billion	-	-
Canadian Infrastructure Bank	1 billion	-	-
Enbridge partnership	1 billion	Indigenous spend	Investment commitment
BC Indigenous Loan Guarantee	1 billion	-	Multiplier struc-ture to advance participation
FNFA	2 billion	-	Multiplier struc-ture to advance participation - accumulative amount across mandate
Federal Indigenous Loan Guarantee	5 billion	-	Multiplier structure
Longhouse Capital	1 billion	-	Indigenous-led investment vehicle
City of Calgary Indigenous Economic Contri-butions Report	2.1 billion	-	-

Keeask Manitoba	2.175 billion	-	-
Wataynikaneyap Power Project	1.9 billion	51% Indigenous ownership	-
Miawtuk	1 billion	-	-
Fortesque	1 billion	-	-
Tukuukuti	1 billion	-	-
Taza Wind Farm	1 billion	-	-
Astisiy	1 billion	-	-
East Tank Farm	1.3 billion	-	-
Fort Chipewyn Wind Farm	1 billion	-	-
Meadow Lake Bio Energy	1.2 billion	-	-
First Nation Power Authority and SaskPower	1 billion	-	-
George Gordon Nation and SaskPower	1 billion	-	-
Keeask Hydro Electric	2.175 billion	-	$8.7 billion with 25% equity ownership
Wood Buffalo Métis	1 billion	-	-
Crown Mountain	1 billion	-	-
Nisga'a LNG	10 billion	-	-
Tahltan Red Cross Mine	1 billion	-	-
Selwyn	1.2 billion	-	-
Kaya	1 billion	-	-
Eagle	1 billion	-	-

Kudz Ze Kayah	1 billion	-	-
Yukon Bell Indigenous Partnership	1 billion	-	-
Casino	3 billion	-	-
Mackenzie	1 billion	-	-
Prairie	1 billion	-	-.
Tlicho	1 billion	-	-
Sixty North Unity Consortium – Northwestel Acquisition	1 billion	-	-
Gazho	1 billion	-	-
Hope Bay Gold	1 billion	-	-
Meliandian	1 billion	-	-
Oneida Energy Storage Project	1 billion	-	-
Membertou / Clearwater	1 billion	-	-
LNG Canada	40 billion	-	Identified direct corporate Indigenous economic spend across projects

The following identifies a series of key points in the emerging $100 billion Indigenous economy:

- This profile summary focuses on Indigenous projects with values over $1 billion only, not below.
- The number of projects below $1 billion is sizable, and there is no clear pathway for tracking and determining these numbers or value.
- Total project value and percentage of Indigenous equity ownership are identified where possible.

- This summary does not include the identification of Indigenous Nations' own-source revenues, investment and trust values, or assets under management across Canada, which are significant but remain unmeasured.
- Corporate Indigenous spend is not clearly identified, representing a sizeable amount of Indigenous economic activity and partnerships.
- This list is not within a specific fiscal year; however, the most recent were identified within the timeframe of the establishment of the $100 billion Indigenous economic target, which was established in 2019.

Finally, this is not an exhaustive list; it only highlights identified projects to advance the narrative of the emerging beyond $100 billion Indigenous economy.

Indigenous Economic Contribution Profile

A growing trend is the increasing economic narrative is of Indigenous Nations and businesses as net contributors to the regional and national economies. Table 3 outlines a series of national and regional Indigenous economic contribution reports that frames the rise of Indigenous economic power.[102]

Table 3: National and Regional Indigenous Economic Contribution Reports

Study	Year	Estimate ($)	Notes
Stats Can National Indigenous GDP Study	2020	48.9 billion	2.2% of Canadian GDP
Indigenous contribution to Atlantic Canada	2020	3.6 billion	Atlantic Economic Council
Indigenous contribution to Manitoba	2016	9.3 billion	3.9% of Manitoba's GDP
Indigenous contribution to Saskatchewan	-	Unmeasured	-
Indigenous contribution to Alberta	2019	6.74 billion	The GDP generated by the Indigenous economy was equivalent to approximately 2% of Alberta's total GDP in 2019

Indigenous contribution to Quebec	-	Unmeasured	-
Indigenous contribution to Ontario	-	Unmeasured	-
Indigenous contribution to BC	-	7.35 billion	The GDP generated by the FN economy was approximately 2.6%
Indigenous contribution to Yukon	-	Unmeasured	-
Indigenous contribution to Northwest Territories	-	Unmeasured	-
Indigenous contribution to Nunavut	-	Unmeasured	-
Calgary Indigenous economic contribution study	2021	1.5 billion	1.2% of Calgary's total GDP

The following identifies a series of points of significance in the emergence of the $100 billion Indigenous economic target:

- Every single province and territory should be measuring Indigenous economic growth consistently.
- Achieving "par" is based on the Indigenous population being approximately 5 percent of the total population.
- The gap between the contribution percentage of total GDP and the Indigenous population is the investment and the partnership opportunity.

Indigenomics is the process of reclaiming Indigenous economic space. The rise of Indigenous economic power is a parallel process of advancing Indigenous economic jurisdiction and facilitating the structures for economic self-determination.

An example of this is the Squamish Nation LNG regulatory assessment. This environmental assessment process was the first legally binding Indigenous-led environmental assessment of a project in Canada. This landmark agreement advanced the Squamish Nation's full and independent environmental oversight of a project on their Traditional Territory. With a focus on innovation, consent, risk management, and collaboration, the agreement identifies specific conditions applicable to Woodfibre LNG, FortisBC, and the Province of British Columbia. Woodfibre LNG is responsible for meeting a series of conditions identified in the agreement. What is of particular significance is that it establishes a return to Indigenous-led stewardship and risk management, with the Nation at the decision-making table instead of a prescribed externalized regulatory process. By advancing Squamish regulatory jurisdiction, this process created economic space through authority, collaboration, and project de-risking.

Shifting Meaning in the Rise of the Indigenous Economic Power

$100 billion is an Indigenous economy marker. It is an insertion into this country's consciousness, to acknowledge Indigenous Peoples as having a place at the economic table.[103] Beyond a $100 billion economic agenda imagines a future national economy that embodies Indigenous worldviews, an economy in which Indigenous Peoples are the drivers of partnerships, investment, and long-term economic growth—by design. Economic equality must be designed. It doesn't just happen by itself. The $100 billion target is working to re-story Indigenous economic growth in Canada. By increasing the visibility of Indigenous business success and framing beyond the $100 billion Indigenous economic target, Indigenomics is counteracting the false narrative of invisibility, deficit, and dependency. Through building Indigenous economic equality, Indigenous Nations are unlocking hundreds of billions of dollars of economic output in the Canadian economy. The focus is on bringing visibility to economic activity by Indigenous Nations and shaping the narrative in a way that supports investability, partnership, and reconciliation outcomes.

Building a Policy Response to Beyond the $100 Billion Indigenous Economy

A key inquiry in the process of deconstructing Indian Act economics is to ask the core question: How can Canada prepare for exceeding the $100 billion Indigenous economy?

The work of the First Nations Financial Management Board is building exemplary results in the Indigenous economy. Centering the fiscal relationship is a central objective of this organizational structure. Harold Calla, Executive Chair, describes this work: "Ultimately, a new relationship means a sharing of power between Canada and First Nations and a transfer of wealth to First Nations. But First Nations wealth creation should not be based on fiscal transfers from Ottawa to First Nations but rather through First Nations economic development and the sharing of revenues between Canada and First Nations for the benefit of all Canadians."[104]

Indigenous business leader Wil Jimmy offers this perspective: "Canada can prepare for the Indigenous economy to exceed the $100 billion target through public policy interventions and building tools for Nations to access capital, or through procurement outcomes, for example."

Cadmus Delorme reflects further that "the Indigenous economy is an untapped market. Indigenous economic growth has the potential to raise the national GDP while at the same time lifting up our children and our children's children. This will have an impact on building economic opportunities for Indigenous nations.

Hillary Thatcher outlines a key perspective to this question:

Moving beyond the $100 billion Indigenous economic target is inevitable. There is a huge swell of growth in the Indigenous market and the Indigenous economy right now, and it's time for Canada to get ready for that. Canada can do a better job of supporting communities in all regions and reimagine, refocus, and innovate around how to provide capital for Indigenous businesses.

Rose Paul describes a policy response to exceeding the $100 billion Indigenous economic target:

Canada needs to prepare that the Indigenous economy requires more tools to support participation for Nations to meet the huge project investement requirements. Whether it be more access to capital for entrepreneurs or the Canada loan guarantee programs to support the billion-dollar industries of the projects that Nations are now undertaking. Corporate Canada needs to really emphasize and be available to be able to see that we're looking at bigger portions of projects now.

How Can Corporate Canada Respond to the Rise of Indigenous Economic Power?

This is a pivotal moment for building an understanding of how corporate Canada can respond to the rise of Indigenous economic power. Interview participants reflect on this question.

Hillary Thatcher identifies three main areas in building a corporate response:

First, corporate Canada needs to view Indigenous Nations as a growing part of the market. Indigenous Peoples are customers, they buy broadband services, they buy cell phone services, they buy homes, they drive on toll roads. They're using water and wastewater systems and electricity to their homes, they're customers. So, build a customer-base focus that also is culturally appropriate and sensitive to the unique needs of the customers that you are serving and take advantage of this growing market. It is important to build strategies on how to serve these communities.

Second, there is a growing Indigenous market that requires capital. So, whether you're a lender or a private investor or venture capital fund, there's a growing market that's requiring capital. It is important to understand the needs of Indigenous borrowers for larger economic opportunities. It is important to understand the existing barriers of the Indian Act, but also how do you work around it to be creative, be innovative so that you can find solutions rather than just putting up a no and adhering and being a part of the barriers.

And the third thing for corporate partners to understand is be a buyer and act as a partner. Work with the Indigenous partners through procurement, through training and other types of capacity supports. It's a changing environment, so it's no longer about Impact Benefit Agreements (IBA) where you identify this many jobs without being held accountable to it and no jobs ever go to the Indigenous People to set up training. Projects can be the training ground for young Indigenous Peoples in the region. And so rather than shipping up all the project workers, why aren't you training local communities and helping them set up their own businesses so that they can be a part of the procurement process and they can grow and flourish while staying at home, where they often want to be and being a part of their community. And part of that culture. These are a number of elements that private sector can incorporate.

Rose Paul reflects on her work on leading Indigenous economic development regionally:

This is the time for corporate Canada to walk the talk with Indigenous People. Corporate Canada can respond to the rise of Indigenous economic power in several ways, such as meaningful partnerships and collaboration engagements with Indigenous communities, businesses, and entrepreneurs to foster economic development opportunities that benefit both parties. This can include joint ventures, supply chain partnerships, and capacity-building initiatives. Building a knowledge base and leadership space for respect for Indigenous rights and the exercising of Indigenous sovereignty is foundational. This includes land rights, self-governance, and cultural autonomy, while Nations are building billion-dollar project participation levels through our rightful land ownership and participation mechanisms. Corporate Canada must consult and collaborate with Indigenous communities on projects and initiatives that may affect them.

Sometimes, corporations move too quickly, causing the tires to spin. Then, the frustration starts, and a project could be shelved or watered down. Corporations go through this because they don't spend enough time on building an understanding of the Indigenous relationship, shifting legal requirements, or the rise of the Indigenous economy.

Cadmus Delorme describes:

If you're generational Canadian in this country, our education system put us in this moment to not know truth. Baby boomers were not taught the truth in the education system. Generation X was not taught the truth in our education system. Generation Y was not taught the truth in this in our education system, and those three generations are the decision-makers in this country today.

In today's economic environment, responding to the Truth and Reconciliation Commissions Call to Action #92 on business and reconciliation means changing our norms, frameworks, and policies; building an understanding of what partnership means; understanding what equity ownership means; and transferring real generational wealth to Indigenous Nations. This must be the corporate response to the rise of Indigenous economic power.

Cadmus Delorme refers to the growing trend of Indigenous equity ownership as a corporate response:

One example of this is in Saskatchewan with the Crown corporation called SASK Power, which is the purchaser and seller monopoly of power in the province of Saskatchewan. Now it is established within organization, any party that wants to get into renewable energy project at minimum have to have 10 percent Indigenous equity ownership in any application they're going to do.

In the Indigenous economic development process today, long-term sustainability is the key to building long-term relationships. Partnerships with Indigenous communities are based on trust, transparency, and mutual benefit. Sustainable partnerships require patience, cultural understanding, and a willingness to listen and learn from Indigenous perspectives. By embracing these approaches, corporate Canada can contribute to the economic empowerment and self-determination of Indigenous Peoples while also fostering economic growth and sustainability for the country.

It is time to get ready for beyond the $100 billion Indigenous economy. In the narrative of the rise of Indigenous economic power being reflected in the media, archaic thinking is still perpetuated. As an example, the Fraser Institute is an independent, nonpartisan research and educational organization, and although in a position of influence and leadership, it entirely misses the significance of the rise of Indigenous economic and legal power. An article titled "B.C. Plans to 'Reconcile' by Giving First Nations Veto on Land Use" leads with the element of fear by describing, "We live in strange times. A new generation of political leaders seem determined to cripple their own societies."[105] The article continues:

> NDP Premier David Eby is preparing to bring the province to its knees. The B.C. government plans to share management of Crown land with First Nations. The scheme will apply not to limited sections of public land here and there, but across the province. The government quietly opened public consultations on the proposal last week. According to the scant materials, the government will amend the B.C. Land Act to incorporate agreements with Indigenous governing bodies.
>
> These agreements will empower B.C.'s hundreds of First Nations to make joint decisions with the minister responsible for the Land Act, the main law under which the provincial government grants leases, licenses, permits and rights-of-way over Crown land. That means that First Nations will have a veto over how most of B.C. is used. Joint management can be expected to apply to mining, hydro projects, farming, forestry, docks and communication towers, just to start. Activities at the heart of B.C.'s economy will be at risk.

The nature of this archaic thinking is irresponsibly spreading fear and perpetuating the colonial shenanigans that "power" is to be given to the Indians. The doomsday-style reporting offers a narrative of colonial fear of giving the Indian too much.

> For many, it is likely to change for the worse. B.C. could become an untenable host for land-based, resource-related enterprise. Impenetrable layers of red tape would entangle applications for leases and licenses. The price for First Nations approvals could be an increasing share of royalties and kickbacks, without which consent will be refused. Both governments and First Nations will siphon an ever-larger piece of a shrinking pie.[106]

This grand finale of fear mongering of the evolution of the Indigenous relationship continues:

> If you are feeling grateful not to live in B.C., don't count your chickens. In 2021 the federal government passed its own version of B.C.'s Bill 41, the federal United Nations Declaration on the Rights of Indigenous Peoples Act. It requires the federal government to "take all measures necessary to ensure that the laws of Canada are consistent with the Declaration.[107]

In complete opposite to the above fear mongering, by placing Canada in the context of the advancement of global Indigenous rights, legal expert Bill Gallagher offers an important perspective:

> The advancement of Indigenous Rights is a worldwide phenomenon and Canada has got the best story to tell. We have the best toolbox. We have Indigenous constitutional rights, we have got the Charter of Rights and Freedom, we have got all these Indigenous court cases wins, we have two Royal Commissions on Indigenous Peoples. What other country in the world has this as a focus on the Indigenous relationship?

It is in this space that the deconstruction of Indian Act economics is also occurring. Cadmus Delorme offers this perspective:

> The Indian Act was created for one purpose—to brainwash the Indigenous worldview away. And so why Canadians should care about understanding of the purpose of the Indian Act is because we are in a moment of reconciling. The Indian Act segregates the rights holder in this country, which are First Nation People. And so once we understand the purpose of the Indian Act and how it still is implemented and today, it is possible to speak to it collectively. Canadians are asking, "How did I not know about this? Why did they still have the Indian Act? Why don't they delete the Indian Act?" We must understand what we collectively inherited from the Indian Act.

Indigenous business is shaping meaning in the national economic narrative. Rose Paul's work leading the Bay Street Development Corporation is advancing the question: How might a Mi'kmaq worldview better support the economic development process than the Indian Act?

> In every economic initiative we undertake, we strive to honor these gifts, ensuring that our present actions nurture and preserve their sanctity for the generations yet to grace this world. This philosophy of living in harmony with and nurturing these fundamental elements of life is the bedrock upon which we build our economic future. In weaving these principles into the fabric of our economic policies and initiatives, we are not only revitalizing our own community but also offering a model of development that is holistic, just, and deeply respectful of the intricate web of life. This is the path we walk as Mi'kmaw, as stewards of our land, and as global citizens in an ever-changing world. In the dance of economic progress, each step is a deliberate imprint upon the soil of our lands. As we move through the intricacies of economic development, we carry with us the profound understanding that we are the custodians of a legacy that transcends mere transactions and figures. It is a legacy that intertwines the delicate strands of conservation, environment, and the vibrance of our culture into a holistic vision that respects and nurtures our Earth Mother. The world in which we engage economically is not a series of isolated islands but a vast interconnected ecosystem. Every decision we make, every partnership we form, and every project we embark upon is evaluated through the lens of this deep interconnectedness. Our economic practices are not just about ensuring the financial well-being of our people today; they are about maintaining the ecological sanctity and ensuring the prosperity of those yet to walk this Earth. We must not compromise ecological integrity, and we must always look into the future so the next generations have expanded opportunities.

This Mi'kmaw worldview depicts a common worldview of weaving Indigenous values and principles into the way we do business and why we use business as a tool.

Building Economic Outcomes Through Modern Indigenous Economic Design

As the value in the Indigenous economy is unlocking, it is important to examine the economic outcomes that are being created. While this is not an exhaustive list, it provides some key outcomes in the rise of Indigenous economic power.

1. Establishes wealth transfer mechanisms derived from own-source revenue, revenue-sharing agreements, settlements, and trusts.
2. Increased project and financing certainty that creates stronger pathways for Indigenous consent to de-risk project financial models.
3. Increased recognition of the Indigenous legal and economic position.
4. Advances economic value translation through land transfers, settlement values, and leveragability.
5. Builds equality/inclusion through reconciliation pathways that create tangible economic benefits, including increasing Indigenous participation in decision-making and governance and increasing numbers of Indigenous corporate directors.
6. Increases accessibility to the financial markets through access to financial tools such as loan guarantees, regional Indigenous capital programs, and financial sector collaborations for capital alignment.
7. Facilitates the development of financial structures and tools that increase accessibility to capital.
8. Building Indigenous economic institutions.
9. Advances a shift in the regulatory environment that sees Indigenous inclusion and the re-centering of Indigenous approaches to environmental stewardship and risk management.
10. Implementation of UNDRIP that creates a stronger economic foundation for Nations to participate in the economy.
11. Implementation of Call to Action #92.
12. Increases the development of corporate economic reconciliation action plans.

Conclusion

Beginning to plan beyond the $100 billion Indigenous economic target is essential as Indigenous Nations are taking their seat at the economic table and increasingly advancing economic self-determination and pathways for Indigenous economic inclusion.

In the process of advancing Indigenous economic space, what is being reclaimed is Indigenous worldviews, inclusion, risk management, and governance structure/process for Indigenous Nations in the economic development process. What is emerging is a new economic space for Indigenous-led ownership, Indigenous-led decision-making, risk management, and stewardship responsibility. In advancing this new Indigenous economic space, a core question that is emerging: What do Indigenous partnerships bring to the economic table? The answer is certainty.

Reflective Questions

1. How is the emerging $100 billion Indigenous economy an opportunity?

2. What is important about building positive Indigenous economic outcomes today?

3. How can corporate Canada respond to build radical Indigenous economic inclusion today?

8

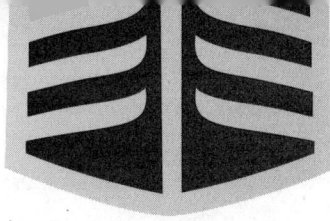

The Rise of Indigenous Economic Power

It's time for Indigenous Peoples to be at the center
of Canada's economy

—David McKay, RBC

THE $100 BILLION Indigenous economic value proposition offers a compelling business case. Indigenous economies can achieve transformative scaling by leveraging cultural capital, advancing sustainable development, fostering the entrepreneurial spirit, building social impacts, creating innovative partnerships, and enhancing community well-being outcomes. This growth benefits Indigenous Nations but also contributes to the national broader economic goals.

The tension between the long-term outcomes of the Indian Act and the value proposition for scaling the Indigenous economy is particularly significant in the recovery from Indian Act economics. Breaking down the behavioral dynamics of Indian Act economics becomes an important exercise.

The original objective of the Indigenous relationship has shifted from the policy of eradication to accommodation and recognition through the ongoing pressures of the evolving legal field and the incredible legal victories driven by Indigenous Nations. Today, Canada exists somewhere in the middle of the story of cause and effect. It actively contributes to the awkward defining question: What is the root cause of Indian Act economics, and what are the effects? With the escalating costs based on historical injustices, the absence of accountability for results is astounding in the evolution of the Indigenous legal and economic relationship.

Author and strategist Bill Gallagher describes the current economic field as having three significant core narratives. The first narrative is identifying how to develop a revenue-sharing scheme with Indigenous Peoples properly.

Until this happens, the Indigenous legal wins are only going to intensify. The second core narrative stems from the understanding that resourcing the future of the clean economy with Canadian critical minerals must be centered in the realization that all these resources go through Indigenous territories and require Indigenous consent. Lastly, the emphasis on UNDRIP implementation is critical to advance the Indigenous relationship. Gallagher describes that "while I personally think there is a lot of undermining going on in the implementation process, the actual level of power in the United Nations Declaration is maybe 10 percent of what is available in the full spectrum of the streak of Indigenous legal wins in this country."

Indigenous business leader Rose Paul brings forward a strong perspective in describing the work of economic reconciliation today that must work alongside the growth of the Indigenous economy.

> It is clear that the path forward requires tangible actions and a commitment to a deeper understanding between Indigenous and non-Indigenous Peoples. This is where the concept of reconciliation becomes paramount. It is a process that embodies the dialogue and the shared commitment to righting the wrongs of the past and moving forward with a collective purpose.

In the experience of framing the rise of Indigenous economic power in the region, Paul further frames the process of economic reconciliation:

> The legacy of victimization and oppression that has shadowed our people for generations is now giving way to a new narrative—one where the economic perspectives of the Mi'kmaw Nation are recognized as vital to the renaissance of our community and culture. Our Nation's approach to building regional economies is that when we are engaging with potential non-Indigenous partners, we approach the table with a clear message: recognizing and honoring our status as right holders is non-negotiable. We seek partners who are not only willing to communicate but are also prepared to act—partners who understand that rebuilding trust is a journey that requires both patience and perseverance.

In building the foundation of Indigenous economic growth for Nations, Cadmus Delorme offers a perspective of what that process looks like today.

We, as Indigenous People, we have to control our destiny, and it all starts with political sovereignty and governance. That is foundational to our approach to both Nation-building and economy. We have to be able to think beyond the Indian Act elections system of every two or four years as outlined in the Indian Act. Instead, we have to think and plan for 10, 20, 100 years ahead. As an example, in my Nation, we have parcels of land that we purposely will not develop because we want to leave that to the next generation to utilize. We don't have to develop all of our prime lands now, we can leave parcels of land that we know are good return on investment and for the next generation might see. That is long-term generational planning—to be able to operate from here is success.

Delorme continues reflecting on the Indian Act, noting it all starts with advancing our Indigenous governance structures. In the process of nation-building as the recovery to the Indian Act, he describes that:

It is important to consider the purpose and role of Chief and Councils from a true Nation-building perspective. We need to define for ourselves and ask, "What role do Chief and Councils play? What is the duty of care?" And once we understand this, as a Nation, the duty of care of governance is to create Nation-building portfolios that create an economic arm that has business-minded people on those boards. Then we can determine and set the path for the success of our future as a Nation.

Delorme articulates that the foundation for building a strong local Indigenous economy is good governance and self-determination.

We need to look at our systems and ask, "Where are the supporting financial institutions? Where are our investments going to come from to be equity owners?" These are the essential structures to recover from Indian Act economics because we do not want to just hold the shovels, and we don't want to just have the gas stations on the reserve type of economic development. We want equity participation in everything across all sectors in our territories.

In continuing to frame the foundation of strong governance in building strong Indigenous economic participation, Delorme draws on his experience as a past Chief of his community: "Quasi jurisdiction development is foundational to this. That is what UNDRIP and reconciliation must do—advance the institutions and frameworks to ensure we are building jurisdiction based on our Indigenous worldview."

Framing Success in the Indigenous Economy

In recent years, the dominant narrative of the Indigenous economy has been largely deficit based, focusing on the costs, lack of access to opportunity, and the experience of gaps, barriers, limitations, the socioeconomic gap, and challenges. Today, in the context of the rise of the Indigenous economy, building an Indigenous economic foundation that focuses on the structure of success is important in shifting the narrative to focus on growth, participation, inclusion, reconciliation, and designing outcomes in the Indigenous economy.

Bringing visibility to the rise of Indigenous economic power is essential to shaping a narrative of success. Figure 6 brings focus to visualizing the emerging $100 billion national Indigenous economic narrative through the perspective of global billionaires.

While visualizing this series of global billionaires within the context of the emerging $100 billion Indigenous economy in Canada, it is important to reflect on several key insights.

First, extreme wealth accumulation is largely viewed as the undermining force working against poverty alleviation, equality, and climate change. Second, while the UN set a goal to end poverty by 2030, a Canadian Poverty Institute report has identified that Indigenous Peoples in Canada continue to experience elevated levels of poverty. In 2021, 9 percent of persons of Indigenous identity were reported to be living in poverty compared to 7 percent of non-Indigenous persons.[108] And finally, the growing strength of

100 Billion in Perspective
$ in USD

Bernard Arnaut	LVMH $220B
Jeff Bezos	Amazon $207B
Elon Musk	Tesla $190B
Mark Zuckerberg	Facebook $168B
Larry Page	Google $156B
Bill Gates	Microsoft $154B
Sergey Brin	Google $148B
Steve Ballmer	Microsoft $145B
Warren Buffett	Berkshire Hathaway $138B
Larry Ellison	Oracle $138B
Michael Dell	Dell $113B
Mukesh Ambani	Reliance Industries $110B
Carlos Slim	Grupo Carso $106B
Gautam Adani	Adani Group $100B
CDN Indigenous Economy	Indigenous Economic Target $100B
Jim Walton	Wal-Mart $87B
Rob Walton	Wal-Mart $86B

0   50   100   150   200

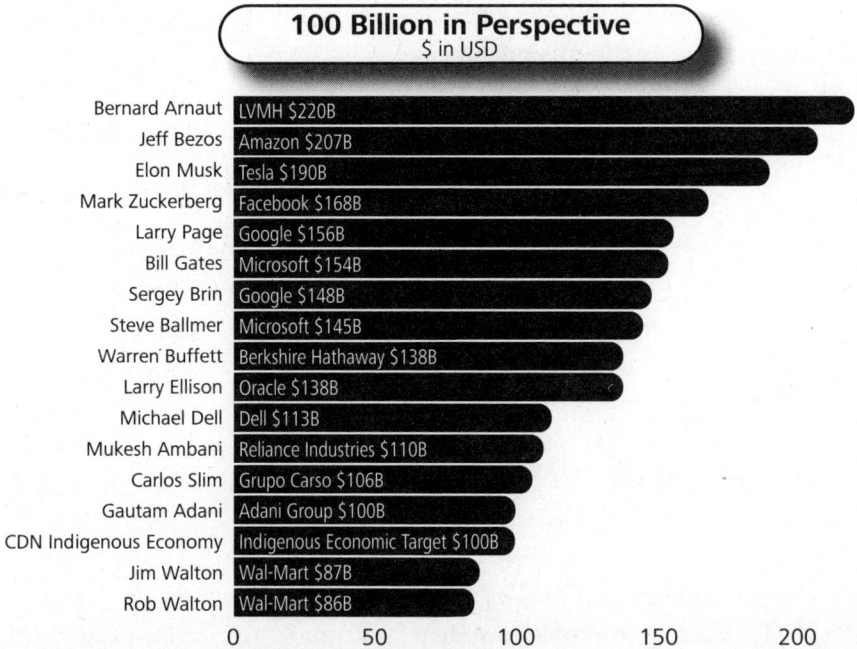

Figure 6: *$100 Billion indigenous economy in perspective. Source: Indigenomics Institute.*

the Indigenous economy visualized here must be understood through several key concepts. This growth represents a very short generational period of Indigenous business activities. Indigenous business is grounded outside the capitalist norm of extreme accumulation, greed, and profit. The foundation of the growth of the Indigenous economy is only at the beginning stages of taking shape. The distinction of the growth of the Indigenous economy is that economic development is an equalizer. Indigenous economic reclamation is a wealth builder but for much different reasons than wealth accumulation. Indigenous community economic value is perceived uniquely in terms of return on investment in culture, Elders, youth, and stewardship.

Framing Indigenous Economic Success

While there are many facets and dimensions of success at individual, national, and collective levels, the following frames this success narrative of the rise of Indigenous economic power.

In an interview with Rose Paul, she describes the shaping of Indigenous business success in the Atlantic region.

> Success in the Indigenous economy today looks like increasing Indigenous-led and Indigenous-owned projects that are able to provide long-term return on investments for our communities. We are sitting in seats at tables that we've never been able to sit at before. Now we are major players in the economy. This is happening now.

Indigenous legal wins are shaping Indigenous economic success in a new ways. Across the consistent stream of Indigenous legal wins, some of these represent massive shifts in the evolving Indigenous relationship. Bill Gallagher describes this development in the context of the rise of Indigenous economic power.

> It is easy to forget that the Native empowerment movement shut down the Canadian transportation system for a month prior to the pandemic in 2020. We barely even recall that event today, yet it was hugely newsworthy. The train system was stopped all around the country, and ports were closed due to Indigenous protests nationwide. This transportation corridor shut down brought a new perspective of the sense of importance the natural resources economy to both the Canadian economy and Indigenous Rights. This movement only slowed because of the beginning of the pandemic but was a major shake-up.

In the rise of Indigenous economic power, Indigenous economic data must be foundational to Indigenous economic success. A national Indigenous labor market study must build a profile of the actual number of Indigenous businesses and the jobs created and ask critical qualitative questions: How many of the Indigenous businesses have partnerships? How are the partnerships evolving? With the rise of the Indigenous economy, there should be a solid data set on the benefits of collaborating and creating economies of scale for working with Indigenous businesses. Without this, we are fumbling in the dark.

In an interview with Indigenous business leader Wil Jimmy, he brings forward an important context in framing the rise of Indigenous economic success:

It is important to understand that when looking at the growth of Indigenous companies and their labor forces, Indigenous businesses generate opportunities for all Canadians. To date, the Canadian government has never funded a national Indigenous labor market survey. An Indigenous labor market survey which would affirm that Indigenous businesses have done more for the local and regional economies and the jobs of their fellow Canadians than we would ever think possible.

This is a pivotal moment to build insights into the rapid growth of the Indigenous economy. The rise of the Indigenous economy is a force to be reckoned with today. Peering through the lens of how Nations are building successful business outcomes, Indigenous leaders are reflecting on this growth. In an interview with Indigenous business leader Hillary Thatcher, she reflects that:

In terms of success in the Indigenous economy, there are more and more economic development projects where large revenue bases are being generated for the community and more major projects that hit the bank that have Indigenous partners already. That is success when Indigenous communities and people are included in major project financing and project development projects that get built on time, on budget, typically, and our communities are better for it.

Thatcher describes what the rise of Indigenous economic power looks like today:

It has been gradually shifting. Today, it is about increasing economic participation and economic inclusion of Indigenous communities where projects are on their territory. Communities are leaning in and making investments in major projects and building their own strengths and abilities to participate and actively engage in the economy. We're seeing it in other ways, not just investments in major infrastructure projects but also in the sort of training and education solutions to engage young people.

It is important to focus on the foundation of what is driving the rise of Indigenous economic power. Today, Nations are using their growing legal interests to build inclusion at the economic table for inclusion in these major projects that are being built on their lands. These opportunities are becoming unlocked, and communities are better able to create businesses, partnerships, and investments that align with the community's values. Hillary Thatcher describes this further:

> The biggest contribution to the rise of the Indigenous economy is the crystallization of Indigenous Rights and that these Rights have then been translated into economic opportunity. So when a community can slow down or stop a project because they haven't been adequately consulted or accommodated for the impacts or potential impacts on rights, companies, developers, investors, and governments are paying closer attention. It has taken a long time to get to this point and a lot of case law to get here. This is the foundation of Indigenous economic power today.

Today, Nations can increasingly leverage the legal tools that have created new space for Indigenous interests to better advance business opportunities. The fiery spirit of economic justice expresses itself in the courtroom and is further activated in the economy. Thatcher continues:

> In this shifting legal environment, the federal and regional governments now have to meet these legal obligations, which has resulted in the increased resolution of land claims. This is significant because when land claims have been resolved, it is providing for more certainty in business activities on Indigenous lands.

The foundation of Indigenous economic success is an increased opportunity to participate. Further insight into the increasing resolution of land claims is important; it is important to understand that these often come with significant cash settlements. So now, the Nations have access to capital and a better structure to leverage and make investments in projects, which was not possible under the Indian Act.

In an interview with Indigenous business leader Cadmus Delorme, he discusses the Cowesses Nation's economic development process, which is based on self-determination and nation-building.

> When I was a Chief, we had three core pillars—economic self-sustainability with a focus on balancing culture rejuvenation and political sovereignty. As an example of our approach, we started with agriculture. In this context, it is important to understand that a non-Native farmer will have access to a lot of potential investment, security and can establish a low-risk profile, whereas on-reserve farming land is registered under the Indian Act and does not get these same benefits or structures and requires external decision-making. Cowesses Nation was able to advance 7,000 acres of their existing lands for farming. As community we did that with a lot of policy change, a lot of advocacy, and a lot of telling the financial institutions to not let Section 87 of the Indian Act scare them away from working with us. A second project was in renewable energy where we have A1 turbine with supporting solar panels valued at about $9 million. We developed a second project of 10 megawatts of thousands of solar panels valued at $20 million. The community finished a project of thirty-six turbines valued at $400 million. This has helped position Cowessess as an Indigenous leader in Canada's clean energy sector. Cowesses owns equity in all three of these projects, but the equity came from two options: grants or bank loans. Private equity and other forms of capital were unattainable for us. There are currently ceilings for Indigenous businesses, and it is our responsibility today to address those ceilings so that Indigenous businesses can have parity with non-Indigenous businesses. Success in business to us is that, in these types of project developments, we don't have to give up our Indigenous worldview to do business. This speaks to the opportunity for private equity to engage with Indigenous projects and to realize the growing size and

scale and pace of them. It is time to see Indigenous business as an opportunity.

This scale of Indigenous business development outcomes is a defining feature of the rise of Indigenous economic power. However, the ability to operate from within an Indigenous worldview is an essential dimension of this success. Indigenous business leader Rose Paul describes this further when asked, "What does Indigenous economic power look like today, and how is that shifting?"

> For my Nation, governance and economic reconciliation are not static concepts but a reawakening of our traditional laws and knowledge systems. Our customs are not simply a set of rules; they are a living testament to the process of sustainability and reconciliation, evolving from shared models of conduct. Rooted in oral traditions and teachings, they reflect our daily life, encapsulating our shared experiences of hardship and joy from operating in the natural world and in relationship to each other. Our ways are a celebration of our heritage, expressive in its nature, and deeply performative. They have matured through centuries of oral storytelling, a cherished practice where every narrative shared is a strand in the tapestry of our collective identity. They hold the laughter and tears of our ancestors, their trials and triumphs, and through them, we celebrate our resilience, our culture, and our connection to this land, long before the first European footprints marked our soils. To be able to operate from this center— that is our economic power.

An essential question at this moment in time is: What is contributing to the rise in Indigenous economic power? Rose Paul describes in her work of leading Indigenous economic development corporations to unprecedented economic success.

> As we navigate profound transformations since the recent arrival of settlers, we draw on our ancestors' wisdom for governance and economic reconciliation, reawakening traditional laws and customs. Our

practices, rooted in oral traditions, celebrate our resilience and connection to the land, predating European settlement. This will be
foundational to our success.

The rise of Indigenous economic power is in motion and is activated
within the national and regional economies. Cadmus offers another important reflection point in describing what has contributed to this rise of
Indigenous economic empowerment:

It's the Indigenous leadership and Indigenous entrepreneurs and
Indigenous spiritual leaders that just won't take no for an answer.
Our business ethic is a response so deeply rooted in a time and systems long before the Indian Act. Our people will continue long after
the Indian Act—that is both our success and the gift that has been
given to us and that we bestow within our future.

What is being described here is the economic worldview that is activated
and shaping the pathway forward based on Indigenous economic self-determination today. The activation of the right to an economy is expressed in the
advancement of Indigenous-led equity ownership. This is the power of the
Indigenous economy—from coast to coast, Indigenous self-determination,
stewardship, and ownership are expressing themselves through creating a
seat at the economic table that has so long been denied. This is the opposite
of Indian Act economics.

It is important to recognize the significance of this moment—right
now—as the majority of the Big Five Banks, as well as the Bank of Canada, all
have Indigenous directors on their corporate boards. This a power moment,
a defining space for Indigenous economic power when we see Indigenous
Peoples sitting in corporate board seats alongside equity ownership positions.
The rise of Indigenous economic power is representative of the fact that we
are winning in spaces that were never made for us. This is Indigenomics in
motion. In the words of Cadmus Delorme:

Indigenous Peoples were never meant to exist at the margins, nor are
we a cost burden to the system. We are not a liability on the balance

sheet. We are rights holders. We belong at the equity table. Today, the future of Canada is inextricably linked to Indigenous business success.

Twenty-five Trends in the Indigenous Economic Value Creation Process

Twenty-five key themes come into focus when the narrative of the rise of Indigenous economic power is centered. Through this lens, a core driving question is: How is value creation happening in the Indigenous economy? Understanding the emerging trends that are facilitating value creation in the Indigenous economy is an important way of framing the advancement of Indigenous economic power.

Indigenomics serves as a departure from the common narrative of gaps and barriers and the reliance on the socioeconomic gap. It also shifts focus away from GDP as the primary metric of the Indigenous economy. The following section frames three key narratives:

1. It is important to move away from the existing dependency on limited Indigenous economic data sources.
2. Focus on the narrative shift away from the Indigenous economy being measured solely against the backdrop of GDP metric.
3. The Indigenous economy is unique and needs to move away from the common narrative of the Indigenous economy being viewed solely as a contribution to the regional or national economies.

The following set of trends demonstrates how value creation is happening in the Indigenous economy, using the Canadian media narrative to advance these insights.

1. Land Transfer

The growing estimate of Indigenous-controlled or -owned lands is a significant development in the Canadian and the Indigenous economy. A significant portion of this Indigenous land base acquisition has been established over time through self-government agreements.

Indigenous land transfers are facilitated through specific claims or settlement cases that address historic wrongs against Indigenous Peoples and are catalyzing economic growth today. The federal and provincial governments have a duty to consult with Indigenous communities, and historical and current land and resource disputes are creating a wave of upcoming legal claims at the regional and national level. This is particularly true where treaty obligations have been contravened historically. Historical land seizures under the Indian Act are a source of increased legal challenges driving land transfer settlements. What is significant here is that the acquired land values now hold economic value that was denied through the structure of the Indian Act.

Another way land can be repatriated to Indigenous Nations is through the addition-to-reserve process. This was a historically burdensome process in which land could be added to existing reserves either through the upholding of a legal requirement, community population growth, or a Specific Claims Tribunal decision.

Nations will often use a land transfer trust structure that will hold the acquired lands in private ownership, ensuring a better ownership structure beyond the Indian Act system. This land trust structure serves to ensure several key outcomes: 1) an increased role for Indigenous-led conservation processes, 2) removing the lands from the fee simple market, 3) fostering the Nation's leadership in sustainable development, 4) increased access for economic activity and investment, 5) establish space for Indigenous-led land use planning, and 6) provide a stronger wealth-building structure for the Nation.

The following outlines several examples of this development. One example of the land transfer process is with the Fox Lake Cree Nation. The Nation legally addressed the historical impacts of Manitoba Hydro's development, which resulted in extensive flooding and profound environmental and social impacts on their lands, waters, and culture since the 1960s. The Nation negotiated with Manitoba Hydro and various levels of government for compensation and justice. The nation is looking to acquire up to 26,000 acres of land transfer to address the historical injustices.[109]

In another example, a *CBC* article titled "B.C. Transfers 312 Hectares of Land on Vancouver Island to Lyackson First Nation and Cowichan Tribes" brings into focus the modern treaty settlement process. The article notes that the Province purchased the private forestry land parcel valued at $8.55 million, and the lands are being made available through an incremental treaty agreement. "We've been misplaced for four generations and this is the time for us to start moving forward," says Lyackson First Nation Chief Pahalicktun.[110]

Another example of this land transfer process is the City of Nanaimo transferring 81 hectares of Mount Benson land to the Snuneymuxw Nation, which builds upon the original 212 hectares transferred as part of a 2020 agreement. The article cites the Chief: "The Mount Benson lands hold much opportunity for the Snuneymuxw First Nation to strengthen their connection to land and culture, create new economic activity, and protect wildlife habitat."[111]

This example highlights the significance of land transfer in advancing the rise of Indigenous economic power. A *CBC* article reports that Cowessess First Nation in Saskatchewan is being transferred over 3,800 acres of Crown mineral rights under the Cowessess Treaty Land Entitlement (TLE) Settlement Agreement. The article references the "TLE agreements provide First Nations with entitlement money to purchase land anywhere in Saskatchewan on a 'willing buyer-willing seller' basis to add to reserves lands noting that the agreements support community growth and traditional land use."[112] Of further insight of this land transfer process, "since 1992, the Government of Saskatchewan and the federal government committed $687 million for TLE settlements in the province. About 888,806 acres have been transferred to date and 1.48 million acres are outstanding."

These streams of media stories weave a common thread in the ongoing narrative of increased Indigenous land tenure, which is foundational to the value creation process within the Indigenous economy.

2. Indigenous Funds

Increasingly, Indigenous Nations and businesses are identifying the space and structure for Indigenous-led capital. This development provides a significant opportunity for financial partners to create collaborative structures that advance investment accessibility, alignment, and economic reconciliation outcomes. It also allows insight into the Indigenous impact of invested dollars in ways that uphold Indigenous participation and impact in new ways.

A *Globe and Mail* article titled "Indigenous-run Longhouse Capital Targets $1-Billion Fund" brings insight into this development. "Longhouse

Capital was created to generate superior risk-adjusted returns for investors while having a lasting positive impact on Indigenous communities as owners," says founding partner Fred Di Blasio.[113] Longhouse will look for investment opportunities in both Indigenous projects and traditional private-equity markets. The article highlights the significant developments that are an increasing number of private sector utilities, such as Innergex Renewable Energy and Ontario's Hydro One as examples who have established equity stakes in infrastructure projects with Indigenous groups as part of the corporate strategy to gain community license for major developments and advance reconciliation. The article further identifies that "as an investor, the fund plans to back businesses or projects with $500 million to $1.5 billion in revenues, and $50 million to $150 million of earnings before interest, taxes, depreciation and amortization. Its investment criteria and fee structure are similar to established private-equity shops." This fund upholds the growing realization that the potential market for Indigenous property assets, infrastructure, and private debt investments is increasingly significant to pay attention to.

The next Indigenous fund to highlight is Raven Indigenous Capital Partners, an early mover in the space that prioritizes Indigenous-led capital for early-start Indigenous entrepreneurs. Acting as an intermediary, the pilot fund's success was followed by the most recent oversubscribed $100 million venture capital fund, which includes an expansion to the US Indigenous market.

Raven Capital excels in a unique value space driving Indigenous system design by inviting asset managers and investors to include Indigenous voices and methods in measuring impact. Raven Capital has created a remarkable leadership space in the financial sector that tells a story where every dollar invested is linked explicitly to improved outcomes and well-being for Indigenous Peoples. The Raven Impact Measurement (RIM) framework reflects:

> The driving force behind an Indigenous-led impact measurement journey that ensures that everything we do at Raven ultimately contributes to the improved well-being of Indigenous Peoples. The release of the impact framework furthers our commitment to be in

service to Indigenous Peoples and their well-being. We as a company hold ourselves accountable to this purpose and are honoured to advance this work in a way that speaks to our mission to decolonize and re-culturalize investment practices.[114]

Another example of building innovative approaches to Indigenous capital is the development of an Indigenous capital consortium called Iskum Investments, which was formed by a collective of BC Coastal First Nations as an investment vehicle for driving regional economic impact. In an article titled "Coastal First Nations Are Open for Business and Looking for Investment Opportunities," it is noted that twenty Coastal First Nations on Vancouver Island and the Sunshine and Central Coast have formed a new investment coalition to increase Indigenous involvement in various business enterprises. "The mandate of the Iskum Investments as a new Indigenous-led investment coalition is 'to explore economic opportunities that will create new self-generated revenues and support certainty for continued investment in B.C.'"[115] The article articulates the significance of this financial structure in advancing Indigenous economic growth. "Iskum Investments is a groundbreaking partnership that aims to advance economic reconciliation—taking hold of our future and making our own decisions, to improve the lives of our Nations' citizens and members now and for future generations," said Hegus John Hackett, Chief of Tla'amin Nation.

Indigenous-led capital and fund structures will play a pivotal role in fostering economic growth and empowerment within Indigenous communities across Canada. An important structure that is advancing Indigenous-led capital is the recently established Indigenous Growth Fund spearheaded by the National Aboriginal Capital Corporations Association, which was identified as a strategic priority within a federal mandate. The fund's purpose is to provide access to capital for the network of Indigenous Financial Institutions (IFIs) and Indigenous small and medium-sized enterprises. With an initial $153 million investment, the fund is structured to help address the historical barriers of access to capital by increasing loan values to Indigenous enterprises and accelerating the scaling of Indigenous businesses. These examples follow an increasing trend of the role of Indigenous-focused capital in advancing Indigenous economic outcomes.

3. Indigenous Legal Developments

The tension between the advancement of Indigenous Rights and the advancement of Indigenous economic space in the Canadian economy is constantly being expressed. This tension can be viewed in Atlantic Canada with Indigenous-led fisheries undergoing an intense legal evolvement regarding Mi'kmaw treaty rights to fish without approval from the Crown. In 1999, the Supreme Court affirmed the community's treaty right to fish, hunt, and gather in pursuit of a moderate livelihood. The First Nation launched its own Mi'kmaq-regulated rights-based lobster fishery, which was the first of its kind in the province. A headline news article describes that:

> The fishery was launched 21 years after the Supreme Court ruling that affirmed a treaty right to hunt, fish and gather in pursuit of a "moderate livelihood." The legal decision affected 34 Mi'kmaq and Wolastoqiyik First Nations in New Brunswick, Prince Edward Island, Nova Scotia and the Gaspé region of Quebec. The problem is moderate livelihood was never clearly defined.[116]

It is important to articulate that, through the underlying thinking of Indian Act economics, no other group in Canada is defined by the language of "moderate living" except the Indians. This is expressed in the highly charged tension in the fisheries sector, which serves to demonstrate the "Indian can't make money" mentality behind the high-profile racially focused clash as Indigenous Nations are rightly taking a seat at the economic table of this region and sector.

Indigenous participation in the cannabis sector is also experiencing a similar legal battle for economic space. An interesting development that ties Indigenous Rights to an emerging industry is a CBC article titled "Cannabis Is Emerging as a New Battleground Over Mi'kmaw Rights." While the federal Cannabis Act delegated the regulation of the sale and distribution of cannabis to the provinces and the federal government, the absence of a consultation process with Indigenous groups has created a significant legal space. The article notes that "the court viewed economic development as a generic right that was shared by pretty well all Indigenous peoples."[117] In doing so, "the judge rejected the standard pre-European-contact test, which has been criticized for being difficult to meet and for 'freezing' certain rights in time by ignoring their evolution," according to lawyer Lara Koerner-Yeo regarding the case.

In the absence of the federal government upholding its responsibilities to the original treaties in Canada across time, this is giving rise to new legal definition that is creating economic opportunities for Indigenous Nations that were previously unavailable through the Indian Act. It is the foundation of economic sovereignty that is being built that allows Indigenous Nations to self-govern, essentially to manage access to business opportunities better and better manage impacts on the land and resources through economic development. As an example, a significant legal development of the Blueberry River First Nation legal case confirmed and defined a new legal space. Here, the BC Supreme Court ruled that the British Columbia Government breached Blueberry River First Nation's Treaty 8 Rights by over-developing lands and waters in its territory and that the government did not take into account the long-term cumulative impacts of industry on the Nation.

The media narrative was shaped by a *Narwhal* article, "Blueberry River First Nations Win Precedent-setting Treaty Rights Case," which describes that the BC government breached its obligations under Treaty 8 by permitting forestry, oil and gas, hydro, and mining developments without consideration of its Treaty 8 obligations.[118] The Court ordered the BC government to establish co-management rules and a structure to protect Blueberry River's Treaty Rights. The case required the BC government to stop issuing licenses that infringed on the Nation's Treaty Rights and to stop allowing new developments that negatively created long-term cumulative impacts. In line with the Indigenomics principles, that what is won in the courtroom expresses itself in the economy, the defining moment of impact in this legal case was a clear outcome that government and industry have to shuffle over at the economic table and make room for Indigenous Rights.

4. Increasing Indigenous Project and Partnership Values

One trend to pay attention to on the path to Indigenous economic empowerment is the increasing project values of Indigenous business partnerships. Partnerships are foundational to creating outcomes in Indigenous economic reconciliation.

A write-up titled "Canada's Indigenous Peoples Eye Big Energy Deals, Await Trudeau Loan Promise" outlines that at least thirty-eight Canadian energy projects were announced with Indigenous investment between 2022 and 2024, ranging in value from $13 million to $14.5 billion ($10.69 billion), according to the Fasken law firm, which has worked on some of the projects.[119]

A well-known example of increasing partnership values is the Clearwater partnership deal in the Atlantic fisheries sector. In a particularly volatile time of Mi'kmaq fisheries, which was mired by regulatory barriers and increasing racial tensions on the waters, it garnered international media attention. At a time of significant destruction of Mi'kmaq assets, including Indigenous fishing boats being destroyed and warehouses burned, came the surprising story of Indigenous economic power and resilience. The "First Nations Partner with B.C. Company in $1 billion Purchase of Clearwater Seafoods" article by *CBC* described in detail that:

> Halifax-based Clearwater Seafoods announced a billion-dollar deal Monday to sell the company to a partnership between Premium Brands of British Columbia and a coalition of Mi'kmaw First Nations. It is "the single largest investment in the seafood industry by any Indigenous group in Canada." The coalition will be led by the Membertou band in Cape Breton and Miawpukek in Newfoundland and Labrador. Membertou Chief Terry Paul said the Mi'kmaq will hold Clearwater's Canadian fishing licences within a fully Mi'kmaq-owned partnership. This deal is a transformational moment for all participating communities. We will now have access to the offshore fishery from an ownership position.[120]

This development is well regarded as the largest single investment that an Indigenous group in Canada has ever made in the fisheries industry. In particular, it fully entered Indigenous Nations into the value chain of the regional fisheries sector as major players.

A second example of the increasing partnership value is in Alberta. The news headline reads "Alberta Indigenous Opportunities Corporation Closes Second Largest Deal With $150 Million Loan Guarantee for 12 Indigenous

Communities." The deal outlines twelve Indigenous communities' purchase of equity in oil and gas midstream infrastructure in the Marten Hills and Nipisi areas of the Clearwater clay in Northern Alberta. The article identifies that:

> Through this partnership, the Nations will be able to realize the benefits of the revenues brought in by the infrastructure, providing long-term and stable financial resource streams for the participating communities. Revenue generated may also provide opportunities for reinvestment and possibilities to pursue other profit-generating ventures, further supporting and improving communities and setting up future generations for success.[121]

A third example of outlining the increasing partnership values is a article further depicting this partnership advancement: "Five Indigenous Nations in Northwestern Alberta Make $20.5 Million Investment in Greenhouse Gas Emission-reducing Cogeneration Unit for Alberta Gas Plant." Again, an investment through the Alberta Indigenous Opportunities Corporation under its loan guarantee mandate facilitated the deal, allowing a collective of Nations to economically benefit from building a stable income stream. This deal will provide the Nations referred to as Niyanin Nations LP (Niyanin) with the opportunity to partner as investors in a 15-megawatt cogeneration unit. The article cites that "with this investment, the Niyanin and NuVista partnership will own a majority interest in the project. The terms of the transaction ensure long-term economic benefit to the participating Nations."[122]

A fourth example, EverWind in Atlantic Canada is forming a hydrogen hub with Mi'kmaq partnerships, which is poised to bring substantial economic benefits to the three Indigenous partners with a proposed renewable power generation that includes wind and solar energy production. The power generated will then be converted to green hydrogen-to-ammonia production. The economic contribution during the construction period for Phase 1 of EverWind's Nova Scotia Project is estimated to be over $2.3 billion in Canadian GDP, with approximately half accruing to Nova Scotia. This is the new face of Indigenous economic power.[123]

These demonstrated partnerships and project values reflect a growing recognition of the importance of Indigenous participation in natural resource management and resource development projects and emerging sectors across Canada. By emphasizing collaboration and inclusion, these initiatives aim to address historical injustices, empower Indigenous communities, and ensure sustainable and culturally sensitive approaches to resource stewardship.

Further, Ontario's Ring of Fire region provides particular insights into the relationship between resource development and Indigenous Rights. This area is known for substantial deposits of minerals such as chromite (used in stainless steel production), nickel, copper, and platinum, which are essential for industries ranging from manufacturing to green technologies like electric vehicles. However, the Ring of Fire's development has raised complex issues concerning Indigenous Rights, environmental protection, and economic opportunity. Indigenous economic inclusion in the resource sector signals a shift toward more equitable and mutually beneficial relationships between governments, industry stakeholders, and Indigenous Nations. This catalyzes economic development outcomes while respecting Indigenous Rights and protecting the environment.

While only a few examples are noted here, there is a constant stream of news stories depicting the changing tides of Indigenous partnership development and inclusion, which must be viewed as a key trend line in the rise of Indigenous economic power.

5. Infrastructure Development—Major Projects

The First Nations Major Projects Coalition (FNMPC) supports Indigenous Nations in participating in major infrastructure and resource projects across Canada. The collective mission is to focus on building capacity for Nations to achieve economic self-determination through equity ownership, environmental stewardship, and governance over large-scale developments. The coalition provides tools and guidance on negotiating agreements, securing financing, and ensuring community benefits. FNMPC has been successful in helping Indigenous communities secure substantial ownership stakes in projects, like energy developments, while emphasizing sustainability and cultural integrity. The advancement of Indigenous-led major projects is creating new opportunities in the Indigenous economy at an increasing rate.

In the example of the Minto Mine in the Yukon, the Yukon Supreme Court granted the Selkirk Nation control of the abandoned mine, marking a significant step in Indigenous economic participation.[124] This brings the Nation into the value chain of future exploration potential. The acquisition opens possibilities for exploration and potential reopening of the mine, benefiting Selkirk First Nation with economic opportunities. This also opens up for Indigenous-led exploration. This acquisition could lead to the first Indigenous-owned exploration company operating in the Yukon. With an increased emphasis on environmental responsibility, Selkirk Nation can better ensure current and long-term environmental integrity at the mine site.

6. Indigenous Trade

Indigenous trade structures and agreements are modern tools that are an important area of advancement in the Indigenous economy. Canada's Trade Diversification Strategy has advanced an inclusive approach to trade that ensures Indigenous Peoples in Canada benefit from the opportunities that flow from international trade and investment agreements.

The Indigenous Peoples Economic and Trade Cooperation Arrangement (IPETCA) is a collaborative initiative advancing Indigenous businesses' capacity to capitalize on trade and investment opportunities. The agreement enhances Indigenous participation in trade, fosters economic development opportunities, and facilitates cooperation between participating economies and Indigenous representatives. Initially endorsed by Canada, Australia, New Zealand, and Chinese Taipei, IPETCA is facilitating Indigenous economic inclusion through inclusive trade practices and removing systemic barriers that have prevented Indigenous businesses' participation in international trade.

The Indigenous Peoples Economic and Trade Cooperation Arrangement reaffirms the significance of existing Indigenous-specific international instruments like the UNDRIP. It underscores the crucial role of the environment in Indigenous economic, social, and cultural well-being. The arrangement acknowledges the importance of preserving Indigenous knowledge and practices that contribute to environmental conservation while striving to identify and eliminate obstacles faced by Indigenous businesses in international trade. Through the IPETCA Partnership Council, cooperation activities are developed collaboratively with Indigenous representatives, with the overarching goal of sharing knowledge, implementing best practices, and enhancing

Indigenous Peoples' participation in the economy and trade, highlighting a commitment to fostering sustainable and inclusive economic development for Indigenous communities globally.[125]

The inclusion in Indigenous trade stems from Canada's federal Indigenous trade mandate that promotes Indigenous economic inclusion, self-determination, and sovereignty by supporting Indigenous businesses in national and global markets. This mandate aligns with reconciliation commitments, such as the Truth and Reconciliation Commission's Calls to Action and UNDRIP, recognizing Indigenous Rights and aiming to reduce economic disparities. Canada supports Indigenous-led economic growth, community development, and poverty reduction through this mandate.

7. Capital Alignment

The majority of the national Indigenous economic narrative to date has named the very real experience of the systemic barriers of access to capital as problematic in the business development process. In establishing a strengths-based narrative of Indigenous economic growth, it is important to use language that shifts away from this singular narrative of "capital access" as a barrier toward positive action that instead examines the alignment of capital to the growth of the Indigenous economy. This is a significant space for building economic reconciliation outcomes. The following outlines the trend of capital alignment.

A Canadian newswire press release, "Scotiabank Partners with Nch'ḳay' Development Limited Partnership, Des Nedhe Financial LP and Chippewas of Rama First Nation to Establish a New Investment Dealer in Canada," describes that:

> Scotiabank has entered into an agreement with two Indigenous development corporations and one First Nation to seek regulatory approval to create and operate a new investment dealer in Canada. The proposed investment dealer, to be named Cedar Leaf Capital Inc. ("Cedar Leaf Capital"), will be majority-owned by three Indigenous shareholders Nch'ḳay' Development Limited Partnership, Des Nedhe Financial LP and Chippewas of Rama First Nation and controlled initially by Scotiabank. Subject to regulatory approval, Cedar Leaf

Capital will be the first-to-market majority Indigenous-owned investment dealer in Canada.[126]

Indigenous business leader Clint Davis, who was selected as the new CEO, is quoted in this development of this capital alignment in the Indigenous economy:

> Cedar Leaf Capital will actively seek to establish roles in dealer syndicates on new bond offerings, acting in broadly syndicated offerings with the ambition to grow into lead roles. In addition, we will seek to identify, attract and develop Indigenous talent, serving as a training ground for Indigenous young people who are considering a career in capital markets and finance. Cedar Leaf Capital will exemplify reconciliation in action.[127]

Another example of leadership of Indigenous capital alignment, as described in a national newswire press release, is the BMO for Indigenous Entrepreneurs lending program, which is specifically designed to provide Indigenous business owners with greater access to working capital, educational resources, and professional partnerships to start up, scale, and accelerate their businesses.[128] The bank describes listening to the experience of Indigenous entrepreneurs and building a responsive program to support Indigenous business capital access and the economic empowerment of Indigenous businesses and communities.

Another example of the advancement of capital alignment as a pivotal trend is described in a *Windspeaker* article, "First Indigenous Equity Loan from Canada Infrastructure Bank Supports Mi'kmaw Investment in Green Energy." Facilitated by the Canada Infrastructure Bank's Indigenous Equity Initiative, this $18 million loan went to the Wskijinu'k Mtmo'taqnuow Agency (WMA), an economic limited partnership owned by thirteen Mi'kmaw communities in Nova Scotia.[129] Understanding the leadership space of driving capital alignment to project development, the CIB is developing success in investing in significant Indigenous projects countrywide.

Finally, CIB and the First Nations Bank of Canada (FNBC) announced signing a $100 million deal to help Indigenous communities borrow money to build infrastructure. "For decades, Indigenous leaders and business experts have said limited access to affordable loans with flexible terms have held back important development projects in Indigenous communities across the country."[130]

The organizations have identified the collaborative development of the financing deal as a means for First Nations, Métis, and Inuit communities to "be able to get loans more quickly and easily for projects ranging from roads, to water and wastewater management, utility connections, as well as housing, commercial and industrial developments."

8. Procurement

Indigenous procurement has rapidly ascended as a core economic enabler in designing outcomes in the Indigenous economy. The policy space for Indigenous procurement as an economic design tool for government and industry is a significant advancement in the Indigenous economy. Several key examples bring this trend line into focus.

Article 24 of the Nunavut Settlement Agreement mandates the Government of Canada to support Inuit businesses by providing procurement opportunities within the federal government. This directive aims to address the historically low participation of Inuit businesses in the procurement processes while fostering the growth and sustainability of Inuit enterprises in the Nunavut Settlement Area. By facilitating access to federal procurement opportunities, the directive specifically aims to 1) enhance the competitiveness of Inuit businesses, 2) promote long-term viability, and 3) align with broader efforts to strengthen economic relationships with Indigenous entrepreneurs and communities.

The Government of Canada affirmed its commitment to bolstering economic opportunities for First Nations, Inuit, and Métis businesses through the federal procurement process by introducing a mandatory requirement for federal departments and agencies to ensure that a minimum of 5 percent of the total federal department's contract value is awarded to Indigenous businesses. This requirement includes provisions for a phased approach and the requirement of public reporting of the annual target. This mandate signals a proactive approach to advancing Indigenous economic participation and empowerment within a clear mandate for federal procurement outcomes.

Following this development, the Yukon Territory government committed to a 20 percent Indigenous procurement target annually, while the City of Regina is committing to an Indigenous Procurement Policy that will award 20 percent of city contracts to Indigenous businesses.

Procurement is an essential tool for both government and industry to advance Indigenous economic participation and build reconciliation outcomes. It is a key trend to watch in the rise of Indigenous economic power.

9. Indigenous Assets Under Management

The pathway to asset management in the Indigenous economy has had serious setbacks in the context of the impacts and limitations of Indian Act economics. With noted chronic underfunding of the upkeep and the development of core infrastructure such as offices, schools, houses, roads, and other capital assets of Nations, further complications such as difficulty in accessing insurance for assets on reserve have uniquely slowed this development process.

The establishment of the First Nations Financial Management Board's structure for developing Financial Administration Laws is advancing a capital planning structure for assets that provides an avenue to create a foundation of leverage value for Indigenous communities.

In perspective of the growing context of Indigenous assets under management as a significant space in the Indigenous economy, other key institutions such as the First Nation Bank of Canada reported in 2023 $4 billion in holdings, while its FNB Trust identified $1.2 billion trust assets under administration upon settlement.[131]

The context of Indigenous land purchases and asset acquisition merge here as well. A *Newhouse* article titled "Mohawks Use New Casino Wealth to Buy Back Ancestral Land" describes the Nation's approach to asset acquisition. "We're not waiting on the state or federal government to come and help us. We're going to fix our own roads. The gaming operation gives us those dollars to do just that."[132] A 240-acre plot of land that extends off the highway is land the Mohawks reclaimed from New York State. The acreage was lost in 1824 in the treaty and was recently repurchased with casino revenue.

Another example of this trend is TIPI Insurance Partners, which is owned by sixty First Nations across Western Canada.[133] The company is the insurance broker on over $1 billion in assets in ninety First Nations communities from BC to Ontario. It is also growing over $200 million in pension assets under management and $40 million in group insurance premiums. While still a modest number, the asset development trajectory path is shifting substantially as Nations increase their asset base as their communities and businesses grow.

A development in BC is aligned with this trend and is of particular significance to advancing the growth of the Indigenous economy. A *CBC* article highlights this development:

> British Columbia's government has introduced a bill that would give federally recognized First Nations the legal right to acquire and hold land in the province. B.C.'s Ministry of Indigenous Relations notes that "the changes to land title and property laws would allow Nations to register at the land title office, reducing discriminatory and racist barriers" for them to own land. First Nations in the province are currently not able to acquire, hold or dispose of land in their own names unless "enabled by specific legislation" such as a modern treaty. It means that Nations without those pathways could set up corporations or alternative arrangements for land acquisition and holding purposes.[134]

Of further note, within the context of Indigenous asset management, there are no recent statistics on the rise of Indigenous impact investing; however, a 2018 report from the University of British Columbia estimated that of the $10.5 billion of impact assets under management in Canada, at least $1.2 billion of that was directed toward Indigenous communities. While this is a dated number, realizing the need to measure assets under management overall is important to connect to the rise of Indigenous economic power. Specifically, the report identifies that:

> This underscores the growing recognition of the potential for impact investing to drive positive social and economic change within Indigenous communities. Through strategic investment and asset management, Indigenous communities can leverage these funds to address key priorities such as infrastructure development, education,

healthcare, and economic empowerment, fostering sustainable growth and prosperity for future generations.[135]

10. The Rise of Indigenous Entrepreneurship

The rise of Indigenous entrepreneurship in recent years is a powerful phenomenon to witness. Recent research suggests Indigenous Peoples are creating new businesses at five times the rate of non-Indigenous peoples, and those businesses are worth billions. According to Statistics Canada, there are nearly 19,000 businesses located in Indigenous communities (approximately 17,000 in First Nations communities and 2,000 in Inuit communities), which together generate just over $10 billion in total revenue.[136] Besides revenue generation, Indigenous-owned businesses are creating significant impacts within community, such as providing essential goods and services, along with creating jobs. More than one in three Indigenous businesses create employment for others.

An RBC article notes on the rise of Indigenous entrepreneurship that:

> The number of Indigenous business owners is growing at five times the rate of self-employed and Indigenous women are starting businesses at twice the rate of non-Indigenous women. Indigenous people represent the fastest growth segment of the population and given the tremendous growth projections for the Indigenous economy, Indigenous entrepreneurship is and will continue to be a driving force of Canada's long-term economic stability. Indigenous businesses contribute more to the Canadian economy than the economic output of PEI and Newfoundland combined.[137]

Indigenous entrepreneurs are building a powerful generational shift today. Examples of Indigenous initiatives such as Pow Wow Pitch create the space for Indigenous entrepreneur pitch competitions that highlight Indigenous businesses from all backgrounds and industries, whether they're just starting or looking to grow. Over 2,400 Indigenous businesses have pitched their business idea through the Pow Wow Pitch platform to date.

Equally important in understanding the rise of Indigenous entrepreneurship are some staggering numbers that are being revealed regarding access to capital. As identified in a Business Council of Canada article titled "It's Time for Indigenous Peoples to Be at the center of Canada's Economy,"

> Less than 20 percent of Indigenous businesses have accessed capital from a financial institution or government program. Loan conditions, some Indigenous business leaders have noted, are based on shorter terms and higher interest-rates than received by other applicants. Qualifying for a loan is also more challenging for on-reserve Indigenous businesses because, technically, reserve land is owned by the federal government and therefore cannot be used as collateral for the capital required to start and grow their enterprises. Despite this, many Indigenous communities, and specifically development corporations, have found ways to start and build multi-million dollar enterprises.[138]

The article further identifies that "lack of connectivity, lack of federal funding, lack of education and over all the stigma in our society surrounding what being Indigenous means, it's often plagued with negative stereotypes versus seeing Indigenous people as they are and the way they are currently thriving."

Indigenous entrepreneurs are also increasingly doing business beyond Canada's borders and utilizing the opportunities that digital commerce and trade mechanisms are creating to reach international customers at a new pace. It has been identified that 24 percent of Indigenous-owned small and medium enterprises (SMEs) are selling products and services internationally, which is double the overall percentage of Canadian SME exporters.[139] Over half of those Indigenous exporters are reaching markets beyond the US.

A *Globe and Mail* article titled "Empowering Indigenous Entrepreneurs: Sustainable Success Through Equal Partnerships" identified the establishment of the "At the Table" roundtable series that connects Indigenous business owners and industry leaders to discuss solutions to some of the most pressing challenges Indigenous entrepreneurs are facing. The article notes that:

> Expansion plans by Indigenous-owned businesses in Canada, including among women and younger entrepreneurs, underscores the importance of economic reconciliation for the benefit of Indigenous

communities and Canada at large. Mastercard recognizes that creating opportunities for those who have historically been excluded does not take away from anyone, it lifts everyone up. "We believe in doing well by doing good, and we see a future where people can reach their full potential with inclusive economic growth," Sloan said, emphasizing that Mastercard prioritizes diversity, equity and inclusion, recognizing them as essential elements in fostering a more inclusive digital economy for all Canadians.[140]

Indigenous entrepreneurship is rapidly increasing. Statistics Canada highlights a notable trend of higher representation of women in Indigenous-owned businesses compared to non-Indigenous ones. Despite this growth, Indigenous entrepreneurs still face significant challenges, constituting just 1.4% of Canadian SMEs, according to Export Development Canada (EDC).[141] Funding hurdles, including institutional bias and misinformation regarding perceived lending risks, contribute to a lower loan approval rate for Indigenous businesses compared to their non-Indigenous counterparts. This highlights some of the systemic barriers that slow Indigenous businesses' full participation within the entrepreneurial landscape.

Efforts to address these inequalities are critical for ensuring greater inclusivity and support systems for Indigenous entrepreneurial success. Reconciliation initiatives aimed at providing tailored financial resources, alignment of capital for Indigenous businesses, addressing institutional bias, and promoting awareness and visibility of Indigenous entrepreneurship can play a key role in leveling the playing field and creating positive Indigenous economic outcomes. By overcoming these systemic challenges through thoughtfully designed approaches and tools, Indigenous entrepreneurs can actualize their full potential and contribute to regional economic growth, community development, and cultural preservation. Ultimately, realizing Indigenous business aspirations can allow for sustainable and prosperous businesses that reflect Indigenous identities and values.

11. Indigenous Trusts

Trust structures are commonly used to safeguard assets for future generations of Indigenous Nations. While Indigenous trusts are directly connected to both the settlement process and asset management, the quickening pace of Indigenous trust development has made this trend a highly competitive arena with financial partners seeking to confirm Indigenous business.

Understanding the scale and scope that these trusts are creating is an important context in the growth of the Indigenous economy. The Sisika Nation clearly demonstrates this in a public statement regarding successfully settling a historical claim against the federal government:

> Settling this case, which dates back to 1910, is long overdue for the People of Siksika Nation. I want to make that clear: Canada is not giving $1.3 billion to Siksika. Canada is righting a wrong committed over a century ago when Canada illegally took 115,000 acres of lands provided to Siksika along with other illegal acts. Now that this case has been settled, the compensation from the settlement can assist Siksika to develop true financial sovereignty and provide more opportunities for our People. Chief Ouray Crowfoot, Siksika Nation[142]

Understanding the development of this significant settlement outcome goes back to the forced 1910 surrender claim of 115,000 acres of Siksika's reserve and mineral rights taken by Canada at the time. This settlement addresses long-standing claims, including the Canadian Pacific Railway Claim and other land-based historical grievances, and included Canada breaking the Blackfoot Treaty obligations when the government took almost half of Siksika's reserve land, including some of its agricultural lands, to sell to people who settled in the area. Over time, the Nation will acquire up to 115,000 acres of land to select for addition to reserve land. The $1.3 billion settlement amount is, to date, one of the largest agreements of its kind reached in Canada.

Understand that the size, scale, and pace of Indigenous settlements are building the pathway for Indigenous Nations to advance key social, cultural, and economic outcomes for today and for future generations. These trust structures are also shifting Nations' financial presence in regional economies.

Other examples of settlements that established the pathway for Indigenous trust developments include a national news article titled "Federal Government Reaches $59M Settlement with First Nation in B.C. Over Land Seizure."

The federal government reached a $59-million settlement with a First Nation in British Columbia for compensation for imposing a right-of-way to be built through its reserve more than 110 years ago. The compensation package addressed the wrongs of the federal government in seizing the land in 1908 for the Vancouver Power Company right-of-way. The construction of the corridor effectively severed access to some reserve lands on the Sahhacum Indian Reserve 1 and Matsqui Main Indian Reserve 2. A government statement says Canada was supposed to make sure the crossings were built and maintained on the right-of-way, but it didn't keep that agreement and the nation's access to its reserve lands was cut off.[143]

The pathways for the increasing pace of Indigenous trust developments are based on Nations challenging historical injustices, which is creating new economic space for Nations through financial leverage and increasing influence within the financial sector. Another example is the Mitaanjigamiing First Nation, where Canada and Ontario reached a settlement on the historical Treaty 3 Flooding Claim.[144] This settlement provides the Nation with $84.45 million in compensation, with Canada paying $45.05 million and Ontario paying $39.4 million. The claim was filed in response to the unauthorized and uncompensated flooding of reserve land due to the building of a dam across the Rainy River at Fort Frances-International Falls in the early 1900s. The dam has continued to cause ongoing flooding on the Nation's reserve lands.

An exponential rise in trust fund investments reflects the large claim settlement amounts of the federal and provincial governments. In 2013, the National Aboriginal Trust Officers Association estimated that roughly $20 billion of trust assets and investments were being managed on behalf of Indigenous Nations.[145] Since then, claim settlements have exceeded $20 billion, suggesting that this Indigenous intermediation gap is likely in the range of tens of billions of dollars and growing.

12. Indigenous Sovereign Wealth Funds

A sovereign wealth fund establishes a structure in which international governments invest state-earned revenues. What makes a wealth fund "sovereign" is that it is created through an act of legislation (law) within a sovereign government (a country) for its purposes and within its culture and language. This financial mechanism is being adapted today by Indigenous Nations as an increasing trend in the Indigenous economy.[146]

The development of Indigenous sovereign wealth is a trend to pay attention to. A news article, "Ontario First Nations Groups Form New Sovereign Wealth Fund," describes this trend:

> In this development, 129 First Nations groups in Ontario have created a new joint sovereign wealth fund called the Ontario First Nations Sovereign Wealth Fund which will be funded by C$29 million in seed capital from the Ontario government. It will also hold the 14 million shares, or a 2.4 percent stake, in Ontario electric utility Hydro One that the 129 groups acquired from the provincial government for C$259 million in a deal that closed Tuesday.[147]

Another interesting development in the increasing trend of Indigenous sovereign wealth structures, as described in the headline "Indigenous-led Project Reconciliation Fast-Tracks $1 Billion Sovereign Wealth Fund Launch," is advancing access for equity ownership in a major national asset.[148]

The Kahnawake Sovereign Wealth Fund (KSWF) is another example of this trend, which is structured to generate long-term wealth, reduce financial risk, and put the Nation in a better position where own-source revenue can fulfill the actual operational needs of the community. The fund's long-term goals are supported by the Council of Chiefs, which included a key objective of a minimum ten-year period where all capital and income will remain within the fund to grow capital for the longer term.

"The KSWF is now ready to start working on building capital for our community," said Michael Delisle Jr., who holds the Economic Development Portfolio and is the Chair of the Investment and Revenue Committee.

> We have approximately $32 million of investment capital, and the fund will primarily be invested in public securities, as we work towards

our long-term financial goals of putting our community in a better financial position for future generations and putting us on a path of self-reliance. At the outset, approximately 80% of the initial capital will be invested in public portfolios that will be overseen by the Investment and Revenue Committee. The remaining 20% will be deployed into other areas, allowing the KSWF the flexibility to invest in community ventures or businesses.[149]

The Mohawk Council launched their first ever Indigenous Sovereign Wealth Fund while celebrating with the TMX Group as a progressive leap in self-determination to manage the Nation's wealth on their own terms and across generations.

13. ESGI Reporting—Changing the Context of Corporate Reporting

A growing area of interest is the emergence of the ESGI narrative, which focuses on Indigenous inclusion as an essential addition to the traditional ESG (Environment, Society, Governance) acronym. Indigenous issues in Canada are increasingly being reflected in corporate relationships and public reporting. There is a growing perspective in identifying how Indigenous issues can be better integrated into existing ESG standards and ratings.

The ESG framework is widely criticized for its limitations in having a "check box" or greenwashing approach that does not truly reflect the need for meaningful engagement, consultation, or the legal requirements for free, prior, and informed consent (FPIC) with Indigenous Nations. There is a wide spectrum of Indigenous Rights and impacts on Nations within the corporate realm; however, what can and cannot be quantified is important to understand within the ESG framework. This has created the need for the "I" in the acronym.

With the increasing complexity of addressing Indigenous issues, there are some factors that can be measured. These include the number of Indigenous employees, Indigenous representation on the board of directors, number of contracts with Indigenous businesses, and support for Indigenous community organizations. However, many aspects of a company's record of dealing with Indigenous Nations are much more relationship-oriented and qualitative versus quantitative, making measurements and tracking more difficult to align with the ESG ratings framework. Thus, adding "I" to the acronym—ESGI—has emerged as a significant trend, ensuring that the complexity of the Indigenous relationship can be better tracked across a company's approach.

As noted in a CPA article titled "Indigenous Involvement and Values Are Key to ESG Investing," as companies move forward with their ESG initiatives:

> It is essential to prioritize Indigenous involvement, knowledge, leadership, and practices, to ensure these initiatives are successful for all stakeholders involved. Upfront inclusion of Indigenous values and input results in more successful, robust, and resilient initiatives, projects, and investments, as well as contributes to reconciliation and self-determination.[150]

An "Indigenous Rights and ESG Reporting" article describes the key context that companies today must play a significant role in advancing reconciliation with Indigenous Peoples. The article specifically references, "A recent 2022 review of Canadian ESG reporting conducted by PwC revealed that less than 30% of companies report policies to attract and retain Indigenous employees, managers and board."[151]

While the legal domain of Indigenous Rights is constantly evolving and expanding, Indigenous Rights are not explicitly addressed within ESG standards. The formative shift from the use of ESG to ESGI encompasses the growing recognition of the requirement for Indigenous participation and consent and the growing need for accountability in corporate reporting.

14. Corporate Response to Economic Reconciliation

It is a growing trend for corporations engaging with Indigenous Nations to measure and report social and economic outcomes through partnerships with Indigenous businesses and communities. While these indicators have largely focused on Indigenous spend, impact, or contracts extended to Indigenous businesses within these projects, measuring economic outcomes is an important exercise to build visibility, accountability, and transparency in major projects with Indigenous communities and businesses.

An example is Enbridge, which established a billion-dollar commitment and target for Indigenous business spending. Formed from the company's commitments in its Indigenous Reconciliation Action Plan (IRAP), Enbridge has established a target for current and future spending with Indigenous businesses.

> From January 2023 to the end of 2030, Enbridge has committed to an additional $1 billion in Indigenous spending across its North American projects and operations. This refers to the total spend with Indigenous businesses on both direct and indirect subcontracting opportunities, as well as wages paid to Indigenous workers by Enbridge contractors.[152]

Through the public announcement of this commitment, the company identified that "setting a meaningful, time-bound spending target demonstrates our continued commitment to engagement and inclusion of Indigenous communities and businesses in the execution of Enbridge projects and operations," notes Kim Brenneis, Enbridge's Director of Community and Indigenous Engagement in Canada.

In the same sector, a report by the Canadian Association of Petroleum Producers identified the industry spending by type of Indigenous businesses, with construction at $1.4 billion and equipment services at $992 million, respectively, as an example.[153]

Another example of a corporate response in advancing economic reconciliation is the Cenvous approach in establishing a $50 million initiative as a collaborative effort with six Indigenous Nations to address one of the biggest problems facing the communities today, the chronic shortage of adequate housing. The investment program is expected to result in about 200 new homes built over five years. The company's leadership is a great example of building a corporate response for Indigenous inclusion based on truly listening to the Indigenous community's needs and responding with collaborative innovations.

Another example of building a corporate response to advancing Indigenous economic empowerment is BMO's commitment to doubling the size of its Indigenous banking business from $4 billion to $8 billion by 2025.

Finally, a rapidly expanding trend is the development of Corporate Reconciliation Action Plans. This trend is designing plans that advance the business of reconciliation within a company through a strategic, accountable, results-based approach. A corporate reconciliation action plan builds an organization or corporation's framework to advance key social and economic outcomes for reconciliation with Indigenous Peoples. Corporate Reconciliation Action Plans help to design the delivery of tangible and substantive social and economic benefits for Indigenous Peoples. An important aspect includes a plan to support increased cultural safety in the workforce or identify how the company engages with the community. The activated plans allow organizations to develop their reconciliation commitments continuously and provide companies with a structured approach to advance reconciliation and be accountable for the results over time.

There are several powerful examples of corporate reconciliation leadership in action. The defining feature is that it is public, accountable, measurable, solution or innovation oriented, and focused on value generation. This is an emerging trend that is demonstrating value creation in corporate business relationships with Indigenous businesses. One example is TELUS, an early leader in establishing a public, accountable, and measurable Corporate Economic Reconciliation Action Plan that lays out core priorities to advance connectivity, culturally responsive relationships, economic reconciliation outcomes, and AI technology advancements with Indigenous communities.

15. Indigenous-led Economic Institutions

The dynamic space of how Indigenous economic value creation is happening brings a series of key trends to the forefront. The development of Indigenous-led institutions is integral to establishing the foundational structures that support Indigenous economic growth, self-determination, and avenues for participation.

The First Nations Fiscal Management Act (FMA) is optional First Nations legislation that came into effect on April 1, 2006. The FMA established four First Nation institutions to develop modern financial and governance tools for First Nations governments. The FMA framework and institutions have enabled Nations to collectively secure an international investment-grade credit rating and have accessed over $2 billion in private capital through the First Nations Financial Authority while creating over 17,000 new jobs. This financial platform was built to move away from the Indian Act and has further empowered Nation governments to generate over $1 billion in tax revenues through the First Nations Tax Commission. To date, close to 350 Nations have signed on. The objective of designing a new fiscal relationship between the Crown and First Nations is to improve the transfer-based fiscal relationship by establishing long-term funding arrangements and a reduced reporting burden while increasing access to financing tools.

The institutional space the FMA framework has created supports a new collaborative institutional approach for advancing wealth development and sustainable First Nations economies. The new institutional framework includes the following features:

- Advances strong governance, and administration systems
- Develops property rights certainty through the Framework Agreement on First Nations Land Management
- Establishes a legal framework to support markets, including certainty of rules, processes, dispute resolution, and timelines
- Establishes a fiscal framework and relationship with the federal and provincial/territorial governments for revenues and services, including clarity over how jurisdictions raise revenue
- Establishes competitive Nations and financing

The newly established First Nation Infrastructure Institute is an Indigenous-led initiative that supports Indigenous communities and organizations in planning, procuring, owning, and managing their infrastructure assets on their lands.

UNDRIP affirms the right of Indigenous Peoples to establish and control their own institutions, a key element of self-determination and cultural autonomy. Specifically, Article 5 of UNDRIP states that Indigenous Peoples have the right to "maintain and strengthen their distinct political, legal, economic, social, and cultural institutions,"[154] while also retaining the option to participate fully in the broader governments institutional systems if they choose.

Key aspects of the right to establish Indigenous institutions include:

Self-Governance and Decision-Making
Indigenous Peoples can create and manage institutions that reflect their governance traditions and systems, enabling them to make decisions aligned with their values and laws. This right is foundational for Indigenous sovereignty, allowing Indigenous Nations to govern themselves without external interference in their internal affairs.

Preservation of Culture and Identity
Indigenous-controlled institutions help maintain and strengthen cultural practices, languages, and identities. For example, educational institutions can integrate Indigenous knowledge, history, and languages, supporting cultural revitalization and passing down Traditional Knowledge to future generations.

Economic and Social Development
By establishing their own economic and social institutions, Indigenous Nations can develop programs, policies, and services that directly address their community's needs. This includes areas like health care, housing, and economic initiatives, fostering economic independence, and improving overall well-being.

Legal and Justice Systems
Indigenous Nations can establish justice institutions that operate according to their traditional laws, values, and restorative principles rather than solely relying on state-based legal systems. This provides a culturally appropriate means of resolving disputes and maintaining social order within their communities.

Control over Resources and Development
UNDRIP supports Indigenous institutions' role in managing and protecting lands, resources, and the environment, ensuring that development aligns with Indigenous priorities and consent. This ensures Indigenous Nations can control their natural and economic resources sustainably and with sovereignty.

Indigenous-led institutions will create stronger, more reliable, and more effective results than through the current process of Indian Act economics.

16. Government Policies, Agreements, and Reconciliation Arrangements

Government policies and agreements are effective tools for building nation-to-nation and government-to-government relationships and are a central structure for advancing Indigenous economic outcomes.

The BC government, in particular, has established a considerable volume of reconciliation agreements with Indigenous Nations that focus on closing the socioeconomic gap and building the foundation for an inclusive and prosperous economy while addressing historical injustices with Nations. BC led the implementation of UNDRIP into law, even before Canada, and laid out an action plan to uphold the implementation process that specifically describes that:

- Indigenous Peoples freely determine their economic development goals, priorities, and strategies, and exercise their right to maintain and develop their economic systems and institutions to support self-governance, along with traditional and other economic activities.
- The Province and Indigenous Peoples collaborate and participate in ongoing, meaningful, and enduring dialogue to achieve a more inclusive, innovative, and sustainable economy for the benefit of present and future generations that reflects Indigenous values, interests, goals and worldviews.[155]

Also in BC, the Forest Consultation and Revenue Sharing Agreement (FCRSAs) is another example. It provides First Nations with economic benefits that return directly to the community based on harvest activities in their asserted Traditional Territories. With nearly 160 specific agreements negotiated and representing over half the Nations in BC, the continued advancement of resource agreements represents a positive step toward building the foundation for other resource revenue-sharing agreements as a mechanism for economic reconciliation.[156]

Revenue-sharing agreements are a key element in the design of the rise of the Indigenous economy. In 2021, Natural Resources Canada (NRCan) was directed to develop a National Benefits-Sharing Framework (NBSF) as part of its economic reconciliation strategic mandate within the natural resource sector. This framework advances the federal government's commitment to uphold and recognize Indigenous Rights by advancing meaningful participation of Indigenous Peoples in decisions that affect their communities and territories. The plan aims to develop and implement actions to ensure Indigenous Peoples receive equitable participation and benefits from natural resource development on their Traditional Territories. The mandate establishes four pillars of focus: capacity, inclusion, partnerships, and economic benefits. The approach to the pillars addresses the barriers preventing Indigenous Nations from fully benefiting from the natural resources sector. The status of implementation of this mandate is unclear as it is not reported on the website.

Also along this trend line, the Indigenous Natural Resource Partnerships (INRP) federal program aims to increase the economic participation of Indigenous Nations in the development of natural resource projects that specifically support the transition to a clean energy future while increasing the capacities of Indigenous Nations to engage in, benefit from, actively participate in economic development opportunities, and improve the investment collaboration environment between Indigenous Nations and stakeholders.

While there are numerous examples to draw from, these initiatives and agreements provide initial insight into the significance of this trend, which is increasing Indigenous inclusion and outcomes. Government-structured responses and leadership in designing tools and programs that advance Indigenous economic inclusion are key trends in the growth of the Indigenous economy.

Finally, BC established a revenue-sharing structure for First Nations, which included amendments to the Gaming Control Act to establish that 7 percent of BC Lottery Corporation's net income is shared with First Nations until 2045. The funds flow through the First Nations Gaming Revenue Sharing Limited Partnership, established by the First Nations Gaming Commission. Many smaller remote Nations described this as the first time they had any leverageable income source.

17. Financial Architecture—Designing Tools for Indigenous Economic Growth

The concept of Indigenomics emphasizes modern Indigenous economic design, which builds the tools and financial architecture for increasing Indigenous economic inclusion and outcomes. In emphasizing the need for financial architecture and tools to enable the full participation of Indigenous Nations in the economy to advance economic reconciliation, the federal government is establishing an Indigenous Loan Guarantee Program. The initiative will enable Indigenous Nations and businesses to access affordable capital to increase economic efficiency, reduce risk perception, and help unlock key opportunities for Indigenous equity ownership in major resource projects.[157]

Four provinces—Alberta, British Columbia, Saskatchewan, and Ontario —have established Indigenous loan guarantee programs. This leaves significant leadership space for the remaining provincial and territorial governments to build Indigenous financial architecture and tools to advance regional Indigenous inclusion and capacity to participate at the equity level in major projects.

18. UNDRIP Implementation into Law

Implementing the United Nations Declaration on the Rights of Indigenous Peoples (UNDRIP) establishes new economic space across governments and the corporate sector as emerging leadership responses are activated. A *CTV News* article highlights the City of Vancouver's leadership in the implementation and connects this as a key trend in advancing Indigenous economic reconciliation. The "Vancouver Releases 5-Year Action Plan to Implement UNDRIP" article notes that "the five-year action plan is meant to solidify Indigenous Rights in the city and was crafted alongside the Musqueam, Squamish and Tsleil-Waututh First Nations. It's about putting our identity back on the map. It's also about the rebuilding of Indigenous economies," said Dennis Thomas-Whonoak, Tsleil-Waututh First Nation Councillor.[158]

The current economic reality is that uncertainty around Indigenous Rights and Title has significantly hindered investment and resource development in this country for years. In the context of Indian Act economics, the trifecta of the honor of the Crown, Indigenous Rights and Title, and Treaty Rights brings into focus the duty of the federal government to accommodate Indigenous Nations and engage them in decision-making. UNDRIP offers a pathway forward for the economic space for value creation in the Indigenous economy.

19. Indigenous Clean Energy Revolution

A *Globe and Mail* Accelerating Transition series report titled "Economic Impacts of Indigenous Leadership in Catalyzing the Transition to a Clean

Energy Future Across Canada" identifies an estimation that there are over 200 medium-to-large renewable energy generating projects with Indigenous involvement now in operation.[159] Further, there are close to 200 projects in the final stages of planning or construction, and most of these projects involve partnerships between Indigenous communities and energy sector companies, utilities, or developers. The report highlights that medium-to-large Indigenous renewable energy projects have experienced a 29.6 percent growth rate across Canada since 2017. It is estimated that, in 2020, there were 1,700–2,100 micro or small renewable energy systems in place with Indigenous leadership/partnerships. Further, smaller-scale Indigenous clean energy projects are accelerating, with many Indigenous Nations developing community-scale or small-generation systems supplying regional grids.

In framing the acceleration of the Indigenous clean energy revolution, the Accelerating Transition report scanned Indigenous participation and the increasing Indigenous ownership in clean energy projects. The report outlines three common approaches: 1) minor project participation reflective of single-digit ownership percentages or equivalent financial benefit; 2) a significant increase in minority ownership, which is trending toward 25–50 percent project participation; and 3) 100 percent Indigenous community ownership, which is becoming increasingly common.[160]

The rapid escalation of Indigenous participation in the clean energy sector is a key trend in the Indigenous economy. It is particularly important in understanding the increasing market space and leadership Indigenous Nations are engaged in within a clean energy future.

20. Call to Action #92 Implementation

Call to Action #92 of the Truth and Reconciliation Commission report specifically outlines adopting UNDRIP as a reconciliation framework and applying its principles, norms, and standards to corporate policy and core operational activities involving Indigenous Peoples and their lands and resources. This includes the following:

I. Commit to meaningful consultation, building respectful relationships, and obtaining the free, prior, and informed consent of Indigenous Peoples before proceeding with economic development projects.

II. Ensure that Indigenous Peoples have equitable access to jobs, training, and education opportunities in the corporate sector, and that Indigenous communities gain long-term sustainable benefits from economic development projects.

III. Provide education for management and staff on the history of Aboriginal Peoples, including the history and legacy of residential schools, the United Nations Declaration on the Rights of Indigenous Peoples, Treaties and Aboriginal Rights, Indigenous law, and Aboriginal-Crown relations. This will require skills-based training in intercultural competency, conflict resolution, human rights, and anti-racism.[161]

The Business Council of Canada, the Canadian Chamber of Commerce, the Conference Board of Canada, the Canadian Council for Public-Private Partnerships (CCPPP), and numerous business associations have all made recommendations and commitments that align with building outcomes to the Call to Action #92.

This Call to Action facilitates a pivotal space for advancing Indigenous economic value creation. It specifically addresses what changes are needed in the corporate sector to achieve steps toward reconciliation with Indigenous communities. When implementing Call to Action #92 strategies in any organization or company, it is imperative that the change is implemented across the whole spectrum of the organization, from the boardroom to the frontline of working with communities.

As an example of responding to this corporate sector Call to Action, the Mining Association of Canada launched an updated "Toward Sustainable Mining Indigenous and Community Relationships Protocol," which is designed to facilitate strong relationship building through collaborative engagement and decision-making processes with Indigenous Nations and establish measurable criteria.[162] This protocol sets a standard for what is considered good practice in sustainable mining that includes achieving free, prior, and informed consent (FPIC) before proceeding with development where impacts to Indigenous Rights occur. The protocol builds on the mining sector's leadership in prioritizing Indigenous employment, workforce development, business partnerships, and support for education and skills-training initiatives. These serve to advance criteria focused on corporate and community collaboration mechanisms that ensure Indigenous Peoples have equitable access to opportunities with mining companies. Additionally, the protocol includes criteria that aim to ensure that management and staff are provided with education and awareness training on the history, traditions, and rights of Indigenous Peoples. The Mining Association members are required to evaluate, publicly report, and independently verify their performance against these new criteria at each of their Canadian mine sites.

21. Indigenous Equity Participation

Equity participation facilitates an Indigenous group's ownership, whole or in part, of a company or project. This rapidly evolving Indigenous economic trend unlocks new levels of control and influence over developments on Indigenous Territories and is a key mechanism for cross-generational wealth generation for Nations.

Indigenous groups are negotiating ownership rights with project proponents and typically purchase their equity stake using a combination of their own capital and debt financing. The Conference Board of Canada describes this development as moving beyond the status quo, and that by Nations developing equity positions in major projects, Indigenous communities are expecting more from the economic development process than the usual employment, training, and procurement opportunities that come with impact and benefit agreements (IBAs).[163] Through equity ownership, Nations are driving new economic outcomes that include long-term stable revenue streams, decision-making powers over major economic projects in their territory, and capacity and skills development opportunities.

In today's legal and economic environment, it is nearly impossible for any energy, resource, or infrastructure project to be developed without securing the support and consent from local Indigenous Nations. Indigenous Nations are increasingly advancing equity participation in these major projects. Project developers and owners understand the strategic objective of partnering with Indigenous Nations to manage project risk better, increase financing efficiency, and facilitate stronger economic reconciliation outcomes.

An Indigenous Law Bulletin by Fasken Law describes that the number of Indigenous groups involved varied by sector. What is emerging is a clear demonstration of Indigenous energy sector dominance, with many of the projects involving multiple Indigenous groups. For example, projects like pipelines often involve numerous Indigenous Nations. Due to tax advantages and liability protection, these major projects establish limited partnerships as the most common structure for Indigenous equity participation. Further, increasing minority ownership ensures Indigenous Nations can hold minority stakes, with an overall average of 21 percent equity interest. In the project analysis by Fasken Law, the article outlines the average number of Indigenous groups involved and includes the following breakdown:

- Linear infrastructure (e.g., pipelines, transmission lines): 15.4
  - Transmission lines: 12.7
  - Oil & gas pipelines: 19.5
- Non-linear infrastructure (e.g., electricity generation facilities): 1.9
  - Hydroelectricity generation: 2.5
  - Solar generation: 2
  - Wind generation: 1.6
  - Other: 2.1[164]

Another demonstration of this equity participation trend can be seen in the media headline "'A Special Moment in Our History': Mohawk Council of Kahnawake Inks Deal with Hydro-Québec." The agreement will establish Indigenous co-ownership of a $1.1 billion transmission line exporting electricity to New York City.[165]

Indigenous equity ownership is a trend to watch as it combines investment and partnership opportunities with economic reconciliation outcomes.

22. Indigenous Fee Simple Land Purchases

Indigenous Nations purchasing fee simple land has become a solution to securing key land parcels for cultural, conservation, or economic development purposes. This is a growing trend that sees an ongoing narrative that it is faster for a Nation to purchase than to go through land claims or a negotiation process through the Indian Act.

A recent example demonstrating this trend is the Tsawout Nation on Vancouver Island in BC. A *CTV* article titled "Land Back: Tsawout First Nation Buys 40-Hectare Agricultural Property" identifies that the Nation has expanded its existing land base by 15 percent more than what is set out within the Indian Act.[166] Tsawout First Nation purchased a property adjacent to the community for $5.6 million. This land expansion process is creating a new economic base for Nations.

Another media story highlighting this trend is "'This Is Just the Beginning': First Nations' Real Estate Megaprojects Game-Changing for Metro Vancouver." The article describes the Musqueam Nation in Vancouver, which, as Indigenous developers, is building 25,000 new homes in Metro Vancouver with purchased property.[167]

This land purchase trend is particularly significant as it also highlights Nations' own-source revenue strategies, which are creating expansion opportunities beyond the established reserves. Real estate purchases are a key value-creation process in the Indigenous economy, posing significant development and financial opportunities in working with Indigenous Nations.

Of further interest within this trend is a recent major development in BC that is setting out to reduce the barriers that First Nations currently face that add time and cost to the land registration process with the BC land title office. Nations may now choose to acquire, hold, and dispose of fee simple land under a corporation or proxy or have the option to choose to hold fee simple land in the name of the First Nation. This aligns with the administrative steps that First Nations must take with that of individuals, corporations, and modern treaty Nations. This development removes barriers to Nations' experiences regarding land holdings within the Indian Act.

A Victoria news story titled "B.C. Property Act Changes Allow First Nations to Purchase, Hold and Sell Land" further articulates this development, noting that prior to this development, First Nations were only able to legally hold land through various proxies.[168]

This trend is also creating value in new ways in the Indigenous economy, as Nations increasingly have own-source revenue streams that ensure real estate purchases are a strategic objective for the return of traditional lands.

23. The Net Zero Agenda and the Indigenous Economy

An emerging central narrative reinforced across the Indigenous business development process is the pivotal point that the road to net zero crosses Indigenous Territories and requires consent to access the resources needed to fuel a low-carbon future. This narrative advances Indigenous economic participation and uniquely situates the importance of Indigenous partnerships in Canada's low-carbon economic future.

Canada's road to net zero will rely heavily on vital sources of capital held by Indigenous Nations. An RBC report articulates this point further. With an estimated $2 trillion in capital required over the next 25 years, with resources coming from Indigenous territories—this capital will essentially be unlocked by Indigenous partnerships, including ownership.[169] The report identifies that an Indigenous-led approach to the climate transition and economic opportunities toward net zero will be essential to economic reconciliation. Furthermore, to achieve net zero and economic reconciliation, Canada needs to leverage four forms of Indigenous capital:

1. **Natural Capital:** Indigenous lands hold vast resources essential to green energy systems, the cleantech revolution, and a low-carbon economy. RBC estimates that at least 56 percent of advanced critical mineral projects, 35 percent of top solar sites, and 44 percent of the better wind sites involve Indigenous Territory.

2. **Financial Capital:** Indigenous Nations' growing wealth includes an estimated $20 billion in trust assets and up to $100 billion in outstanding land and other claims. RBC identifies that this capital will be critical to "crowding in" billions of dollars in private and public clean energy investment for net zero initiatives.

3. **Intellectual Capital:** Incorporating Indigenous values and Traditional Knowledge in the net zero transition will lead to more sustainable and profitable outcomes. Indigenous conservation can establish Canada as a leader in regenerative techniques, the preservation of critical biodiversity, and advance nature-based carbon solutions. The RBC report has identified this as a powerful strategic advantage as Canada competes with other countries for capital to finance the energy investment into the net zero economy.

4. **Human Capital:** With a rapidly growing young population, emerging young Indigenous leaders and entrepreneurs will be critical activators for shaping the innovative thinking needed to fuel the green transition. As the fastest-growing youth cohort, Indigenous Canadians can help

power a net zero workforce, including valuable jobs in skilled trades, advanced technology, business ventures, and more.

24. Settlement Values

A *Globe and Mail* article titled "Wealth Managers Seek to Help Indigenous Communities Balance Spending and Investing Settlements" describes that there are over 627 outstanding First Nations claims actively under assessment or being reviewed by the Canadian government, according to data published by Crown-Indigenous Relations and Northern Affairs Canada.[170] Known as specific claims, these legal challenges deal with historical wrongs against Nations, including the administration of lands and the absence of the fulfillment of historic treaties and other agreements. The article details that another 675 specific claims have already been settled through negotiations, with the most recent 264 claims resolved for close to $8.9 billion in compensation. These totals do not include the $20 billion federal settlement over discrimination in the Indigenous child welfare system or the recent $10 billion between the federal and Ontario governments and the twenty-one Robinson Huron First Nations over unpaid annuities, which have been addressed through separate out-of-court processes. This summary provides important insights into the acceleration of legal claims, settlement outcomes, and the investment environment through which Nations can now generate long-term wealth through past wrongs and create significant economic value as an outcome. An important reference point is that, between April 2022 and March 2023, fifty-six claims were resolved for $ 3.5 billion.

Understanding this process and outcome can be seen through the example of the Chippewas of Rama First Nation in negotiating a land settlement. In 2012, it was part of the Chippewa Tri-Council settlement claim with the federal government for the Coldwater Narrows Lands in Ontario. This was one of the largest specific claims settlements in Canadian history and, at that time, provided the Nation with an $80 million settlement. In addition, the Nation has received more than $140 million for a land deal with Casino Rama and over $100 million in the Williams Treaties settlement of 2018.

Righting historical wrongs is creating a significant new investment environment for Nations. In an article titled "Manitoba First Nation Clears Final

Hurdle in $200M 'Cows and Plows' Case Massive Historical Treaty Legal Settlement," a northern Manitoba First Nations community has finalized a massive legal settlement that will see more than $200 million injected into the Nation, and each individual member receive a $30,000 payout, based on the promises made more than a century ago that the federal government did not keep.[171] Pine Creek First Nation is part of Treaty 4. When the treaty was originally signed in 1874, the federal government promised to supply agricultural equipment and livestock to families and individuals to assist them in adjusting to an agricultural-based economy and society. (Also called "forced assimilation" within the context of Indian Act economics.) The federal government has admitted that it did not supply the agricultural equipment or the livestock agreed upon in the treaties, including Treaty 4, and is now working to compensate the Nations with financial settlement values adjusted to today's currency.

The ongoing connected pattern of increasing settlement values creates new financial leveragability from land, asset, and investment value. It is a significant trend that must be paid attention to in the rise of the Indigenous economy. According to a federal news release, to date, Canada has settled over 590 specific claims through negotiated settlements with First Nations across the country. This includes over 180 claims settled through negotiations since 2016.

Another example of Indigenous settlement value is depicted in the media story "Five First Nations Reach Settlement with B.C., Federal Governments on Treaty Land Entitlement Claims," which highlights the specific context that the Nations signed Treaty 8 in 1899 but did not benefit from the use of their land while others developed it for resources. Under the settlement agreement, BC will provide $800 million in compensation in response to the claim.

> For more than 100 years, the First Nations were deprived of the use and benefit of thousands of acres of land owed to them under Treaty 8, while the resources on and under those lands were taken and developed by others. Under the settlement agreements, Canada will provide the First Nations compensation for these losses and costs relating to the claims. In addition to monetary compensation from the

Government of Canada, the Province of British Columbia will provide approximately 44,266 hectares (109,385 acres) of Crown land
to the First Nations. In a related agreement, the Province of Alberta
has also agreed to provide an amount of land to the Doig River First
Nation in that province.[172]

As part of the press release for this settlement, several interesting facts
were identified: 1) from April 2022 to 2023, fifty-six specific claims were
resolved for $3,515,647,357 in compensation; 2) of the sixty-four claims
that were filed, Canada made an offer to negotiate fifty-six claims; and 3)
working in partnership with First Nations, Canada has resolved more than
665 specific claims since 1973.[173]

With the rise of Indigenous economic empowerment, the facilitation of
value creation through cash value settlements and land transfers has been a
consistent development and is providing Nations with increasing economic
presence within Indigenous Territories.

25. Urban Reserves

A *Municipal World* article describes an Indigenous urban reserve as similar to a municipal property but is a section of reserve land within a larger
municipality. The article cites that "generally, urban reserves are created to
stimulate business activity, generate revenue, and create investment and
employment opportunities that would otherwise be unavailable on other
reserve lands."[174] Urban reserves can be described as "First Nations economic zones." To create such an economic zone, municipalities and First Nations
negotiate municipal service agreements to agree on important development
factors such as bylaw compatibility and service fees. An important distinction is that urban reserves are under the jurisdiction of the First Nation,
not the city or town. For example, two urban reserves are owned by the
Long Plain First Nation in Portage La Prairie and Winnipeg, Manitoba. The
urban reserves have significantly stimulated the economies of both cities
by providing new businesses and a greater number of skilled people in the
workforce.

First Nations people are moving away from reserves to urban centers in
increasing numbers, often due to a lack of housing, education, and economic

or employment opportunities. Urban reserves have catalyzed that trend by providing better opportunities in the city. These land structures create a means of bridging cultural divides and fostering better social, cultural, and economic relationships between Indigenous Peoples.

Another example of an urban reserve in Winnipeg, Naawi-Oodena, has been officially identified as the largest urban reserve in Canada, and it was acquired through the repatriation of the Winnipeg barracks. Manitoba Keewatinowi Okimakanak (MKO) is a political advocacy organization that provides a collective voice on issues of inherent, treaty, Indigenous, and human rights for the citizens of the sovereign First Nations. The MKO Nations are signatories to Treaties 4, 5, 6, and 10. The MKO Chief explains, "We no longer want to be spectators of economic prosperity in Manitoba."[175]

Further outlining this economic trend, a *CBC* article titled "Saskatoon Signs Agreement with Lac La Ronge Indian Band to Create Urban Reserve" describes the Nation's progress. Once the property is designated as a reserve, it will become the tenth urban reserve in Saskatoon. When a property transfers to reserve status, it is no longer under City jurisdiction.

> The Lac La Ronge Indian Band is in the process of creating six new urban reserves including one in Saskatoon. "The goal is to have these urban reserves provide our community the opportunity for economic development including commercial, residential and industrial activities. The intention is to establish the urban reserve in Saskatoon to ensure the Lac La Ronge Indian Band members who are studying science, technology, engineering and math at the post-secondary level have a landing place upon completion of their degree," says Chief Tammy Cook-Searson.[176]

This collective set of trends is actively creating new economic value in the Indigenous economy, previously unavailable through the structure of Indian Act economics. These trends set out to identify the opportunity for capital activation and partnership opportunity in the emerging Indigenous economy. While this is set out in the context of the existing emerging Indigenomics $100 billion Indigenous economy, it is essential to view these trends as strategic opportunities beyond the $100 billion Indigenous economic target.

The Greatest Breakaway

In conclusion, these trends are facilitating value creation in the Indigenous economy in new and powerful ways. Drawing from Canada's favorite game, the rise of Indigenous economic power is the greatest breakaway this country has ever seen. The players with the puck (Indigenous Nations) are the offensive players, and the defensive player is the federal government. In the exhilaration of the breakaway dynamic is the fast-paced turnaround play in which the offensive player breaks free of the defending line and rushes toward the goal. This is the depiction of the rise of Indigenous economic power. While Canada has been so busy defending its position, it has left a gaping hole of opportunity where Indigenous Nations have rapidly turned the play around offensively. Indigenous Nations excel at the breakaway dynamic, with over 370 Indigenous legal wins at the time of writing. Score!

The Indian Act upholds the experiences of denialism, extinction, economic isolation, narcissistic control, and belief systems of the archaic structure of Eurocentric superiority that, ironically, today is helping to shape Indigenous economic futurism. Indian Act economics is a failed system. The rise of Indigenous economic power is a legendary comeback that will be referred to for generations to come.

This is a historic moment in witnessing the rise of Indigenous economic power. History is being made. These are stories of the undeniable evidence of our time—we are witnessing the rise of the Indigenous economy through the ongoing media narrative of the Indigenous relationship in Canada. The rise of the Indigenous economy is the greatest breakaway this country has ever seen. This is Indigenomics in action.

Reflective Questions

1. What can a prosperity-focused agenda look like for advancing Indigenous economic growth?
2. How can the financial sector respond to the growth of the Indigenous economy? Other sectors?

3. How can Indigenous-focused equity partnerships create space for Indigenous economic inclusion?
4. What do the twenty-five trends of Indigenous growth demonstrate about the process of Indigenous economic value creation today?

Conclusion—The Happiest Future

INDIGENOMICS IS A PLATFORM for designing Indigenous economic growth and inclusion by leveraging cultural identity, addressing historical challenges, establishing a forward-looking economic target, and building a strengths-based economic narrative of inclusion.

Designing from a place of strength essentially means to leverage Indigenous cultural assets and knowledge systems to integrate traditional ways of being into modern business practices while integrating community strengths, stewardship, resilience, and responsibility within the economic development process. Addressing the deficit thinking and status quo of the Indigenous economic relationship requires building the leadership and structural responses for advancing Indigenous economic opportunities. This is economic reconciliation.

Indigenomics is future-pacing the story of Indigenous economic power through a forward-looking target and re-storying Indigenous prosperity by driving the national economic narrative to amplify positive action, leadership, and outcomes. Indigenous economic power is the creation of space at the economic table that expands economic opportunities for Indigenous Nations and businesses, and advances the development of partnerships for expanded market access.

The business case for the growth of the Indigenous economy brings into focus the increasing business activity not just as a contribution to GDP but as a metric of value creation. Using GDP as the only measurement of Indigenous economic strength misses key insights into how value creation is happening that are directly related to how the Indigenous relationship is centered in Canadian governance and legal and economic reality. The growth of the Indigenous economy must be re-storied in a narrative beyond barriers, gaps, limitations, and the socioeconomic gap.

Indian Act economics is the absence of the core functioning of the economy itself. Can you imagine the national economy functioning without any structure for value creation, no institutions, no commerce, with the consistent undermining of value through externalized decisions and limitations, the absence of a labor force, no land base, and no resources? How could the Canadian economy function in the absence of the structure of return on investment, absence of mortgage, or future time value of money, the very basics of the structure of finance? This is Indian Act economics. For Indigenous Peoples to rise to economic power in the same generation where the last residential schools closed in 1996 and establish the foundation for $100 billion of Indigenous economic activity, that is Indigenous power. We are a powerful people.

The fire of Indigenous economic resurgence has been lit. While still mourning our old ways, still reeling from the effects of the denial of justice, and upholding in our families and communities the stories of the Survivors, this generation has stood with feet planted firmly in the narrative of our continued existence, picked up the tool of business, and defiantly proclaimed, "We are still here."

In deconstructing Indian Act economics, we define our modern Indigenous space and existence, legal win by legal win, partnership by partnership, and investment by investment. It is time to take account of the truth of our times; the original policy directive of extermination within the Indian Act has not only failed, it is fuel to the fire of Indigenous economic power. The rise of Indigenous economic power is the great equalizer of economic justice. This is an Indigenous economic renaissance we are witnessing unfold daily, with all the odds stacked against us as Indigenous Peoples.

There are no truer words on the reflection of the rise of Indigenous economic power than that of Frederick Douglass, an American activist, social reformer, and abolitionist who became an important leader of the movement for African American civil rights in the early 19th century.

> Power concedes nothing without a demand. It never did and it never will. Find out just what any people will quietly submit to and you have found out the exact measure of injustice and wrong which will be imposed upon them, and these will continue until they are resisted with either words or blows, or with both. The limits of tyrants are prescribed by the endurance of those whom they oppress.[177]

This is the space that Indigenous existence demands today, the activation of social and economic equality, the deconstruction of the systems of economic exclusion, and the designing of our rightful space at the economic table. All while advancing self-determination and building the economic value that has so long been denied and, at the same time, demanding the upholding of the honor of the Crown and the activation of its self-proclaimed fiduciary duty. This is foundational to shaking off the losing foothold of the power dynamics of Indian Act economics.

Power is taken. The rise of the Indigenous economy and Indigenous Peoples taking our seats at the economic table is a beautiful expression of "We are a powerful people." In all the space and structures that were denied to us, in the darkest shadows, in the survival of residential school Survivors, we pick up the tool of business and hold our future clearly in sight with our responsibility to ourselves, to each other, to the Earth, and to our future in our site. This is our response.

It is time to revisit my orientation as the author and in the practice of centering myself in this unfolding story. Reaching deep into my existence, in this lifetime, I am removed—not only once through my mother's lineage into the foster care system, but denied twice in the absence of my father's lineage as prescribed through the Indian Act.

I uphold the central truth of my existence—the Indian Act holds the burden of proof of the denial of Indigenous existence. It must address simultaneously and continuously over time the truth of the denial of the continuation of Indigeneity itself, the denial of the matriarch, the continuation of the patriarchy and the upholding of the mechanisms of ultimate control over the Indian over time. It is failing.

As an author and Indigenous woman, my survival mechanism describes the idea that there must be another possibility other than what is in front of me. Indigenomics is the response. From fragmentation to wholeness, the journey is in front of us, calling us to our truths, telling our stories, and honoring the fallen tears for the experience of being told it is not okay to be who you are.

In revisiting my orientation as an author in this story, I defy the rules placed on my existence. And I revisit the terms of my engagement. We, as Indigenous Peoples, work, play, sing, and dance beyond the darkest shadow and the watchful eyes of the original Indian agent and all the rules prescribed for the continued offence of our existence. The Indian Act is the metaphor of the darkness prescribed to our existence, and our freedom is our choice today. We must build, construct, and design our continued existence. I choose beauty, I choose kindness, I choose respect, I choose well-being, I choose abundance. Indigenomics is my response to Indian Act economics. Indian Act economics is a hallucination.

The rise of Indigenous economic power brings the space for reflection and a focus on leadership and action. Is the Indian Act ethical? What role does the Indian Act play in the continued suppression of Indigenous economic activity today? The activation of these two powerful questions are entirely relevant in Canada's precarious economic landscape. The choice is in front of us. If it's ethical, choose. If it's not ethical, choose. Every action and inaction have consequences, but the rise of Indigenous economic power is only beginning to take shape and form meaning. In this early foundational phase of its development, it is set for exponential growth. This is the opportunity.

In the elegance of the words of Iain McGilchrist in *The Master and His Emissary: The Divided Brain and the Making of the Western World*:

> The model we choose to use to understand something determines what we find. If it is the case that our understanding is an effect of the metaphors we choose, it is also true that it is a cause. Our understanding itself guides the choice of metaphor by which we understand it. The chosen metaphor is both cause and effect of the relationship. Thus, how we think about our selves and our relationship to the world is already revealed in the metaphors we unconsciously choose to talk about it. That choice further entrenches our partial view of the subject. Paradoxically we seem to be obliged to understand something—including ourselves—well enough to choose the appropriate model before we can understand it. Our first leap determines where we land.[178]

In upholding the narrative of the absence of ethics within the process and structure of Indian Act economics, the contrasting metaphor alive at this moment is the fire of Indigenous economic resurgence. The fire burns both as the representation of restitution and reclamation and the fiery experience of its cause of collective economic trauma. Much like the ceremonial burn of the Indian Act upon the signing of a modern treaty, the fire is consuming old beliefs and archaic systems and bringing into focus the rise of Indigenous economic power. The story of now is the rise of Indigenous economic power.

Returning to the burning question of John Burrows: "How can we take account of the seventh generation if the Indian Act continues to remove this from us?" This is our time; this is the response. This is the summation of the calling into the open the consequences of our actions and inaction. Our inherent ability as Indigenous Peoples to take account for the seventh generation lives on through the construct of the sentence, "We are still here, and we are a powerful People."

In the process of moving away from Indian Act economics, this is the return to our inherent responsibility of care for place and care for each other, all activated in our sense of time as expressed in the responsibility to care for our future ancestors and the Earth. This is what we know and what we came to know as Indigenous Peoples. It is activated in our teachings, ceremonies, and ways of living and knowing of our responsibility to the seventh generation.

The combined processes of nation building, economic development, and self-determination upholds the activation of caring for and respecting the old ways that are centered at the intersection of the responsibility of our past and future, the next seven generations—that is, Indigenomics in action. This is a reflection of an Indigenous worldview shaped by thousands of years of success in our practice of being in alignment with the natural world and what it teaches us. This is the true foundation of the concept of Indigenous economic success.

Right now, every invested dollar, every partnership, every relationship with an Indigenous business, every new Indigenous business start-up, and every Indigenous entrepreneur all call into focus another possible future for Indigenous Peoples beyond the trauma of the effects of the Indian Act and the limitations of Indian Act economics and what has been prescribed for our existence as Indigenous Peoples. The rise of the Indigenous economy is poetic justice. It is time to live in a strengths-based economic future that Indigenous Peoples have been denied for so long. As we pick up the tool of business, we do it with the strength of our past and future generations.

In bringing the intention, function, and impacts of Indian Act economics into the light, we must hold the space and responsibility to move through the dark spaces that were created for us without us. By doing so, we give a silent nod to the space that was not and is not safe for us. We must hold the space for the survivors and for the healing of the inheritance of the effects. We hold space.

In the profound words of Jace Meyers, Métis entrepreneur and owner of COYA:

> We are not only the product of our circumstances; we are also the consequences of our actions. To be better ancestors, we have to remember that all of our actions matter. In the story of the mythological snake, eating its own tail, it shows us that we eventually pay for the consequences of our actions. Everything we do and don't do has intended and unintended multi-generational consequences. We must consider this when we doubt our impact on the world. Our impact is sacred. If we grow to evolve in a cosmic spiral, and life is not in a linear form, then there is no end to our potential, only the shedding of old skin and the rise of the next generation. What consequences of our actions will we celebrate?[179]

In the rise of Indigenomics and in the ongoing expression of Indigenous economic power, we face the collective impacts of Indian Act economics, and in doing so, we hold space for the next generation. The fire of economic justice is burning. Burn.

Reflective Questions

1. What are the collective impacts of the Indian Act today?
2. How is economic reconciliation connected to the deconstruction of Indian Act economics today?
3. What is the fuel burning in the fire of economic justice?
4. What are some formative actions that create space for Indigenous Peoples at the economic table of this country?
5. What does moving away from the Indian Act mean?
6. What is your response to Call to Action #92?

Appendix: An Indigenomics Exploration

T HE FOLLOWING SECTION offers a series of explorations that expand on thoughts, insights, and possibilities within the Indigenous economic relationship today. It is centered on the implementation of UNDRIP, human rights, positive reconciliation-focused leadership, and action to activate modern Indigenous economic design. These explorations are centered on the contrasting themes of the deconstruction of Indian Act economics and the rise of Indigenous economic power.

The following section centers powerful questions as an exploration into what is possible. In the words of Anthony Robbins, "Questions are the lasers of human consciousness and can be used to overcome any obstacle or challenge."[180]

These explorations use the custom IndigenomicsAI Indigenous economic intelligence platform as an inquiry engine to advance Indigenous research, data, investment, and legal analytics in Canada and beyond. This prototype has been used to help frame the generative outputs of specific queries to advance these specific explorations and insights.

Powerful questions can inspire, they can invite, and they can build community. Powerful questions can create pathways for positive experiences, invite reflection, and help people to focus on what is valuable. Powerful questions ask what is possible, not what is wrong. They help identify the shift that is being sought. The wrong questions are a destructive force. In the words of Indira Gandhi, "The power to question is the basis of all human progress."[181]

A powerful question generates curiosity and serves to "stimulate reflective insightful conversation, is thought-provoking, draws underlying assumptions out, invites creativity and new possibilities, generates energy and forward movement and new perspectives, channels attention and focuses inquiry, stays with participants, touches a deep meaning and evokes more questions."[182]

Powerful questions are those that:

Curiously explore intentions, values, convictions, hopes, ambitions, and possibilities. Questions that challenge our basic assumptions and create awareness of patterns and connections. Questions that give us new understandings of each other and the world around us and thereby expand our repertoire of possible action.[183]

The Art of Powerful Questions describes questions as generators for a different future. A powerful question is thought-provoking, and helps participants to collectively find deeper meaning. It expands possibilities and focuses attention. It can help to bring underlying assumptions into the light and can stimulate curiosity and innovation. A powerful question can help a group move forward toward a common goal. Questions carry a neutral, generative, or destructive energy. A powerful question offers a common pathway forward into shared understanding, curiosity, and exploration. While "What is wrong with you?" is deemed as a destructive question. "What are we becoming?" is a powerful question.

In the context of the rise of the Indigenous economy, every time Indigenous People win a pertinent legal case, it advances the Indigenous relationship and serves to establish unexplored space within the legal, governance, and economic realm and offers the shared space for answering the question "What are we becoming.?" The following explorations delve entirely into the realm of possibility by imagining the pathways toward Indigenous economic freedom and self-determination through the process of moving away from Indian Act economics.

Exploration 1. The Misalignment of the Indian Act with UNDRIP

The following exploration compares the 1985 version of the Indian Act with the United Nations Declaration on the Rights of Indigenous Peoples, highlights key areas of misalignment, and identifies suggestions on how to advance the Indian Act to comply with UNDRIP as currently mandated.

The 1985 revision of the Indian Act was an important beginning in addressing the more discriminatory aspects of the original Act. However, when compared to the United Nations Declaration on the Rights of Indigenous Peoples (UNDRIP), which upholds the rights of Indigenous Peoples to self-determination, cultural integrity, and land rights, significant misalignments are clearly identified. In response to the federal mandate of implementing UNDRIP in law, it is time to ask better questions. Advancing the Indigenous economy today requires asking the important questions such as: How can we design for Indigenous economic growth? What isn't working? Why isn't it working? How can we fix it? Where are the opportunities for increasing Indigenous economic activity? What is my leadership response?

The following context is essential to frame the necessity of this exploration:

1. The lack of implementation of the recommendations from the Royal Commission on Aboriginal Peoples since 1996.
2. The failure of the government to fully implement the Truth and Reconciliation Commission's Calls to Action to date.
3. Canada's endorsement of UNDRIP in 2010 and the current mandate for its implementation into law.

Since the release of the federal government's report on the consultation and engagement process regarding the implementation of UNDRIP, it has been several years since the implementation mandate was established, with no clear alignment approach in sight. In the context of Indian Act economics and the rise of Indigenous economic power, the experience of the cost of doing nothing is very real—the Indigenous economy is growing rapidly, and the Indigenous legal relationship is constantly evolving. While the federal government released an initial progress report on the implementation of the United Nations Declaration on the Rights of Indigenous Peoples Act, full alignment has not yet been met, nor is it close. It is in this context that this exploration is framed.[184]

Existing Misalignments of the Current Indian Act to UNDRIP

1. Self-Determination and Governance (UNDRIP Articles 3 and 4)
   Misalignment with UNDRIP: The Indian Act allows for limited self-governance but still places significant aspects of governance under the

control of the Canadian government, particularly in financial management and land use decisions.

Suggestion for Alignment with UNDRIP: Advance the Act to ensure full governance rights to Indigenous Nations to manage all internal affairs and local matters without federal interference, unless requested by the Nation itself.

2. Land Rights (UNDRIP Articles 26 and 27)

Misalignment with UNDRIP: The Indian Act controls the management and disposition of reserve lands. Indigenous communities do not have full autonomy over their lands and cannot freely use, develop, or control their resources.

Suggestion for Alignment with UNDRIP: Advance the Indian Act to recognize and affirm the inherent land rights of Indigenous Nations as perpetual and inalienable except by their free, prior, and informed consent. Establish mechanisms to return or compensate for historically taken lands.

3. Cultural Rights (UNDRIP Article 11)

Misalignment with UNDRIP: While not as restrictive as previous versions, the current Indian Act does not fully protect the right to maintain, protect, and develop the past, present, and future manifestations of their cultures, such as archaeological and historical sites, artifacts, designs, ceremonies, and the arts.

Suggestion for Alignment with UNDRIP: Introduce provisions that explicitly protect cultural practices, languages, and traditions and support the revitalization of Indigenous cultural practices and languages through education and cultural centers.

4. Free, Prior, and Informed Consent (UNDRIP Article 19)

Misalignment with UNDRIP: The Indian Act does not require free, prior, and informed consent in legislative or administrative decisions that affect Indigenous Peoples, often leading to conflicts over land development projects.

Suggestion for Alignment with UNDRIP: Legally mandate the requirement of free, prior, and informed consent in all dealings with Indigenous Lands and Nations, ensuring that all negotiations are conducted transparently and respectfully, honoring Indigenous governance structures.

5. Rights to Traditional Knowledge and Intellectual Property (UNDRIP Article 31)

   Misalignment with UNDRIP: The Act does not address the protection of Indigenous knowledge and intellectual property.

   Suggestion for Alignment with UNDRIP: Enact specific protections for Traditional Knowledge, genetic resources, and traditional cultural expressions against exploitation and unauthorized use.

To effectively implement the advancements of UNDRIP into law, the governments must engage in meaningful consultations with Indigenous Nations while upholding the right to self-determination and ensuring that any legal reforms are co-designed with Indigenous Nations. This can be facilitated through a joint legislative review process that includes Indigenous leaders, legal experts, and other stakeholders. These advancements must be part of a broader strategy to harmonize Canadian laws with UNDRIP. Implementing a monitoring and evaluation framework to assess the ongoing compliance of the Indian Act with UNDRIP principles will help to guide and ensure that the rights of Indigenous Peoples are progressively realized.

To ensure that the Indian Act complies with the United Nations Declaration on the Rights of Indigenous Peoples (UNDRIP), key provisions need to be revised or added. The following exploration provides examples of rewritten clauses that serve to align with the implementation of UNDRIP with a focus on self-determination, economic freedom, land rights, and the requirement for free, prior, and informed consent.

Proposed Clauses for the Alignment of the Indian Act to UNDRIP

Title: Recognition of Indigenous Rights and Self-Determination

1. Recognition of Indigenous Governance: Indigenous Nations in Canada are recognized as possessing the inherent right to self-determination. This right includes the freedom to govern themselves in matters related to their internal and local affairs and ways and means to finance their autonomous functions.

2. Land Rights and Territories: Indigenous Nations have the right to own, use, develop, and control the lands and waters and territories, Traditional

Knowledge, and other resources which they have traditionally owned, occupied, or otherwise used or acquired. Any use of these lands and resources by others must only occur with the free, prior, and informed consent of the Indigenous Peoples concerned.

3. Free, Prior, and Informed Consent: No legislative or administrative measures that may affect Indigenous Peoples shall be undertaken without obtaining their free, prior, and informed consent. This includes, but is not limited to, legislative or administrative measures related to resource extraction, land development, or significant cultural, social, or economic impacts.

4. Cultural Rights and Intellectual Property: Indigenous Nations have the right to maintain, control, protect, and develop their cultural heritage, Traditional Knowledge, and traditional cultural expressions. Additionally, they have the right to maintain, control, protect, and develop their intellectual property over such cultural heritage and Traditional Knowledge.

5. Economic Development: Indigenous Nations have the right to an economy. This means establishing support for economic initiatives that ensure fair access to economic opportunities, including training and resources necessary for sustainable development.

6. Environmental Stewardship and Protection: Recognize and support Indigenous roles of governance, decision-making, and revenue sharing in environmental stewardship and sustainable management of natural resources.

7. Implementation and Enforcement: The government shall establish a monitoring body that includes representation from Indigenous Nations to oversee the implementation of these rights and to address any disputes or grievances arising from noncompliance. This body will also be responsible for providing regular reports on progress and challenges in implementing these rights.

8. Dispute Resolution: In the case of disputes between Indigenous Nations and the government or third parties, an independent and impartial tribunal shall be established to resolve disputes according to the principles of justice and international human rights standards. Indigenous legal traditions shall be respected in the process of dispute resolution.

Additional Considerations

To fully integrate these alignments, the governments must undertake a comprehensive review of the Indian Act in partnership with Indigenous Nations to ensure all aspects of the Act respect and promote the specific rights outlined in UNDRIP. Legislative advancements must be complemented by policies that support governance capacity building within Indigenous Nations to govern effectively and exercise these rights fully.

These revisions represent a transformative approach that shifts away from the original Indian Act as a framework of control and assimilation to one of recognition, respect, and partnership with Indigenous Nations. This exploration serves to shape the meaning of the Indigenous relationship in Canada, placing emphasis on rights, respect, recognition, and cooperative development.

Exploration 2. What Are Ten Easy Steps to Bring the Indian Act into Compliance with UNDRIP?

Bringing the current version of the Indian Act into compliance with the United Nations Declaration on the Rights of Indigenous Peoples (UNDRIP) is a complex process that involves significant legal, political, and cultural advancements. The Declaration emphasizes the rights of Indigenous Nations to self-determination, autonomy, and control over their lands, resources, and traditional cultures. The following section identifies ten easy steps that can be taken to align the Indian Act with the principles and intent of UNDRIP:

1. Conduct Thorough Consultations and Engagement with Indigenous Nations
   Engage with Indigenous Nations, leadership, and key stakeholders to advance a meaningful consultation process to understand their needs, aspirations, and suggestions for legislative alignment.
2. Legislative Review and Amendment
   Review the Indian Act comprehensively to identify specific provisions that conflict with UNDRIP, particularly those affecting self-determination, autonomy, and economic participation.

3. Repeal Discriminatory Clauses
   Eliminate any remaining discriminatory clauses in the Indian Act, ensuring all Indigenous Peoples have equal rights and opportunities under the law.
4. Advance Self-Governance
   Amend or introduce provisions that enable Indigenous Nations to adopt governance structures that reflect their traditional practices and cultural values without needing approval from federal authorities.
5. Undertake Land Rights and Management Reform
   Reform land management provisions to ensure Indigenous Nations have greater control over their lands and resources, in accordance with UNDRIP's articles on land rights.
6. Advance Economic Development and Resource Sharing
   Facilitate frameworks for equitable access to economic opportunity, resource management, and revenue sharing that support Indigenous-led economic development initiatives and ensure the Nations benefit directly from resources on their territories.
7. Ensure Cultural Protections
   Enact protections for Indigenous languages, cultural practices, and heritage, ensuring these can flourish and be preserved for future generations.
8. Address the Effects of Gender Disparities of the Indian Act
   Specifically, address and rectify any gender-based disparities that arise from the Act's provisions, ensuring women and men have equal status and rights in all aspects of Indigenous law and life.
9. Education and Awareness
   Implement educational programs for both Indigenous and non-Indigenous Canadians about UNDRIP, the rights of Indigenous Peoples, and the historical and contemporary impacts of the Indian Act.
10. Establish Monitoring and Reporting Mechanisms for Accountability
    Create independent oversight bodies to monitor the implementation of advancements and compliance with UNDRIP, with regular reporting to Parliament and Indigenous Nations.

Implementation Considerations

These steps require careful planning, adequate funding, and sustained political will and leadership to build self-governance and economic self-determination. It is critical to ensure that the pace and nature of these advancements are agreed upon with the full participation of Indigenous leadership. Moreover, the process should be transparent and accountable to Indigenous Nations and the broader Canadian public. Aligning the Indian Act to be in accordance with UNDRIP involves legislative changes and a broader shift in the relationship between the Canadian government, regional governments, and Indigenous Nations that move toward true partnership and respect for Indigenous sovereignty, rights, and self-determination, as well as at the original treaties.

Exploration 3. House Motion: "We Have Pointed the Way"

Like Murray Sinclair's resounding words upon the presentation of the Truth and Reconciliation Calls to Action: "We have pointed the way; it is up to you to do the climbing." The intention of drafting a conceptual motion for the parliament is to actively engage in closing the proximity for action on the pathway forward.

This motion serves as a demonstration of the need to uphold the current mandate of UNDRIP implementation and the existing shortcomings of the Indian Act.

A. Draft Motion for the Immediate Alignment of the Indian Act with UNDRIP

In December 2019, the Minister of Justice and Attorney General of Canada, with the support of the Minister of Crown-Indigenous Relations, was mandated by the Prime Minister to introduce co-developed legislation to implement UNDRIP by the end of 2020. Drawing directly from the theme of Bill C-15 House motion with a clear target for implementation,

> Whereas the United Nations Declaration on the Rights of Indigenous Peoples provides a framework for reconciliation, healing and peace, as well as harmonious and cooperative relations based on the principles of justice, democracy, respect for human rights, non-discrimination and good faith; Whereas the rights and principles affirmed in the

Declaration constitute the minimum standards for the survival, dignity and well-being of Indigenous peoples of the world, and must be implemented in Canada.[185]

This Bill draws from the earlier 2017 private motion by Romeo Saganash, who in the House speech, refers to addressing the wrongs described:

> We are only now beginning to discuss the fundamental rights of Indigenous peoples as human rights. That does not happen a lot, very rarely as a matter of fact, so it is important that we remind ourselves that the Indigenous Peoples' fundamental rights in this country are indeed human rights. Bill C-262 would also allow us to begin to redress the past wrongs, the past injustices that were inflicted on Indigenous people. This is the main objective of Bill C-262, to recognize that on one hand they are human rights but on the other hand that we begin to redress the past injustices that were inflicted on the first peoples of this country.[186]

On June 21, 2021, the United Nations Declaration on the Rights of Indigenous Peoples Act received Royal Assent and came into force. The following concept House motion builds on that directly in regard to the advancement of the specific alignments of the Indian Act to this mandate.

Title: Motion for the Immediate Amendment to the Indian Act to Be in Compliance with the United Nations Declaration on the Rights of Indigenous Peoples

Motion Text:

Whereas the United Nations Declaration on the Rights of Indigenous Peoples (UNDRIP) establishes the minimum standards for the survival, dignity, and well-being of Indigenous Peoples worldwide;

And whereas Canada is a signatory to UNDRIP, committing to implement these standards within Canadian law;

And whereas the current Indian Act does not yet fully comply with the principles of self-determination; land rights; cultural integrity; and free, prior, and informed consent as outlined in UNDRIP as set out in Bill C-15;

Therefore, be it resolved that this House directs the Government of Canada to:

1. Initiate comprehensive harmonization of the Indian Act that:
   - Ensures full powers of self-governance to Indigenous governments, removing the Act's oversight requirements that limit decision-making on internal and local matters.
   - Recognizes and affirms the rights of Indigenous Nations to own, use, develop, and control their lands and resources, while requiring free, prior, and informed consent for any use or development of these lands by others.
   - Protect and promote Indigenous cultural rights, including the right to maintain, control, protect, and develop their languages, traditions, and cultural expressions.
   - Ensure that all legislative or administrative actions affecting Indigenous Nations are undertaken only with their free, prior, and informed consent.
2. Establish a timeline of two years for the completion of these amendments, with interim reports to be submitted to this House every six months detailing progress made.
3. Create a joint committee consisting of Members of Parliament, Senators, and Indigenous leaders to oversee the amendment process, ensuring that all changes align with UNDRIP and respect the sovereignty and traditions of Indigenous Peoples.

This motion, as passed, would be a significant step toward reconciling Canadian law with international commitments, ensuring that Indigenous rights are fully respected and upheld in accordance with global human rights standards with a clear timeline for implementation.

Exploration 4. Human Rights and Genocide

Since its enactment in 1876, the Indian Act has been globally critiqued for its paternalistic and colonial nature, and despite numerous amendments, it continues to raise significant human rights concerns. The intention of this exploration is to focus on the areas the Indian Act may conflict with the

Universal Declaration of Human Rights (UDHR) as internationally recognized human rights standards:

1. Right to Equality and Non-Discrimination (Articles 1 and 2 of the Universal Declaration of Human Rights): The Indian Act has provisions that differentiate between individuals based on their status as "status Indians," "non-status Indians," and non-Indigenous Canadians. This distinction has led to differential treatment and access to services, potentially contravening the rights to equality and non-discrimination. Historically, the Act contained explicitly discriminatory provisions against Indigenous women, particularly concerning the loss of status through marriage, which have been amended but still result in disparities.

2. Right to Participation in Government (Article 21 of the UDHR): The Indian Act imposes specific regulations on the governance of First Nations communities, including the electoral systems on reserves. These provisions can be seen as limiting the self-determination and autonomy of Indigenous Peoples in managing their affairs. Although amendments have been made to allow communities to create their governance structures, the default rules still reflect a degree of control inconsistent with the self-determination principles in international human rights law.

3. Right to Freedom from Arbitrary Interference (Article 12 of the UDHR): The Act gives the federal government sigznificant powers over land management on reserves and, in some cases, the lives of Indigenous Peoples, which could be seen as arbitrary interference with personal and communal life. This includes restrictions on the sale and possession of property on reserves that do not apply to other Canadians.

4. Cultural Rights (Article 27 of the UDHR): The Indian Act has historically had a role in the suppression of Indigenous cultures and languages through various policies. While current versions of the Act have moved away from these explicitly assimilationist policies, the legacy of cultural disruption and the ongoing control over aspects of cultural expression can still conflict with the right to freely participate in cultural life.

5. Right to an Adequate Standard of Living (Article 25 of the UDHR): Conditions on many reserves, which are influenced by the provisions of the Indian Act relating to land use and resources, contribute to challenges

in accessing adequate housing, clean water, and sanitation. These issues can be seen as inconsistent with the right to an adequate standard of living.

While recent amendments have aimed to address some of these issues, the structure and history of the Indian Act reflect ongoing challenges in fully aligning with the principles of the UDHR. Each of these points would require a detailed legal and sociocultural analysis to fully understand the scope of noncompliance and its impact on Indigenous communities. Such an analysis would also need to consider the perspectives of Indigenous Peoples themselves, who are directly affected by the Act's provisions.

In the 1876 version of the Indian Act, which clauses would lead to genocide as defined by the UN and the UN Convention on the Prevention and Punishment of the Crime of Genocide?

Based on the United Nations definition of genocide, certain clauses of the Indian Act of 1876 could be argued to facilitate acts that could align with genocide under contemporary international law definitions, particularly if these were executed with intent to destroy, in whole or in part, a national, ethnical, racial, or religious group. Key aspects of the 1876 Indian Act that could potentially be related to genocide include:

1. Restricting the movements and rights of Indigenous women: The Act states that any Indian woman marrying a non-Indian man would cease to be considered an Indian "in any respect within the meaning of this act" except for receiving annuities. This could be interpreted as imposing measures intended to prevent births within the group, which is a criterion under the UN definition of genocide.
2. Forcible transfer of children: Although not explicitly covered in the 1876 version, later versions of the Indian Act facilitated the removal of Indigenous children from their families to residential schools, which could be considered as "forcibly transferring children of the group to another group." However, this specific aspect was more explicitly enacted in amendments beyond 1876.
3. Severe restrictions on rights and freedoms: The Act imposed severe limitations on the rights and freedoms of Indigenous Peoples, including

restricting their movements, controlling their economic activities, and enforcing cultural assimilation through various policies. Depending on the execution and impacts of these policies, this could align with "deliberately inflicting on the group conditions of life calculated to bring about its physical destruction in whole or in part."

While the 1876 Indian Act itself does not explicitly call for physical or biological destruction, its provisions laid the groundwork for policies that could lead to significant harm to the culture, rights, and lives of Indigenous Peoples in Canada. The intent behind these provisions, whether they constitute an intent to destroy a group in part or in whole, is crucial for classifying actions as genocidal under international law.

Exploration 5. Terms of Engagement to Uphold UNDRIP

A common misperception of UNDRIP is that Indigenous Peoples have special rights. Another misconception is that it "gives" Indigenous Peoples rights. No, it does not give Indigenous Peoples rights; Indigenous Peoples have always had these rights, only there was a growing urgent need to recognize and uphold these rights in the absence of them being activated. Another misconception is that UNDRIP is only for Indigenous Peoples, so why should I be concerned with it? The following exploration provides the foundation of a response to UNDRIP into building a leadership response for the foundation of Indigenous economic belonging, recognition, and reconciliation.

A. Individual Citizen Leadership Terms of Engagement

As a settler and a citizen with agency and ethics, I understand the importance of adhering to the principles outlined in the United Nations Declaration on the Rights of Indigenous Peoples (UNDRIP). The Declaration is crucial for protecting and promoting the rights and dignity of Indigenous Peoples nationally and worldwide. Here is how I, as a settler and citizen, uphold, activate, and respect the key terms of my engagement with the activation of UNDRIP:

1. Self-Determination and Autonomy
    I recognize that Indigenous Peoples have the right to self-determin-
    ation. I acknowledge that Indigenous Peoples must freely determine their

political status and pursue their economic, social, and cultural development. I support Indigenous Peoples' right to self-determination and self-government.

2. Free, Prior, and Informed Consent (FPIC)

I understand that Indigenous Peoples should not be forcibly removed from their lands or territories. Any relocation must only occur through free, prior, and informed consent by Indigenous Peoples. I understand that all levels of government and other entities need to consult and cooperate in good faith with Indigenous Peoples to obtain consent before adopting any measures or policies that may affect them.

3. Cultural Rights and Identity

I respect Indigenous Peoples' right to practice and revitalize their culture, traditions, and customs. This includes the right to maintain, protect, and develop their own histories, languages, education, oral traditions, philosophies, and literatures. I believe in supporting efforts to preserve and celebrate Indigenous cultures and languages.

4. Rights to Lands, Territories, and Resources

I acknowledge and actively uphold the importance of Indigenous Peoples to maintain and strengthen their spiritual relationship and connection with their traditionally owned lands, territories, and waters. I actively support Indigenous Peoples' right to own, use, and control these lands and resources and advocate for their legal recognition, economic development, stewardship, and protection.

5. Participation and Decision-Making

I believe Indigenous Peoples should actively participate in decision-making processes that affect their rights. Indigenous Peoples must be able to choose their governance representatives according to their procedures and maintain their decision-making institutions. Indigenous Peoples must also be able to determine their strategic development priorities particularly in relation to education, economy, health, housing, and social programs.

6. Equality and Non-Discrimination

I recognize that Indigenous Peoples are free and equal to all other peoples and individuals. Indigenous Peoples should be free from discrimination based on their Indigenous descent and identity. Indigenous Peoples, cultures, traditions, histories, and aspirations should be appropriately reflected in education, health, and justice systems and public and historical information.

7. Protection Against Violence and Discrimination

I understand the need to pay special attention to the rights and needs of Indigenous elders, women, youth, children, and persons with disabilities. Government should take measures, in conjunction with Indigenous Peoples, to ensure that Indigenous women and children are fully protected against all forms of violence and discrimination.

8. Implementation and Redress

I support Indigenous Peoples' right to access just and fair procedures for resolving conflicts and disputes with governments or other parties. Indigenous Peoples are entitled to effective remedies for all infringements of their individual and collective rights. These decisions should respect Indigenous Peoples' customs, traditions, rules, protocols, and legal systems.

By upholding these principles of UNDRIP, I respect and actively support and uphold the rights of Indigenous Peoples by recognizing their distinct cultural identities, dignity, economic sovereignty, and right to self-determination.

B. Terms of Engagement for the Financial Sector and Financial Institutions in Upholding UNDRIP

The financial sector's engagement with the United Nations Declaration on the Rights of Indigenous Peoples (UNDRIP) involves specifically integrating the Declaration's principles into governance practices, investment decisions, corporate policies, and financial practices across the sector. Here is a conceptual Terms of Engagement for the Financial Sector:

1. Respect for Indigenous Rights

Policy Commitment: Financial institutions (such as banks and investment firms) must develop and adopt specific policies that recognize Indigenous Peoples' rights under UNDRIP. These policies should be publicly available and embedded in the institution's core values and action plans.

Due Diligence: Financial institutions must implement a due diligence process that includes detailed assessments of how financial activities could impact Indigenous Peoples' rights. This should involve consultations with Indigenous nations, businesses, and experts.

2. Free, Prior, and Informed Consent (FPIC)

   FPIC Process: Before financing projects affecting Indigenous lands or resources, institutions must work to ensure FPIC is achieved. This involves providing all relevant information to Indigenous Nations, allowing adequate time for decision-making, and obtaining their voluntary agreement.

   Engagement: Establish a framework for ongoing engagement with Indigenous Peoples, ensuring communication is clear, transparent, and culturally appropriate.

3. Cultural and Environmental Considerations

   Environmental and Social Risk Management: The financial sector must serve to incorporate Indigenous cultural and environmental values into the risk management process. This includes respecting sacred sites, gender safety, and upholding traditional practices and protocols.

   Sustainable Practices: The financial sector must prioritize investments in sustainable projects that promote environmental stewardship and respect for Indigenous cultural heritage.

4. Participation and Decision-making

   Inclusive Governance: Include Indigenous representatives in governance structures for projects impacting their communities, such as corporate boards, advisory boards, steering committees, or sectoral representation.

   Capacity Building: Provide funding and resources for training programs that empower Indigenous communities to participate effectively in financial decision-making.

   - Equitable Benefits and Partnerships

     Benefit Sharing: Ensure that financial agreements include provisions for equitable benefit sharing with Indigenous Nations and businesses. This might involve developing profit-sharing, community development funds, or other financial arrangements.

     Partnership Models: Develop joint venture models in which Indigenous Nations and businesses hold equity stakes and have a meaningful role in project management and ownership.

- Transparency and Accountability
Reporting and Disclosure: Regularly publish detailed Indigenous economic and sectoral reports on how financial activities align with UNDRIP principles. These reports should include specific cases and outcomes.
Accountability Mechanisms: Create robust reporting mechanisms to report progress, outcomes, insights, and next steps regarding value creation and risk management processes within the Indigenous economy.
Transparency Mechanisms: Create robust grievance mechanisms that allow Indigenous Nations and businesses to report violations of their rights. These mechanisms should be accessible, fair, and transparent.
- Non-Discrimination and Equality
Inclusive Policies: Develop and enforce policies that prohibit discrimination against Indigenous Peoples in hiring, lending, and investment practices as a sectoral framework.
Supportive Frameworks: Advocate for regulatory changes that enhance the protection of Indigenous rights within the financial sector. This could involve working with governments and international bodies. Create regular and transpartent reports of these outcomes.
- Implementation and Monitoring
Continuous Improvement: Set up a regular review process to evaluate and improve compliance with UNDRIP principles. This could include annual audits and policy updates based on feedback from Indigenous Nations and businesses.
Independent Monitoring: Engage independent auditors or third-party organizations to monitor and verify adherence to UNDRIP principles. Their findings should be made public.
By following these terms of engagement for the implementation of UNDRIP, financial institutions can ensure they respect and promote the rights of Indigenous Peoples, contributing to their sustainable development and well-being across the full spectrum of the financial sector.

Endnotes

Introduction

1 David Williams, "Canada's Post-pandemic Economic Recovery Was the 5th Weakest in the OECD," *Business Council of British Columbia,* 2023, https://www.bcbc.com/insight/canadas-post-pandemic-economic-recovery-was-the-5th-weakest-in-the-oecd

2 Ibid.

3 Alessia Passafiume, "'Diminished' Hope: Yellowhead Institute to End Reports on TRC Calls to Action," *The Canadian Press,* December 20, 2023. https://vancouversun.com/news/national/yellowhead-institute-end-reports-on-trc

4 Ka'nhehsí:io Deer, "Pope Says Genocide Took Place at Canada's Residential Schools," *CBC,* July 30, 2022, https://www.cbc.ca/news/indigenous/pope-francis-residential-schools-genocide-1.6537203#:~:text=In%20his%20multiple%20speeches%20over,%2C%20a%20so%2Dcalled%20race.

5 Gilad Hirschberger, "Collective Trauma and the Social Construction of Meaning," *Frontiers in Psychology* 10, no. 9 (2018): 1441. https://www.ncbi.nlm.nih.gov/pmc/articles/PMC6095989/

6 "Wikipedia: Historical Trauma," last modified November 10, 2024, https://en.wikipedia.org/wiki/Historical_trauma#:~:text=Collective%20trauma%20suggests%20that%20the,to%20make%20sense%20of%20it.

7 Ibid.

Chapter 1

8 N. J. Grove and A. B. Zwi, "Our Health and Theirs: Forced Migration, Othering, and Public Health," *Social Science & Medicine* 62, no. 8 (2006):1931–1942. doi: 10.1016/j.socscimed.2005.08.061.]

9 E. A. Viruell-Fuentes, "Beyond Acculturation: Immigration, Discrimination, and Health Research Among Mexicans in the United States," *Social Sciences & Medicine* 65, no. 7 (2007): 1524–1535.

10   Martin Sandbu, *The Economics of Belonging: A Radical Plan to
     Win Back the Left Behind and Achieve Prosperity for All* (Princeton
     University Press, 2020).

11   John Milloy, "Indian Act Colonialism: A Century of Dishonour,
     1869–1969," *Centre for First Nations Governance,* May 2008, https://
     fngovernance.org/wp-content/uploads/2020/09/
     milloy.pdf.

12   Ibid.

13   Ibid.

14   Ibid.

15   Ibid.

16   Indigenousfoundations.arts.ubc.ca, "John A. Macdonald, 1887,"
     Accessed September 2024, https://indigenousfoundations.arts.ubc.
     ca/the_indian_act/.

Chapter 2

17   John Burrows, "Seven Generations, Seven Teachings: Ending the
     Indian Act," *Centre for First Nations Governance,* May 2008, https://
     fngovernance.org/wp-content/uploads/2020/05/john_
     borrows.pdf.

18   David Williams, "Outlook 2023: Canada's Economy Enters 2023 with
     Serious Structural Weaknesses," *Business in Vancouver,* January 16,
     2023, https://www.biv.com/news/commentary/outlook-2023-
     canadas-economy-enters-2023-serious-structural-weaknesses-8270
     163.

19   David Williams and Jock Finlayson, "Opinion: Canadians Face 40 Years
     of Stagnant Incomes—Government's Economic Strategy Is Failing,"
     The Globe and Mail, September 12, 2023, https://www.theglobeand
     mail.com/business/commentary/article-canada-economic-growth-
     strategy/.

20   John Giokas,"The Indian Act Evolution, Overview and Options
     for Amendment and Transition," *Publications du gouvernement du
     Canada,* March 22, 1995, https://publications.gc.ca/collections/
     collection_2016/bcp-pco/Z1-1991-1-41-130-eng.pdf.

21   Carlo Cafiero and Renos Vakis, "Risk and Vulnerability Considerations
     in Poverty Analysis: Recent Advances and Future Directions," *World
     Bank,* 2006, https://documents1.worldbank.org/curated/zh/4143
     61468142164415/pdf/377190Risk0vul1ity0SP0061001PUBLIC1.pdf

22 Kyle Darbyson, "At the End of Their Lease," *Golf Business: Official Publication of the National Gold Course Owners Association,* May 2017, http://www.golfbusiness.com/article.aspx?id=3720&bq=6yfv%5Eg 433$.

23 Ibid.

24 Ibid.

25 Joan Taillon, "Supreme Court Slashes Rent on Musqueam Land," *Windspeaker* 8, no. 18 (2000), https://ammsa.com/publications/ windspeaker/supreme-court-slashes-rent-musqueam-land-0.

26 Ashifa Kassam, "First Nations." Seek to Raise Canada's Rent After 150 Years of $4 Payments," *The Guardian,* October 15, 2017, https://www. theguardian.com/world/2017/oct/15/canada-first-nations-treaty- annuity-lawsuit.

27 James Hopkin, "Done Deal: $10-billion Robinson Huron Treaty Settlement Finalized," *SooToday.com,* January 23, 2024, https://www. sootoday.com/local-news/done-deal-10-billion-robinson-huron- treaty-settlement-finalized-8151056.

28 Kassam, "First Nations."

29 Jeremy Simes, "Sask. Chief Files Class-action Lawsuit Over $5 Annuity Payments Signed 150 Years Ago," *CBC,* February 11, 2024, https://www.cbc.ca/news/canada/saskatchewan/class-action- lawsuit-annuity-payments-1.7111985.

30 Brody Langager, "14 First Nations Receive $37 Million After Federal Minister Settles Treaty Salaries Claims, *Global News,* August 1, 2023, https://globalnews.ca/news/9869715/first-nations-federal-minister- treaty-salaries-claims/.

31 Ibid.

32 Maxime Faille as quoted in Aidan Macnab, "Manitoba First Nations' Class Action Seeks Treaty Annuity Payments," April 22, 2024, https:// www.canadianlawyermag.com/news/general/manitoba-first-nations- class-action-seeks-treaty-annuity-payments/385652.

33 Macnab, "Manitoba First Nations.'"

34 Ibid.

35 First Nations Financial Management Board. *The RoadMap Project,* 2023. https://fnfmb.com/sites/default/files/2022-11/2022-11-09_ roadmap_chapter_4_unlocking_first_nations_economies.pdf.

36 Ibid.

Chapter 3

37   John Burrows, *Seven Generations, Seven Teachings: Ending the Indian Act*, Centre for First Nations Governance, May 2008, https://fngovernance.org/wp-content/uploads/2020/05/john_borrows.pdf.

38   Peter Koslowski, *Contemporary Economic Ethics and Business Ethics* (New York: Springer, 2020).

39   Manuel Velasquez, Claire Andre, Thomas Shanks, S.J., and Michael J. Meyer, "What Is Ethics?: Markkula Center for Applied Ethics," *Santa Clara University*, 2010, https://www.scu.edu/ethics/ethics-resources/ethical-decision-making/what-is-ethics/#:~:text=Ethics%20is%20based%20on%20well,does%20ethics%20mean%20to%20you%3F%22.

40   Ibid.

41   Markkula Center for Applied Ethics, "A Framework for Ethical Decision Making—Markkula Center for Applied Ethics," *Santa Clara University*, November 5, 2021, https://www.scu.edu/ethics/ethics-resources/a-framework-for-ethical-decision-making/.

42   T. L. Beauchamp and J. F. Childress, *Principles of Biomedical Ethics* (Oxford University Press, 2013), https://www.allisonkrilethornton.com/wp-content/uploads/Medical_Ethics_Readings/BandC-Moral-Dilemmas.pdf

43   "The Indian Act, " Indigenousfoundations.arts.ubc.ca, n.d.

44   Martin Sandbu, *The Economics of Belonging: A Radical Plan to Win Back the Left Behind and Achieve Prosperity for All* (Princeton University Press, 2020): 70.

Chapter 4

45   Canadian Council for Public-Private Partnerships, *P3's: Bridging the First Nations Infrastructure Gap* (Toronto, 2016).

46   Kelly J. Lendsay and Wanda Wuttunee, *The Cost of Doing Nothing*, Royal Bank of Canada, October 23, 1997, https://www.rbc.com/indigenous/_assets-custom/pdfs/The-Cost-of-Doing-Nothing.pdf.

47   Ibid.

48   Assembly of First Nations, "Royal Commission on Aboriginal People at 10 Years: A Report Card," n.d., https://www.cbc.ca/news2/background//pdf/aboriginalsafn_rcap.pdf.

49   Brett Forester, "Federal Liabilities 'Likely' Owed to Indigenous People Grow to $76B Under Trudeau," *CBC*, December 14, 2023, https://

www.cbc.ca/news/indigenous/canada-liabilities-indigenous-legal-claims-1.7058139.

50 Department of Finance, *2023 Fall Economic Statement*, 2023, https://www.budget.canada.ca/fes-eea/2023/report-rapport/FES-EEA-2023-en.pdf.

51 Forester, "Federal Liabilities."

52 Government of Canada, "Chapter 7: Moving Forward Together on Reconciliation | Budget 2022," *Canada.ca*, April 7, 2022, https://www.budget.canada.ca/2022/report-rapport/chap7-en.html.

53 Government of Canada, "Chapter 4: Advancing Reconciliation and Building a Canada That Works for Everyone," December 14, 2023, https://www.budget.canada.ca/2023/report-rapport/chap4-en.html.

54 *CTV News*, "AFN Says Billions Needed to Close Infrastructure Gap," *CTV News*, April 9, 2024, https://www.ctvnews.ca/politics/assembly-of-first-nations-says-349b-is-needed-to-close-infrastructure-gap-by-2030-1.6839930.

Chapter 5

55 Cheryl Crazy Bull, *Changing the Narrative About Native Americans*, https://rnt.firstnations.org/wp-content/uploads/2018/06/Message Guide-Allies-screen.pdf.

56 Derrick Penner, "MST Development Corp. Is About First Nations Becoming 'Powerful in Our Territories Once Again,'" *Vancouver Sun*, February 4, 2020, https://vancouversun.com/news/mst-development-corp-is-about-first-nations-becoming-powerful-in-our-territories-once-again.

57 Nelson Bennett, "Why MST Development Are Elite Vancouver Developers." *Western Investor*, May 27, 2022, https://www.western investor.com/british-columbia/first-nations-are-now-elite-vancouver-residential-developers-5416666.

58 Ben Miljure, "B.C. Development: Squamish Nation Embarks on Ambitious Plan," *CTV News Vancouver*, March 29, 2023, https://bc.ctvnews.ca/squamish-nation-embarks-on-ambitious-plan-to-become-one-of-largest-developers-in-canada-1.6334812.

59 Angela Sterritt, "The Little-known History of Squamish Nation Land in Vancouver," *CBC*, April 21, 2019, https://www.cbc.ca/news/canada/british-columbia/little-known-history-of-squamish-nation-land-in-vancouver-1.5104584.

60   Bennett, "Why MST Development."

61   Taza, N.D, https://togetherattaza.com/.

62   Bill Kaufmann, "Tsuut'ina Nation Announces Multi-billion Dollar Development Plans Along Ring Road," *Calgary Herald,* July 11, 2016, https://calgaryherald.com/business/commercial-real-estate/tsuutina-nation-announces-multi-billion-dollar-development-plans-along-ring-road.

63   Amanda Whalen, "Tech Update: Oneida Energy Storage Project Shows 'True Commitment to Partnerships with Indigenous Business' and Other Venture News," *Toronto Star*, September 30, https://www.thestar.com/business/mars/tech-update-oneida-energy-storage-project-shows-true-commitment-to-partnerships-with-indigenous-business-and/article_e2721a23-aec3-5c7e-a8c8-d976187fc90a.html.

Chapter 6

64   American Psychiatric Association, *Diagnostic and Statistical Manual of Mental Disorders* (5th ed.) (Washington, DC: American Psychiatric Publishing, 2013): 669–670.

65   Natasha Burton, "How Can You Spot a Real Narcissist? 4 Traits to Look For," *DailyOM*, June 5, 2023, https://www.dailyom.com/journal/how-can-you-spot-a-real-narcissist-traits-to-look-for/?aff=910&ad=1&utm_source=google&utm_medium=ppc&utm_campaign=Performance Max&acct=9358138875&campaign_id=16896613381&gad_source=1&gclid=EAIaIQobChMIg5Pgvc OghgMVfi6tBh3-_QqREAMYASAAEgIGT_D_BwE.

66   American Psychiatric Association, *Diagnostic and Statistical Manual,* 659–662.

67   Ibid., 235–237.

68   Government of Canada, "Indian Act," 2024, https://laws-lois.justice.gc.ca/eng/acts/I-5/section-20.html.

69   John Leslie, *Commissions of Inquiry into Indian Affairs in the Canadas, 1828–1858: Evolving a Corporate Memory for the Indian Department* (Ottawa: Treaties and Historical Research Centre, DIAND,1985).

70   Wsanec Leadership Council, "The Creation of Indian Reserves and Their Impact on the Wsanec Nation," N.D., https://wsanec.com/the-creation-of-indian-reserves-and-their-impact-on-the-wsanec-nation/.

71   James Daschuk, *Clearing the Plains: Disease, Politics of Starvation, and the Loss of Indigenous Life* (University of Regina Press, 2019).

72 Wsanec Leadership Council, "The Creation of Indian Reserves."

73 T. J. Morgan, (1889-1893). "Statement on Indigenous Assimilation Policies," U.S. Office of Indian Affairs.

74 Alberta Teachers' Association, "Forced Relocation of Indigenous Peoples in Canda," 2020, https://legacy.teachers.ab.ca/SiteCollection Documents/ATA/For%20Members/ProfessionalDevelopment/ Walking%20Together/PD-WT-16e%205%20Forced%20Relocation %20of%20Indigenous%20Peoples%20in%20Canada.pdf.

75 Wsanec Leadership Council, "The Creation of Indian Reserves."

76 Edgar Dosman, *Indians: The Urban Dilemma* (McClelland and Stewart, 1972).

77 Daschuk, *Clearing the Plains.*

78 Facing History & Ourselves, Canada, "Dispossession, Destruction, and the Reserve," 2020, https://www.facinghistory.org/en-ca/ resource-library/dispossession-destruction-reserves.

79 Tristin Hopper, "Here Is What Sir John A. Macdonald Did to Indigenous Peoples," *National Post,* August 28, 2018, https://national post.com/news/canada/here-is-what-sir-john-a-macdonald-did-to-indigenous-people

80 Government of Canada, "Indian Act," 2024, https://laws-lois.justice. gc.ca/eng/acts/I-5/section-20.html.

81 Daschuk, *Clearing the Plains.*

82 Queen's University, "Sir John A. MacDonald Fact Sheet," N.D., https://educ.queensu.ca/sites/educwww/files/uploaded_files/JAM %20Fact%20Sheet.pdf.

83 Government of Canada, "Constitution Act 1867," 2024, https://laws-lois.justice.gc.ca/eng/const/page-1.html.

84 Library of Parliament, "Bill C-15: An Act Respecting the United Nations Declaration on the Rights of Indigenous Peoples," May 18, 2021, https://lop.parl.ca/staticfiles/PublicWebsite/Home/Research Publications/LegislativeSummaries/PDF/43-2/43-2-c15-e.pdf.

85 *BBC,* "The Wet'suwet'en Conflict Disrupting Canada's Rail System," *BBC,* February 20, 2020, https://www.bbc.com/news/world-us-canada-51550821.

86 Mia Urquhart, "Mi'kmaw First Nations Expand Aboriginal Title Claim to Include Almost All of N.B.," *CBC,* February 15, 2023, https://www.cbc.ca/news/canada/new-brunswick/

mi-kmaq-aboriginal-title-land-claim-1.6749561#:~:text=In%20
2016%2C%20Elsipogtog%20First%20Nation,of%20the%20
province's%20natural%20resources.

87   Ibid.

88   Government of British Columbia, "First Nations Reach Settlement
     with B.C. Federal Governments on Treaty Land Entitlement Claims,"
     April 15, 2023, https://news.gov.bc.ca/releases/2023IRR0019-
     000539.

89   Darryl Greer, "B.C. Signs Agreement Handing Over Title to Haida
     Gwaii," *Vancouver Sun,* April 14, 2024, https://vancouversun.com/
     news/local-news/decades-in-the-making-b-c-signs-agreement-
     handing-over-title-to-haida-gwaii.

Chapter 7

90   John Burrows, *Seven Generations, Seven Teachings: Ending the Indian
     Act,* Centre for First Nations Governance, May 2008, https://
     fngovernance.org/wp-content/uploads/2020/05/john_borrows.pdf.

91   David McKay, "It's Time for Indigenous Peoples to Be at the Centre
     of Canada's Economy," *Business Council of Canada,* 2020, https://
     thebusinesscouncil.ca/publication/its-time-for-indigenous-peoples-
     to-be-at-the-centre-of-canadas-economy/.

92   "Documentary Short Declares Plastic Recycling 'Like a Band-Aid on
     Gangrene,'" *The Energy Mix,* N.D. with July 9, 2019, https://www.
     theenergymix.com/documentary-short-declares-plastic-recycling-
     like-a-band-aid-on-gangrene/.

93   Andreas Kruszakin-Liboska, "Why Challenging the Status Quo Is
     More Important Than Ever," *Medium,* February 6, 2024,
     https://medium.com/design-bootcamp/why-challenging-the-status-
     quo-is-more-important-than-ever-74ca55940459.

94   "Chief Clarence Louie: The Key to the Future Is Building a Strong
     Economy," *Alberta Native News,* August 19, 2014, https://www.
     albertanativenews.com/chief-clarence-louie-the-key-to-the-future-is-
     building-a-strong-economy/.

95   First Nations Financial Management Board, *The RoadMap Project,*
     https://fnfmb.com/sites/default/files/2022-09/roadmap_project_
     chapter_4_unlocking_economies_final_v2.pdf

96   Wendy Stueck, "Canada Infrastructure Bank Unveils Details for
     $1-billion Indigenous Equity Loan Program," *The Globe and Mail,*

November 28, 2023, https://www.theglobeandmail.com/business/article-canada-infrastructure-bank-unveils-details-for-1-billion-indigenous/.

97   Andrew Willis, "Indigenous-run Longhouse Capital Targets $1-billion Fund," *The Globe and Mail,* October 2, 2023. https://www.theglobeandmail.com/business/article-indigenous-private-equity-longhouse-capital/.

98   Assembly of First Nations, *Closing the Infrastructure Gap by 2030: A Collaborative and Comprehensive Cost Estimate Identifying the Infrastructure Investment Needs of First Nations in Canada,* 2024, https://afn.ca/economy-infrastructure/infrastructure/closing-the-infrastructure-gap/.

99   James Dunne, "What Could a $5B Government Loan Program Do? Turn Indigenous Communities into Powerful Investors," *CBC,* April 25, 2024, https://www.cbc.ca/news/business/federal-indigenous-loan-guarantee-program-1.7182528.

100 Maureen McMcall, "The Far-reaching Impact of the Alberta Indigenous Opportunities Corporation," BOE Report, February 15, 2024, https://boereport.com/2024/02/15/the-far-reaching-impact-of-the-alberta-indigenous-opportunities-corporation/.

101 City of Calgary, "New Study Benchmarks Indigenous Economic Contributions and Informs Action Toward Economic Reconciliation in Calgary and Treaty 7 Regions," December 12, 2023, https://newsroom.calgary.ca/new-study-benchmarks-indigenous-economic-contributions-and-informs-action-toward-economic-reconciliation-in-calgary-and-treaty-7-region/#:~:text=Jointly%20commissioned%20by%20Calgary%20Economic,cent%20of%20Calgary's%20total%20GDP.

102 BC Assembly of First Nations, *Economic Participation and Contributions of First Nations in BC,* N.D., https://www.bcafn.ca/sites/default/files/docs/reports-presentations/BCAFN%20Economic%20Participation%20Report.pdf.

103 Carol Anne Hilton, *Indigenomics: Taking a Seat at the Economic Table* (New Society Publishers, 2021).

104 First Nations Financial Management Board, "Chapter One: Creating Paths for Indigenous Prosperity," 2022, https://fnfmb.com/sites/default/files/2022-05/roadmap_project_chapter1_intro_final.pdf.

105 Fraser Institute, "B.C. Plans to 'Reconcile' by Giving First Nations Veto on Land Use," February 1, 2024, https://www.fraserinstitute. org/article/bc-plans-to-reconcile-by-giving-first-nations-veto-on-land-use.

106 Ibid.

107 Ibid.

Chapter 8

108 Canadian Poverty Institute, N.D., "Poverty in Canada," https://www. povertyinstitute.ca/poverty-canada.

109 "How to Transfer Your Land to Indigenous Peoples," *TVO Today*, June 28, 2018, https://www.tvo.org/article/how-to-transfer-your-land-to-indigenous-peoples.

110 *CBC*, "B.C. Transfers 312 Hectares of Land on Vancouver Island to Lyackson First Nation and Cowichan Tribes," May 12, 2024, https://www.cbc.ca/news/canada/british-columbia/bc-land-transfer-first-nations-1.7202221.

111 Nanaimo News Bulletin, "City of Nanaimo Transferring 81 Hectares of Mount Benson Land to Snuneymuxw," *Nanaimo News Bulletin*, February 27, 2024 https://www.nanaimobulletin.com/local-news/city-of-nanaimo-transferring-81-hectares-of-mount-benson-land-to-snuneymuxw-7322922.

112 Caitlin Brezinski, "Sask. First Nation to Receive Almost 3,811 Acres of Crown Mineral Rights," *CTV News*, May 22, 2024, https://regina. ctvnews.ca/sask-first-nation-to-receive-almost-3-811-acres-of-crown-mineral-rights-1.6896848.

113 Andrew Willis, "Indigenous-run Longhouse Capital Targets $1-billion Fund," *The Globe and Mail*, October 2, 2023," https://www.theglobe andmail.com/business/article-indigenous-private-equity-longhouse-capital.

114 Raven Indigenous Capital Partners, "Raven's Impact Measurement Framework," N.D., https://ravencapitalpartners.com/approach/impact.

115 Nelson Bennett, "B.C. Coastal First Nations Form Investment Consortium," *BIV*, April 2, 2024, https://www.biv.com/news/economy-law-politics/bc-coastal-first-nations-form-investment-consortium-8543892.

116 Stephanie Hogan, "Livelihood or Profit? Why an Old Fight Over Indigenous Fishing Rights Is Heating Up Again in Nova Scotia," *CBC*,

September 23, 2020, https://www.cbc.ca/news/canada/mi-kmaw-sipekne-katik-self-regulated-fishery-nova-scotia-1.5734646.

117 Richard Cuthbertson, "Cannabis Is Emerging as a New Battleground Over Mi'kmaw Rights, *CBC*, April 2, 2024, https://www.cbc.ca/news/canada/nova-scotia/cannabis-emerging-new-battleground-over-mikmaw-rights-1.7151120.

118 Emma Gilchrist, "Blueberry River First Nations Win Precedent-setting Treaty Rights Case," *The Narwhal*, June 30, 2021, https://thenarwhal.ca/blueberry-river-first-nations-bc-supreme-court-ruling/.

119 BOE Report, "Canada's Indigenous Peoples Eye Big Energy Deals, Await Trudeau Loan Promise," April 2, 2024, https://boereport.com/2024/04/02/canadas-indigenous-peoples-eye-big-energy-deals-await-trudeau-loan-promise/.

120 Paul Withers, "First Nations Partner with B.C. Company in $1B Purchase of Clearwater Seafoods," *CBC*, November 9, 2020, https://www.cbc.ca/news/canada/nova-scotia/mi-kmaq-purchase-clearwater-seafoods-1.5796028.

121 EnergyNow Media, "Alberta Indigenous Opportunities Corporation Closes Second Largest Deal with $150 Million Loan Guarantee for 12 Indigenous Communities," December 15, 2023, https://energynow.ca/2023/12/alberta-indigenous-opportunities-corporation-closes-second-largest-deal-with-150-million-loan-guarantee-for-12-indigenous-communities/.

122 BOE Report Staff, "Five Indigenous Nations in Northwestern Alberta Make $20.5 Million Investment in Greenhouse Gas Emission-reducing Cogeneration Unit for Alberta Gas Plant," December 18, 2023, https://boereport.com/2023/12/18/five-indigenous-nations-in-northwestern-alberta-make-20-5-million-investment-in-green house-gas-emission-reducing-cogeneration-unit-for-alberta-gas-plant/.

123 First Nation Energy Investment, "EverWind's Atlantic Canada Hydrogen Hub with Mi'kmaq Partnerships," February 17, 2024, https://minogi.ca/insights/f/everwinds-atlantic-canada-hydrogen-hub-with-mikmaq-partnerships.

124 Sara Connors, "Selkirk First Nation Given Control of Minto Mine in Yukon," *APTN News*, September 11, 2024, https://www.aptnnews.ca/national-news/selkirk-first-nation-given-control-of-minto-mine-in-yukon/.

125 Government of Canada, "Indigenous Peoples Economic and Trade Cooperation Agreement (IPETCA)," 2023, https://www. international.gc.ca/trade-commerce/indigenous_peoples-peuples_ autochtones/ipeca-acecpa.aspx?lang=eng.

126 Scotiabank. "Scotiabank Partners with Nch'kay' Development Limited Partnership, Des Nedhe Financial LP and Chippewas of Rama First Nation to Establish a New Investment Dealer in Canada," February 23, 2024, https://www.scotiabank.com/corporate/en/ home/media-centre/media-centre/news-release.html?id=4083& language=en.

127 Ibid.

128 BMO Financial Group, "BMO Introduces BMO for Indigenous Entrepreneurs Program," October 24, 2023, https://www. newswire.ca/news-releases/bmo-introduces-bmo-for-indigenous- entrepreneurs-program-832394622.html.

129 Windspeaker, "First Indigenous Equity Loan from Canada Infrastructure Bank Supports Mi'kmaw Investment in Green Energy," February 15, 2024, https://windspeaker.com/news/windspeaker- news/first-indigenous-equity-loan-canada-infrastructure-bank- supports-mikmaw.

130 James Dunne, "Finance Deal Struck Help Indigenous Communities Build Infrastructure," *CBC*, March 6, 2024, https://www.cbc.ca/news/ business/canada-infrastructure-bank-first-nations-bank-1.7135486.

131 First Nations Bank of Canada, *LinkedIn Post*, February 2024, https:// www.linkedin.com/posts/first-nations-bank-of-canada_indigenous economicdevelopment-fnbc-indigenouseconomicempowerment- activity-7150879498861735936-rBf0.

132 Quinn Gawronski, "Mohawks Use New Casino Wealth to Buy Back Ancestral Land," *The News House*, May 30, 2019, https://www. thenewshouse.com/borderlines/mohawks-use-new-casino-wealth-to- buy-back-ancestral-land-fund-social-programs/.

133 BDC, "Indigenous Owned: A Business Model with a Bright Future," N.D., https://www.bdc.ca/en/articles-tools/business-strategy- planning/manage-business/indigenous-owned.

134 *CBC*, "B.C. Introduces Bill for First Nations Land Acquisition," *CBC*, April 2, 2024, https://www.cbc.ca/news/canada/british-columbia/ bc-first-nations-land-acquisition-1.7161757.

135 Jordan Whitehouse, "The Indigenous Impact Opportunity," *Smith Business Insight,* November 8, 2022, https://smith.queensu. ca/insight/content/The-Indigenous-Impact-Opportunity. php#:~:text=There%20are%20no%20recent%20statistics,was%20 directed%20at%20Indigenous%20communities.

136 Chambers of Commerce Group Insurance Plan, "Resources for Indigenous Entrepreneurs in Canda," November 8, 2022, https:// www.chamberplan.ca/product/blogs/read,article/210/resources-for-indigenous-entrepreneurs-in-canada.

137 Royal Bank of Canada, "Financial Learning Centre," N.D., https:// www.rbcroyalbank.com/healthcare-financial-solutions/royal-college/ advice-and-learning/article/?title=indigenous-entrepreneurship-in-canada-the-impact-and-the-opportunity#:~:text=The%20number %20of%20Indigenous%20business,rate%20of%20non%2D Indigenous%20women.

138 David McKay, "It's Time for Indigenous Peoples to Be at the Centre of Canada's Economy," *Business Council of Canada,* June 8, 2020, https:// thebusinesscouncil.ca/publication/its-time-for-indigenous-peoples-to-be-at-the-centre-of-canadas-economy/.

139 https://publicpolicy.paypal-corp.com/sites/default/files/2021-09/ The_Power_of_Indigenous_Entrepreneurship_in_Canada.pdf.

140 Globe and Mail, "Empowering Indigenous Entrepreneurs: Sustainable Success Through Equal Partnerships," *The Globe and Mail,* April 26, 2024, https://www.theglobeandmail.com/business/adv/article-empowering-indigenous-entrepreneurs-sustainable-success-through-equal/.

141 Statistics Canada, https://www150.statcan.gc.ca/n1/pub/36-28-0001/2022012/article/00004-eng.html.

142 Prime Minister of Canada, Justin Trudeau, "Major Historical Claim Settlement with Siksika Nation," June 2, 2022, https://www. pm.gc.ca/en/news/news-releases/2022/06/02/major-historical-claim-settlement-siksika-nation.

143 The Canadian Press, "Federal Government Reaches $59M Settlement with First Nation in B.C. over Land Seizure," *APTN News,* February 21, 2024, https://www.aptnnews.ca/national-news/ federal-government-reaches-59m-settlement-with-first-nation-in-b-c-over-land-seizure/.

144 Indigenous Affairs, *Mitaanjigamiing First Nation, Canada and Ontario Reach Settlement on Treaty 3 Flooding Claim*, August 23, 2022, https://news.ontario.ca/en/release/1002253/mitaanjigamiing-first-nation-canada-and-ontario-reach-settlement-on-treaty-3-flooding-claim.

145 Lawrence L. Schembri, *The Next Generation: Innovating to Improve Indigenous Access to Finance in Canada*, Fraser Insitute, December 2023, https://www.fraserinstitute.org/sites/default/files/next-generation-innovating-to-improve-indigenous-access-to-finance-in-canada.pdf.

146 Chief Calvin Bruneau, Robert Morin, Harrie Vredenburg, and Liana Wolf Leg, "Striving for First Nations Economic Sovereignty Through a Low-Carbon Indigenous Sovereign Wealth Fund," *The Future Economy*, July 22, 2021, https://thefutureeconomy.ca/op-eds/first-nations-economic-sovereignty-through-a-low-carbon-indigenous-sovereign-wealth-fund/.

147 Rick Baert, "Ontario First Nations Groups Form New Sovereign Wealth Fund," *Pensions & Investments*, January 4, 2018, https://www.pionline.com/article/20180104/ONLINE/180109930/ontario-first-nations-groups-form-new-sovereign-wealth-fund.

148 Tara Weber, "Project Reconciliation Advances Launch of $1B Wealth Fund While Keeping Eye on Trans Mountain," February 18, 2021, https://www.pionline.com/article/20180104/ONLINE/18010 9930/ontario-first-nations-groups-form-new-sovereign-wealth-fund.

149 Mohawk Council of Kahnawa'ke, "MCK Green Lights the Kahnawake Sovereign Wealth Fund," 2023, https://www.kahnawake.com/pr_text.asp?ID=6706.

150 Lori Mathison, "Indigenous Involvement and Values Are Key to ESG Investing," November 27, 2023, https://www.bccpa.ca/news-events/cpabc-newsroom/2023/november/indigenous-involvement-and-values-are-key-to-esg-investing/.

151 Maya Stano and Jennifer King, "Indigenous Rights and ESG Reporting," November 11, 2022, https://www.lexpert.ca/legal-insights/indigenous-rights-and-esg-reporting/370856#:~:text= Notwithstanding%20the%20important%20role%20that,Indigenous %20employees%2C%20managers%20and%20board.

152 Enbridge, "A Billion-dollar Commitment: Target Set for Indigenous Business Spending," 2024, https://www.enbridge.com/projects-and-

infrastructure/public-awareness/indigenous/indigenous-business-spending-target#:~:text=From%20January%202023%20to%20the,North%20American%20projects%20and%20operations.

153 CAPP, "Indigenous Partnerships," 2024, https://www.capp.ca/en/our-priorities/indigenous-partnerships/.

154 Siegfried Wiessner, "United Nations Declaration on the Rights of Indigenous Peoples," 2009, https://legal.un.org/avl/pdf/ha/ga_61-295/ga_61-295_e.pdf.

155 Government of British Columbia, "Reconciliation & Other Agreements," September 20, 2024, https://www2.gov.bc.ca/gov/content/environment/natural-resource-stewardship/consulting-with-first-nations/first-nations-negotiations/reconciliation-other-agreements.

156 Government of British Columbia, "Forest Consultation and Revenue Sharing Agreements," September 15, 2024, https://www2.gov.bc.ca/gov/content/environment/natural-resource-stewardship/consulting-with-first-nations/first-nations-negotiations/forest-consultation-and-revenue-sharing-agreements.

157 Lynn Parsons, "Fall Economic Statement and the Indigenous Loan Guarantee Program," November 28, 2023, https://www.mccarthy.ca/en/insights/blogs/canadian-energy-perspectives/fall-economic-statement-and-indigenous-loan-guarantee-program#:~:text=Following%20on%20the%20heels%20of,Loan%20Guarantee%20to%20enable%20Indigenous.

158 Gabriela Panza-Beltrandi, "Vancouver Releases 5-year Plan to Implement UNDRIP," *CTV News,* June 3, 2024, https://bc.ctvnews.ca/vancouver-releases-5-year-plan-to-implement-undrip-1.6912379.

159 Globe and Mail, "Accelerating Transition: Economic Impacts of Indigenous Leadership in Catalyzing the Transition to a Clean Energy Future across Canada," *The Globe and Mail,* N.D., https://.theglobeandmail.com/files/editorial/News/indigenous-clean-energy.pdf.

160 Ibid.

161 Truth and Reconciliation Commission of Canada, "Truth and Reconciliation Commission of Canada: Calls to Action," 2015, https://www2.gov.bc.ca/assets/gov/british-columbians-our-governments/indigenous-people/aboriginal-peoples-documents/calls_to_action_english2.pdf.

162 Mining Association of Canada, "Response to the Truth and Reconciliation Commission's Calls to Action," 2024, https://mining.ca/our-focus/indigenous-affairs/response-to-the-truth-and-reconciliation-commissions-calls-to-action/.

163 Conference Board of Canada, "Indigenous Ownership: A New Economic Era," 2024, https://www.conferenceboard.ca/in-fact/indigenous-ownership/#:~:text=What%20Is%20Indigenous%20Equity%20Participation,the%20development%20of%20their%20territories.

164 Amy Carruthers and Erin McKlusky, "Four Trends in Indigenous Equity Participation in Canada," March 6, 2023, https://www.fasken.com/en/knowledge/2023/03/6-four-trends-in-indigenous-equity-participation-in-canada.

165 Rene Bruemmer, "'A Special Moment in Our History': Mohawk Council of Kahnawake Inks Deal with Hydro-Quebec," *The Gazette*, https://montrealgazette.com/news/local-news/mohawk-council-inks-deal-with-hydro-quebec-on-electricity-transmission-line-to-new-york.

166 Anna McMillan, "Land Back: Tsawout First Nation Buys 40-hectare Agricultural Property," *CTV News*, June 21, 2024, https://bc.ctvnews.ca/land-back-tsawout-first-nation-buys-40-hectare-agricultural-property-1.6935479.

167 Dan Fumano and Lori Culbert, "'This Is Just the Beginning': First Nations' Real Estate MegaProjects Game-changing for Metro Vancouver," *Vancouver Sun*, https://vancouversun.com/business/real-estate/indigenous-developers-to-create-25000-new-homes-in-metro-vancouver.

168 Wolf Depner, "B.C. Property Act Changes Allow First Nations to Purchase, Hold, and Sell Land," *Victoria News*, April 2, 2024, https://www.vicnews.com/news/bc-property-act-changes-allow-first-nations-to-purchase-hold-and-sell-land-7336672.

169 Royal Bank of Canada, "92 to Zero: How Economic Reconciliation Can Power Canada's Climate Goals," 2024, https://thoughtleadership.rbc.com/92-to-zero-how-economic-reconciliation-can-power-canadas-climate-goals/.

170 Clare O'Hara, "Wealth Managers Seek to Help Indigenous Communities Balance Spending and Investing Settlements" *The Globe*

and Mail, October 11, 2023, https://www.theglobeandmail.com/business/article-tk-with-billions-in-settlements-on-the-line-wealth-managers-seek-to/.

171 Dave Baxter, "Manitoba First Nation Clears Final Hurdle in $200M 'Cows and Plows' Settlement with Feds to Right Century-old Wrong," *The Winnipeg Sun,* March 4, 2024, https://winnipegsun.com/news/provincial/manitoba-first-nation-clears-final-hurdle-in-200b-cows-and-plows-settlement-with-feds-to-right-century-old-wrong.

172 Chad Pawson, "Treaty 8 First Nations in B.C. Celebrate Inking of Treaty Land Entitlement Claims with Province, Ottawa," *CBC,* April 15, 2023, https://www.cbc.ca/news/canada/british-columbia/treaty-land-entitlement-claims-bc-canada-treaty-8-nations-april-2023-1.6812180.

173 Government of British Columbia, "Five First Nations Reach Settlement With B.C., Federal Governments on Treaty Land Entitlement Claims,"April 15, 2023, https://news.gov.bc.ca/releases/2023IRR0019-000539#:~:text=From%20April%201%2C%202022%2C%20to,offer%20to%20negotiate%2056%20claims.

174 Rob Campbell, "How Urban Reserves Support Local Business and Municipal Economies, *Municipal World,* October 2023, https://www.municipalworld.com/feature-story/how-urban-reserves-support-local-business-and-municipal-economies/#:~:text=Generally%2C%20urban%20reserves%20are%20created,unavailable%20on%20other%20reserve%20lands.

175 Ozten Shebahkeget, "Naawi-Oodena Officially Becomes Largest Urban Reserve in Canada After Repatriation of Winnipeg Barracks," *CBC,* December 19, 2022, https://www.cbc.ca/news/canada/manitoba/naawi-oodena-repatriation-winnipeg-largest-urban-reserve-1.6691359.

Conclusion

176 City of Saskatoon, N.D., https://www.saskatoon.ca/news-releases/city-and-lac-la-ronge-indian-band-sign-new-urban-reserve-agreements-0.

177 Frederick Douglass, N.D. "Frederick Douglass Quotes," https://www.goodreads.com/quotes/951719-power-concedes-nothing-without-a-demand-it-never-did-and.

178 lain McGilchrist, *The Master and His Emissary: The Divided Brain and the Making of the Western World* (Yale University Press, 2019).

179 Jace Meyers, conversation.

Appendix

180 Quotewise.com, N.D., http://www.quoteswise.com/anthony-robbins-quotes-3.html.

181 Indira Ghandi, *Goodreads*, 2024 https://www.goodreads.com/quotes/53583-the-power-to-question-is-the-basis-of-all-human.

182 Eric E. Vogt, Juanita Brown, and David Isaacs, *The Art of Powerful Questions: Catalyzing Insight, Innovation, and Action*, 2003, https://www.sparc.bc.ca/wp-content/uploads/2020/11/the-art-of-powerful-questions.pdf.

183 Thomas Johansen, Thomas Specht, and Henry Kleive, *Leadership for Sustainability Powered by Questions: How to Create Sustainable Organizational and Business Development*, MacMann Berg Press, 2020, https://campaigns.macmannberg.dk/wp-content/uploads/sites/74/2020/12/Johansen-Specht-Kleive-2020-Leadership-for-Sustainability-Powered-by-Questions-021220.pdf.

184 Government of Canada, *Annual Progress Report on the Implementation of the United Nations Declaration on the Rights of Indigenous Peoples Act*, June 2022, https://www.justice.gc.ca/eng/declaration/report-rapport/2022/index.html

185 House of Commons of Canada, "Bill C-15," 2020, https://www.parl.ca/DocumentViewer/en/43-2/bill/C-15/first-reading.

186 Romeo Saganash, "Romeo Saganash on Indigenous Rights, 2017," *Great Canadian Speeches*, 2017, https://greatcanadianspeeches.ca/2017/12/07/romeo-saganash-on-indigenous-rights-december-5-2017/.

Index

About Carol Anne Hilton

CAROL ANNE HILTON, MBA, is founder of the Indigenomics Institute, the Global Center of Indigenomics, and the Global Indigenous Technology House, which focuses on the economic empowerment of Indigenous Peoples. She is a Hesquiaht woman of Nuu-chah-nulth descent from the west coast of Vancouver Island, and is from the house of Mam'aayutch, a Chief's house, a name which means "on the edge." Hilton is the first generation out of Canadian residential schools, fifth generation since the establishment of the Indian Act, and comes from over 10,000 years of the Potlatch tradition of giving and the demonstration of wealth and relationship. Her work focuses on building a collective reality that centers Indigenous peoples in social and cultural well-being and economic empowerment today, and is leading the evolution of Canada's $100 billion Indigenous economy. An advisor to governments, business, and First Nations, she is author of the award-winning *Indigenomics: Taking a Seat at the Economic Table*. She lives in Victoria, BC.

ABOUT NEW SOCIETY PUBLISHERS

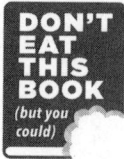

DON'T EAT THIS BOOK *(but you could)*

New Society Publishers is an activist, solutions-oriented publisher focused on publishing books to build a more just and sustainable future. Our books offer tips, tools, and insights from leading experts in a wide range of areas.

We're proud to hold to the highest environmental and social standards of any publisher in North America. When you buy New Society books, you are part of the solution!

- This book is printed on **100% post-consumer recycled paper**, processed chlorine-free, with low-VOC vegetable-based inks (since 2002)
- Our corporate structure is an innovative employee shareholder agreement, so we're one-third employee-owned (since 2015)
- We've created a Statement of Ethics (2021). The intent of this Statement is to act as a framework to guide our actions and facilitate feedback for continuous improvement of our work
- We're carbon-neutral (since 2006)
- We're certified as a B Corporation (since 2016)
- We're Signatories to the UN's Sustainable Development Goals (SDG) Publishers Compact (2020–2030, the Decade of Action)

At New Society Publishers, we care deeply about *what* we publish — but also about *how* we do business.

To download our full catalog, sign up for our quarterly newsletter, and learn more about New Society Publishers, please visit newsociety.com.

ENVIRONMENTAL BENEFITS STATEMENT

New Society Publishers saved the following resources by printing the pages of this book on chlorine free paper made with 100% post-consumer waste.

TREES	WATER	ENERGY	SOLID WASTE	GREENHOUSE GASES
55	4,300	23	180	23,700
FULLY GROWN	GALLONS	MILLION BTUs	POUNDS	POUNDS

Environmental impact estimates were made using the Environmental Paper Network Paper Calculator 4.0. For more information visit www.papercalculator.org

Certified B Corporation

new society PUBLISHERS
www.newsociety.com

MIX
Paper | Supporting responsible forestry
FSC® C016245

SDG PUBLISHERS COMPACT